MW01487711

Freedom for All

FREEDOM FOR ALL

WHAT A LIBERAL SOCIETY COULD BE

● ● ●

ALEX ZAKARAS

Yale

UNIVERSITY PRESS

New Haven and London

Published with assistance from the foundation established in memory of
Henry Weldon Barnes of the Class of 1882, Yale College.

Yale University Press books may be purchased in quantity for
educational, business, or promotional use. For information, please e-mail
sales.press@yale.edu (U.S. office) or sales@yaleup.co.uk (U.K. office).

Set in Adobe Garmond type by Integrated Publishing Solutions.
Printed in the United States of America.

Library of Congress Control Number: 2025932259
ISBN 978-0-300-28176-7 (hardcover)

A catalogue record for this book is available from the British Library.

Authorized Representative in the EU: Easy Access System Europe,
Mustamäe tee 50, 10621 Tallinn, Estonia, gpsr.requests@easproject.com

10 9 8 7 6 5 4 3 2 1

For my students

Contents

INTRODUCTION
Radical Liberalism

I graduated from college in 1998, during the high tide of American self-confidence. The country was basking in the glow of its Cold War victory and enjoying a sustained economic boom. Pundits were declaring the final triumph of liberal democracy and the free market. Surveys found Americans to be overwhelmingly optimistic about their nation's future. The vast majority were confident of their economic prospects, and almost two-thirds expected the federal government to play a major role in "making things better."[1]

A great deal has changed since then. We lived through September 11, 2001, and the two failed wars it provoked. We weathered the financial crisis of 2008 and the Great Recession, which shined a spotlight on the extravagant wealth of the 1 percent and the economic insecurity afflicting so many others. In its aftermath, a majority of young people now doubt that the "American dream" is still possible.[2] We witnessed police officers killing unarmed Black men in broad daylight—over and over again—and mostly escaping justice. We survived a pandemic and a decade of record temperatures and climate disruption, with its steady drumbeat of hurricanes and floods, massive wildfires and deadly heat waves. We watched a violent mob invade and defile the Capitol with the blessing of a sitting president, who now stands triumphant in the White House again, giving vent to his authoritarian impulses.

Seen through the eyes of a late 1990s college graduate, our society today looks alarmingly fragile. The fundamentals that many of us took for granted—our democracy, our promise of widely shared prosperity, our natural environment—now look damaged and brittle. How did we get here? And how do we move forward?

Before we can answer these questions clearly, we need to articulate a vision of what a good society should, ideally, look like. Although this vision may seem like a distant dream, it can help us understand the extent of our society's failures and expose the roots of our current crisis. It can also lend coherence to our political advocacy and guide our diverse efforts to make our country a better, fairer place. This book outlines one such vision, grounded in liberal ideals. It argues that these ideals are our best hope of achieving the political, economic, and ecological realignments we urgently need.

When the Trump administration's cruelty, corruption, and incompetence finally exhaust his credibility with the American electorate and his allies are swept from power, we will have an opportunity to change direction decisively and begin building a better future. To save liberal democracy in this country, we will have to seize that moment. This book aims to prepare us for it.

For over two centuries, social and political reformers—in the United States and elsewhere—have drawn inspiration from the liberal political tradition. Liberal ideals shaped the most important reform movements in the modern world, including the fight to abolish slavery and establish racial and gender equality. They animated the twentieth-century push to end colonial occupation and protect human rights, as well as diverse efforts to expand and improve social services so that fewer people are trapped in poverty. Still, our crises have grown so severe that critics—on both the left and the right—now deny that liberalism can offer an adequate response. Many assert that liberal principles are among the chief causes of our discontents.

The terms "liberalism" and "liberal" often sow confusion because they have several different meanings. In the United States, for example, they commonly refer to the political left or center-left. This is not the meaning I will use in this book. Instead, I use these terms to describe a tradition of ideas that still shapes the way most Americans think about politics. Liberalism, in this older sense, is defined by two things: its commitment to a common goal and its embrace of a shared set of political strategies.

—The *goal* is to create the conditions under which people can live freely. Liberals value *personal* freedom above all: they defend the freedom to speak and associate, to worship, to work and form meaningful relationships, to own property, and to do these and other things securely.

—The *strategies* include the rule of law, constitutional restraints and the separation of powers, individual rights, democratic accountability, economic markets, a free media, and an open and diverse civil society. They also include access to a range of public goods—including education, for example, and health services—designed to widen individual opportunities.

In this sense of the term, a great many Americans across the political spectrum are liberals. They may disagree sharply over policy questions, but they agree about these basic goals and strategies. "Liberalism," as the philosopher Martha Nussbaum puts it, "is not a single position but a family of positions."[3]

How then could liberal ideals have caused our current crises? In our polarized society, it is no surprise that we hear very different answers. Leading intellectuals on the right see liberalism as a ruthlessly disruptive force that undermines traditional values, pulls communities apart, and erodes the cultural and religious identities that make human life meaningful. They accuse liberals of elevating limitless individual choice over anything that might stand in its way, including the moral restraints and family values that have long held human communities together. The result, these critics say, is an increasingly harsh, selfish, and materialistic society devoted to the gratification of individual desire above all else—a society that neither nourishes moral character nor prepares people to govern themselves wisely.

If conservatives view liberalism as a source of corrosive change, critics on the left tend to see it as the ideology of the status quo. They accuse liberals of wielding the language of individual rights and freedoms to entrench existing patterns of privilege—including the privileges of wealthy corporations and dominant racial groups. They see this pattern unfolding in several ways. Climate regulation is scuttled because it interferes with consumer choice or the free market. The push for racial justice is halted by appeals to the rights of white voters or applicants. The effort to invest in our schools and make housing affordable is frustrated by appeals to the rights of taxpayers, property holders, or developers. From these points of view, liberalism looks like a set of strategies designed to impede social justice. Critics on both sides of the political spectrum also maintain that liberalism has grown too stale and dogmatic to meet the urgent challenges of the twenty-first century.

In this book, I set out to answer these criticisms and to lay out a robust defense of liberal ideals and institutions. I do so by recovering a strain of liberalism committed not just to freedom, but also to equality. At its best, liberalism is an emancipatory political project designed to secure freedom for all. Throughout these pages, I explore what it would mean to implement this project in America today, and what it would demand of us. These questions can help us diagnose the injustices at the heart of our economy and society. They can also inspire us to pursue an ambitious slate of reforms designed to empower people, on equal terms, to shape their own lives.

Many prominent defenders of liberal ideals have taken a more cautious approach in recent years. Rather than present liberalism as a recipe for far-reaching reform, they have described it as a humane and pragmatic alternative to the excesses of the authoritarian right. In their eyes, liberal societies thrive because they encourage toleration amid diversity, reasoned compromise instead of violent conflict, and gradual reform rather than sudden upheaval. These writers often harken back, implicitly or explicitly, to a time when our public life was less strident and polarized, and urge us to recover its conciliatory virtues. They write mainly as defenders of the existing institutional order. Their books are full of calls for civility and political restraint.[4]

This accommodating posture is inadequate for the crises of our time. In the face of rampant inequality, climate catastrophe, and political tyranny, liberals must be willing to demand deep change. Moreover, to compete successfully against charismatic critics promising dramatic solutions, liberalism must prove itself capable of inspiring a passionate allegiance in its own right. To do so, it must offer a clear and bold set of principles and present a compelling vision of the future. When confronting grave threats, liberals in earlier times have been audacious in both vision and action. Such audacity is sorely needed now.

This book therefore defends what I will call radical liberalism.[5] Radical liberalism stands apart from other versions of liberal ideas in several ways. First, it embraces an expansive idea of personal freedom. Freedom, I will argue, means *having the power to make choices*. Taken seriously, it requires access to a broad range of resources and opportunities, including affordable education, housing, and healthcare; a clean and resilient natural environment; robust collective bargaining rights, and a great deal more. Embracing this expansive idea of free-dom means rejecting the stripped-down alternative widely accepted on the American right, which holds, essentially, that freedom means *not being told what to do.* This threadbare version is compatible with grinding poverty and inequality, labor exploitation, and discrimina-tion, among other social ills. Its chief function in America today is to protect the powerful from taxation and regulation.

Second, radical liberalism depends on the grassroots power gen-erated by politically active and organized citizens. Without it, liberal governments—like all governments—tend to tilt toward oligarchy. The reason is fairly straightforward: in all modern societies, powerful business interests are continually flexing their political muscle. They are well-organized, have tremendous resources at their disposal, and operate patiently over long time frames. Without sustained counter-pressure, they routinely thwart necessary reforms and rewrite politi-cal and economic rules in their favor.[6] When this happens, most peo-ple become less free: their rights erode, their economic opportunities shrink, and their livelihoods, health, and communities stand increas-ingly at the mercy of the rich. Radical liberalism therefore posits a fundamental relationship between freedom and popular mobiliza-tion: it sees freedom as a goal that must be constantly shored up and protected by channeling ordinary people's voices and interests into the political process.

Finally, radical liberalism stands apart for its belief that freedom is owed to everyone on equal terms, without exception. In domestic politics, which is my focus in this book, "everyone" means everyone living within the nation's borders. For centuries, societies professing liberal ideals have extended them selectively to a privileged slice of their populations—to white men, typically, or to rich people. In our own time there is an intense struggle for the soul of liberalism itself, between those genuinely committed to achieving freedom for all and those using liberal ideas to perpetuate longstanding inequalities and injustices. Any credible defense of liberalism today must confront these realities unflinchingly. It must show that liberalism contains the moral and political resources to identify and correct its own failures and to think clearly about what is owed to those who have suffered from them. Radical liberalism is committed to meeting this challenge head-on.

In exploring what radical liberalism can do for us, I will emphasize four key characteristics that, together, explain why it is uniquely capable of addressing our current crises.

Radical liberalism demands meaningful equality. Profound inequality runs like a bright thread through the metastasizing injustices of our time. It reaches far beyond the maldistribution of income and wealth. Access to political power is overwhelmingly a privilege of the rich and well connected. Public institutions that should moderate inequality—including, first of all, our schools and universities—are deepening it. The escalating effects of environmental degradation and climate change fall disproportionately on the poor and marginalized. And all of these dimensions of inequality intersect with gender and race: women and people of color are more likely to be poor, to lack access to political power, to be victims of violence, to lack adequate medical care, and to live in polluted environments.

Given the overflowing wealth of twenty-first-century America, and given its stark legacies of historical injustice, these inequalities are morally inexcusable. There is simply no credible way of justifying them. Any political outlook that fails to diagnose and condemn these inequalities is not just wrong, but also useless to us in this moment. If critics are right in presenting liberalism as a fundamentally inegalitarian doctrine, then liberalism is in serious trouble.

Fortunately, they are mistaken. Over the past two hundred years, liberal ideas have been repeatedly harnessed by reformers fighting for greater equality and inclusion. These include civil rights activists, labor leaders, human rights advocates, and reformers pressing for women's rights and LGBTQ rights, among others. Their legacies still run strong: many of the philosophers, commentators, and activists writing within the liberal tradition today are egalitarians, and their insights can be found throughout this book.[7] I draw especially on a new generation of scholarly work on the idea of freedom, which emphasizes the deep and necessary connections between freedom and equality. Over and over, sociologists, labor economists, political scientists, and philosophers have shown that societies in which poor and marginalized groups are consigned to second-class citizenship are not truly free. *Some* members of these societies may enjoy a wide field of personal choice, but many more suffer harsh constraints.

This scholarship has taken several forms. Some philosophers have focused on the relationship between freedom and power and shown that unequal distributions of power, by themselves, often leave many people dominated and unfree. Other economists and philosophers have emphasized the link between freedom and *capability:* they have shown that people are free, above all, when they enjoy the power to make choices, and that this power presupposes a range of personal capacities or capabilities, including education, health, and social respect or belonging. Yet another set of scholars—including those advocating a Universal Basic Income—have insisted that there is no meaningful freedom without access to economic resources. They have shown how empty the promise of freedom is, and how constrained the range of options, for those who are economically deprived. Together, these insights point in a sharply egalitarian direction, toward a society committed to equalizing the distribution of power, respect, and opportunity for all its members.

Radical liberalism rests on widely shared values and beliefs. Any vision of the good society rests ultimately on a set of values or ideals, such as justice, equality, harmony, progress, virtue, and freedom. To command broad appeal among voters, these ideals must resonate with the local culture(s). The most powerful political ideals are those that successfully invoke widely shared moral intuitions and collective identities, tap into prevailing stories and myths, and use these to show why political change is necessary.[8]

In the United States, radical liberalism is well suited to this task. Its core values and concepts—including moral equality, human dignity, and freedom—are deeply entrenched in our national culture. Moreover, since the early nineteenth century, this country's dominant national myths have centered on the value of individual liberty.[9] For both better and worse, those who successfully harnessed this cardinal value have gained an important political advantage. Our most effective reformers, from Franklin Roosevelt to Martin Luther King Jr., have understood the power of this approach.

It is vitally important for any society to harbor a wide range of critical perspectives, including some that are sharply at odds with dominant moral and political paradigms. Dissenting social critics play a crucial role: they broaden our sense of what is possible, force us to examine our deeply held assumptions, and help us think more critically about our society and its politics. But anyone trying to correct injustices must first win power, and anyone bidding seriously to win power must use the most effective rhetorical tools available—those that can persuade a broad cross-section of the electorate. In this sense, political leaders and activists are different from social critics. Their role is to win power and use it for good. In the United States, the rhetorical tools most likely to help them achieve this goal are liberal.

When progressives abandon these tools, they cede them to right-wing business moguls, Christian nationalists, antigovernment zealots, and other groups looking to leverage "American freedom" to support inequality and exclusion. We simply cannot afford to boost their political fortunes in this way. Part of my aim in writing this book is to show that we can take back the language of freedom and appeal to the common sense of American voters without abandoning our pursuit of equality. We need not appeal to exotic moral principles or political theories to get where we want to go.

Radical liberalism is realistic. One of the great virtues of liberal thinking at its best is its refusal to indulge in utopian abstraction. This tendency is manifest, most of all, in liberals' attention to institutions. To remain stable and functional, a free society requires well-designed institutions, guided by the best available evidence about what works and what doesn't, and grounded in realistic expectations about how people are likely to behave. These institutions encompass not just legislatures and courts, regulatory agencies, and police who respect people as equals, but also media organizations, labor unions, and other civil society groups. Liberals have long understood that both freedom and equality depend on these institutional foundations.

In these areas, liberalism contrasts sharply with the Marxist tradition, which has offered an alternative vision of human equality for the modern world. Karl Marx himself was famously elusive about the institutions that would structure his communist utopia, and many leading Marxist thinkers since his death have shown little interest in institutional design. Meanwhile, revolutionaries inspired by their ideas often developed hierarchical, exclusive, authoritarian political structures that crushed the emancipatory ideals expressed in Marxist philosophy. This impatience with institutions is not confined to the Marxist left; it also affects other left-leaning thinkers who write in a "poststructuralist" vein as well as academic writers who style themselves anarchists or "radical democrats." Many of these thinkers are housed in English departments, cultural studies departments, and other academic niches where they feel little need to study real political institutions and movements or think through policy details.

When socialists in the early twentieth century began to get serious about institutions and search for alternatives to the Leninist authoritarianism then taking hold in the Soviet Union, many turned to liberalism for inspiration. They embraced the separation of powers, independent judiciaries, the rule of law, democratic accountability, markets and private property, free media, and open civil society. Unlike the "classical" liberals of the nineteenth century, they did not celebrate laissez-faire economics but instead embraced a program of economic regulation and labor empowerment paired with a muscular social-welfare state. They believed these institutions would expand opportunities for workers while also shielding them from the harsh vicissitudes of the market.[10] These reformed socialists asserted the importance of equality and social solidarity alongside the value of liberty. In Europe, they called themselves social democrats, and they achieved significant expansions of human equality and freedom. But their rejection of Marx's utopianism and their embrace of liberal institutions, including their commitment to tame and regulate markets rather than abandon them, brought them firmly into the liberal fold.

Not all versions of liberalism share this realistic bent. Today, its abandonment is most evident in the "neoliberal" thinking—which I will also call market fundamentalism—that has shaped American politics for the past forty-five years. Market fundamentalists tend to treat economic markets as cure-alls that are not only efficient and innovative, but also free and fair. They make a show of caring about institutions and being wise and realistic about the power of incentives, but their policy prescriptions ultimately belie this posture. As their policies have caused or intensified multiple crises—including massive inequality, financial instability, and ecological devastation—many market fundamentalists have adhered with a kind of religious fervor to economic abstractions in the face of empirical evidence. Wedded to a very narrow set of analytical tools drawn largely from economics, they have been willfully blind to the intersecting manifestations of power in American society, and therefore unable to chart a realistic course toward human freedom.

A realistic disposition is essential to both the theory and practice of politics: without it, the loftiest goals and principles go unrealized. But it also carries danger. Time and again, morally urgent reforms have been condemned as *un*realistic. The idea of democracy was widely dismissed as impractical when it was first proffered; so too was gender equality. In our day, the idea that everyone has a right to housing, healthcare, and a livable wage is derided as unrealistic, often by those who benefit most from our savage inequalities. What we need, then, is a radical liberalism that is realistic about its strategies but unwavering in its goals. The pursuit of equal freedom is, morally speaking, nonnegotiable—but as we try to figure out how to achieve it, we should be open to the widest range of experimental evidence. We should also focus on those experiments—both in our own society and abroad— that have shown success in expanding freedom for those who possess the least of it.

Radical liberalism is dynamic and innovative. One of the leading accusations leveled at liberals nowadays is that they are complacent and out of ideas. In the United States, this charge draws strength from the evident dysfunction of our national politics, which too often prevents Congress from addressing the nation's pressing problems. In Europe, it reflects widespread frustration with the bureaucratic morass of EU governance, which seems increasingly inflexible and remote from constituents' needs.

But holding up these two governments as embodiments of liberalism is misleading. The sources of gridlock and polarization in the United States, for example, are complicated and multilayered: they include the effects of cable news and social media on the spread of information, gerrymandering and long-term geographic sorting that have made voting districts uncompetitive, and unique features of the

US Constitution—including the Senate and the electoral college—that were designed to impede political change. Our political system is also hobbled by the tremendous power of money in American politics, which corporate donors have leveraged over and over to block commonsense political reforms, distort the policy agendas of both major political parties, and weaken the government's capacity to act. Is either the theory or the practice of liberalism responsible for these tendencies? The answer is far from clear.

When we take a broader view of liberal society, this line of attack looks even weaker. Far more than any other kind of society on record, liberal societies are incubators of creative solutions. We usually emphasize their tendency to promote private-sector innovation, but this is far from the whole story: liberalism also encourages experimentation within civil society and in state and local governments. In the United States today, many of these experiments adhere closely to the aims of radical liberalism. They include pilot projects offering a guaranteed basic income to help bring families out of poverty; creative mixed-use zoning schemes and other innovations designed to promote affordable housing; community-led restorative justice programs to promote rehabilitation and healing instead of punitive incarceration; regenerative agriculture to reverse the long-term degradation of topsoil and mitigate the effects of climate change; and new legal and financial instruments to facilitate worker ownership of businesses. That these innovations are often resisted by those in power is hardly an indictment of liberalism; such resistance exists in all societies for the simple reason that innovations often disrupt existing patterns of power and privilege.

Two final clarifications are needed before I can begin developing my argument in detail. The first has to do with historical injustice. As I pointed out earlier, any attempt to defend liberal politics in the twenty-first century must come to grips with the legacy of injustice that has tainted liberal institutions for over two hundred years. It is not enough merely to acknowledge that, at various times, thinkers and politicians professing liberal ideals have condoned chattel slavery, colonial subjugation, racial and gender hierarchy, and oppressive economic exploitation. The truth is that societies that styled themselves liberal—including the United States before (and after) the Civil War and the nineteenth-century British empire—not only perpetrated egregious abuses, but also structured their economies in ways that depended on them. In many of these societies, the liberties of white men were substantially enabled by the oppression and exploitation of women and people of color.

How should this legacy of injustice affect our willingness to affirm liberal ideals today? There is a range of possible answers. One is to treat these injustices as hypocritical aberrations that form no central part of the history of liberalism. Another is to consider liberalism wholly irredeemable because of its complicity in profound injustice. This book embraces neither of these extremes. The first approach is clearly untenable, for it tells the history of liberalism—implicitly or explicitly—through the eyes of white men whose experiences are allowed to define the liberal norm. Everyone else's experience becomes an exception. This view of liberal history stands manifestly at odds with the commitments to equal freedom and equal human dignity that are deeply held among liberal egalitarians today.

There are strong reasons, however, to reject the second extreme as well. Liberal history is complex: while it is undeniably true that liberal ideas have been used to rationalize hierarchy and oppression, it is also true that these same ideas have been harnessed continually in the fight for social justice. In fact, liberal ideas have featured prominently in the most important egalitarian movements in modern history. For example, the abolitionist movements that arose in the late eighteenth and early nineteenth centuries—in Haiti, England, Jamaica, and the United States—drew heavily on liberal principles. Abolitionists asserted the equal natural rights of all men (in some cases, of all women too) and lambasted the hypocrisy of those who sang the song of universal freedom while holding human beings as property or profiting from others who did. It was abolitionists who first popularized the language of human rights that became so influential in the twentieth century. More recently, the movement for LGBTQ rights has drawn heavily on liberal principles: on the equal moral dignity of all persons, and the fundamental imperative to leave people free to shape their own lives. Other examples abound.

But the more important reason to try to rescue liberalism from its historical injustices has to do with our current predicament: in rejecting liberalism, we would reject some of the most powerful tools we have to achieve a more just and humane world in the twenty-first century. This point is best made by analogy. Like liberalism, democracy—and the principles and ideas that have justified it—is deeply entangled with historical injustice. Historians have shown very clearly that the birth of mass democracy in the United States coincided with a rising tide of white supremacy. When Americans began defending white male suffrage in the early nineteenth century and rejecting property qualifications for the vote, they often justified this shift in racial terms: superior racial characteristics, they claimed, made white men (or Anglo Saxon men) uniquely qualified for self-government. They drove their point home by denigrating "inferior" races as unfit for self-rule. So as voting rights expanded for whites, they actually contracted for people of color. Historians have rightly described the democratic ideas circulating at this time as *Herrenvolk*—or "master race"—democracy. This racialized view of democracy lasted a long time: it was used to justify Jim Crow as well as colonial interventions in Cuba, the Philippines, and elsewhere, and it survives today in the racial attitudes of many right-wing nationalists.

Should we abandon democratic ideas and institutions because of this pattern of historical injustice? Clearly not. Democratic ideals can be disentangled from white male supremacy and reformulated in inclusive and universal terms, and these inclusive reformulations are powerful forces for good in the world. The same is true of liberal ideals. As I will show throughout this book, liberal and democratic institutions—and the associated politics of human rights—are among the most reliable political tools we have to protect people from oppression, exploitation, and marginalization. And because they resonate so deeply in American culture, liberal and democratic ideas are powerful levers for effective social criticism and reform. To abandon these traditions in search of something purer would be quixotic and self-destructive.

None of this means we should adopt a naive, self-congratulatory, or ahistorical view of liberalism. All credible defenders of liberalism today must remain acutely aware of how liberal ideas have been misused. They must be sensitive to the particular hypocrisies, blind spots, and prejudices that have derailed the liberal project in the past and still derail it today. We cannot fight effectively for equal freedom in our own time without understanding how these distortions entrenched themselves in liberal societies and how people professing liberal ideals came to embrace them.

Throughout this book, then, I will draw attention to the ways liberal ideas have been—and are still—*distorted* or *misused* by powerful people and dominant groups. What I mean is simply that they have been used to defend patently immoral goals. I will not argue at any point that the true essence of liberalism, considered as a historical tradition, is egalitarian or emancipatory. Liberalism has a broad and varied history, and many of its standard-bearers have left us mixed legacies. The radical liberalism I defend in this book is just one version of liberalism. I believe it is the best version, the one that holds genuine promise for the future, but it is hardly the only version that can draw support from liberalism's long and convoluted history.

The second clarification concerns the relationship between liberalism and democracy. It is well known that the two sometimes come into conflict. When the majority decides to use its political power to attack the rights of minorities, for example, or to brutalize and intimidate immigrants, then democratic power is bent to illiberal purposes. This pattern is tragically ubiquitous in American political history, and it is clearly manifest in the ambitions of right-wing demagogues today. Conversely, when judges or bureaucrats intervene in democratic politics to shield individual freedoms from legislative interference, or impose unpopular interpretations of these freedoms, they weaken democratic self-government. Liberal democracies must continually negotiate these tensions. Their resounding success since World War II suggests that, most of the time, liberalism and democracy are mutually reinforcing. But when tensions between them escalate, moments of real peril can arise.

In a deeper sense, however, liberalism—especially radical liberalism—depends on democracy. I have already suggested that radical liberalism cannot succeed without grassroots political power mobilized in support of equal freedom. Many of the landmark expansions of liberal freedom—from workers' rights to civil rights to marriage equality—came only after sustained periods of popular mobilization. It should be obvious that such mobilization draws strength from democracy, which gives people the right to vote, organize, and speak out without being repressed. Democracy, in other words, gives ordinary people powerful political tools with which to expand their freedoms or protect them from encroachment. Without these tools, their rights and freedoms remain exceptionally brittle.

Democracy and radical liberalism also rest on shared principles. Both insist that all members of society should be respected as free and equal persons, and that our laws and institutions should embody this commitment. From the viewpoint of radical liberalism, it is impossible to respect people in this way without giving them the right to govern themselves democratically. When we reduce people to voiceless political subjects with no say in shaping the policies and institutions that govern their lives, we treat them as children or wards, not as free persons. Any credible defense of radical liberalism must therefore be a defense of liberal democracy.

The rest of this book lays out a systematic argument for radical liberalism. I begin, in Chapter 1, with a detailed exploration of the idea of equal freedom. What does freedom actually mean? And what does it mean to assert that everyone has an equal claim to it? In Chapters 2 through 5, I consider the leading dangers that threaten freedom in the United States today—tyranny, economic exploitation, racial hierarchy, and ecological degradation—and outline some promising solutions and countermeasures. Finally, in Chapter 6 and the Conclusion, I ask what these solutions would demand of us, both collectively and individually. Here I return to the grassroots power that lies latent among democratic citizens, and I consider how it can be unleashed to deliver the change we need.

1

Equal Freedom

The term "freedom" is notoriously elastic: it can mean many different things. Some of this variety reflects the complexity of the underlying concept. Some of it reflects the fact that freedom is so widely valued. In liberal and illiberal societies alike, virtually all competing parties claim to be fighting for freedom, and they stretch its meaning to suit their political purposes.

Conceptual clarity can serve as one line of defense against such stretching. More specifically, it can help us resist the persistent efforts to make "freedom" serve the interests of the powerful. Dominant groups have often sought to resist change by seizing control of potent concepts that challenge the existing order of things. Freedom is no exception: in our day, it is routinely deployed by business elites to protect their wealth from taxation, shield their immensely powerful corporations from regulation, and preserve their nearly unlimited access to the levers of political power.[1] It is also invoked to excuse racial hierarchy, thwart sensible public health measures, and rationalize reckless ecological destruction. To recover the radical potentials latent in liberal ideals, we must begin by reclaiming this pivotal concept.

The Idea of Freedom

To be free means, in the broadest sense, to be able to do what you want. The idea of freedom thus conjures up a specific scenario: a person making a choice among a set of options. Imagine, for example, that you are deciding how to spend a sunny Saturday afternoon. You are weighing three alternatives: taking a walk with a friend, attending afternoon mass at the local Catholic church, or joining a political protest in front of city hall. Common sense suggests that you are free in this choice only if you actually have the power to choose among these alternatives.

This idea of *having the power to choose* is more complicated than it looks. First and most obviously, it connotes the *ability* to choose the option you prefer. This requires, among other things, that no one prevent you from choosing it. If you decide, upon reflection, that you want to join the protest, but you find that a government-backed mob has attacked and dispersed the protestors, you have been deprived of freedom. You can no longer choose the option you want because someone has foreclosed it.

Brute force is an obvious way of foreclosing an alternative, but of course there are others. Broadly speaking, alternatives can be foreclosed using two strategies: penalty and deception.[2] Sending a mob to beat up protestors is a way of penalizing them for choosing to protest. Imposing steep fines on protestors, or having their children expelled from school, is another. For many people, the mere threat of such punishments would be enough to foreclose the option of protesting. Deception is another way of foreclosing alternatives: if dissidents were systematically deceived—say, by government manipulation of their social media accounts—about the timing and location of their protest, their power to choose this option would likewise have been substantially reduced.

These examples reveal an important feature of freedom: it is a matter of degree. The harsher the penalties, or the more comprehensive the deception, the more freedom is lost. If you had been jailed as a political prisoner before the protest, for instance, your power to attend it would have been extinguished altogether. The risk of government-backed violence, though still severe, does not eliminate your power in the same way. Though it would require unusual bravery, you *could* still attend the protest, at the risk of serious injury. Fines would be still less burdensome, especially if you could afford to pay them. The same spectrum applies to deception: comprehensive manipulation or brainwashing can extinguish freedom altogether; milder forms of deception might simply diminish it.

So far, we have been considering the ways in which choices can be foreclosed by others. These examples reveal an important and intuitive dimension of freedom: to be free is to be protected from certain kinds of intrusion or interference. It is to enjoy the opportunity to make choices without being penalized or deceived by others. This is part of what it means to *have the power to choose*. But there are other requirements, too. Most importantly, we must possess sufficient resources to follow through on our choice. Even if no one is preventing us, we can lack the power to choose if we lack the resources necessary to think or act.

The resources needed to make choices fall into two broad categories, internal and external. Internal resources—which we might call *capacities*—are the qualities of body and mind necessary to carry out a choice. Imagine now that you have chosen to attend mass, but you are too sick to get out of bed. Or you are haunted by paranoid fears that leave you unable to leave the house. In these cases, you lack the power to choose your preferred alternative because you lack the capacity to carry it out. You are not free to make this choice.

Your power to choose also depends on external resources, which are the natural, social, and economic preconditions of effective action. Some of these are so fundamental that we take them for granted: without a ready supply of oxygen, for example, you will not go anywhere on Saturday afternoon. Others are more complicated and context-dependent. Imagine that the Catholic church lies fifteen miles away, on the other side of the city. To get there, you need access to safe and functional roads, which in modern society presupposes a broader infrastructure: electricity for traffic lights, a functional municipal government to oversee repairs and fund traffic police, and so forth. To travel these roads, moreover, you need access to transportation—which typically requires money. If you cannot afford even a bus ticket, your power to attend mass across town will be greatly reduced.

Some philosophers have rejected the idea that freedom means the power to choose. Anxious about its political implications, they have tried to define freedom more narrowly, as the absence of unwanted interference by other people in our lives. They have called this *negative freedom* or negative liberty.[3] This more limited definition triggers a number of peculiar implications. For one thing, it divorces the concept of freedom in puzzling ways from the experience of constraint. Imagine, for example, that on this particular Saturday afternoon you find yourself trapped in your bedroom closet. The door swung shut while you were inside and is now jammed—as hard as you try, you cannot open it. Your family is away on vacation and your phone is downstairs, so you are stuck there indefinitely. If the negative view of freedom is correct, then as you languish in your closet unable to do any of the things you want, you cannot be sure whether your freedom has been in any way affected. If some intruder shut you in, then your liberty has been taken away. But if the door swung shut because of a sudden gust of wind blowing through an open window, then you are just as free as ever. Any idea of freedom that turns out to be perfectly compatible with the experience of imprisonment should elicit a skeptical response.

To make things worse, the negative conception of freedom runs into an even more fundamental problem: it divorces freedom from responsibility. As a matter of common usage, describing someone as free to make a certain choice implies that they are *responsible* for it. They can be praised or blamed depending on how they handle the decision.[4] As long as you were free to attend mass on Saturday afternoon, for example, your priest might plausibly blame you for failing to attend. But if you were unable to attend—because you were too sick to get out of bed, for example, or because you accidentally got trapped in a closet—such blame would be out of place. To be "fit to be held responsible" for any choice, writes philosopher Philip Pettit, we must actually have the power to choose.[5] Unless we want to rupture the conceptual bond between freedom and responsibility, then, we should reject a strictly negative view of freedom.[6]

So far, I have argued that freedom means the power to choose, and that the power to choose means, first and foremost, the power to select our preferred alternative. But the idea of choice has other connotations too. One is the availability of other desirable options. Imagine now that you decide to take a Saturday afternoon walk with your friend and, unbeknownst to you, the other two alternatives are foreclosed: anti-Catholic rioters disrupt mass and scatter local congregants, and government breaks up the protest. These unwelcome developments clearly have a direct bearing on your freedom. If you had changed your mind and decided, on further reflection, that you should attend mass or protest, you would have been unable to do so.[7] You were, in this sense, less free than you thought you were.

To borrow Pettit's language again, we need a range of desirable options to render freedom *robust:* these options ensure that our freedom would persist even if we happened to choose differently. Here too, freedom is a matter of degree. As the number of desirable options grows, so too does our freedom. And the extent of its increase depends not just on the number but also on the desirability of these newly acquired options. Gaining access to a new and delicious brand of soft drink, for example, increases our freedom far less than gaining the right to speak freely.

Finally, another important measure of freedom's robustness is the reasonable expectation that it will persist through time.[8] When you choose to attend the protest on a Saturday afternoon, you generally do so with the expectation that a comparable range of options will be available to you on future Saturdays. You expect, for example, that the law will continue to protect citizens' ability to stage peaceful protests, as well as worshippers' right to assemble. You believe these options are guaranteed to you and that this guarantee is a matter of common knowledge in your society; or to put it another way, you feel *secure* in your access to these options. Things would feel very different if, for example, you had been granted an extraordinary, one-time permission by some powerful official to protest on this particular Saturday, with no guarantees beyond it.

To think about freedom's robustness is to shift our attention from free choices to free people. If the idea of freedom invites us, at first, to imagine an individual making a particular choice, the politics of freedom invites us to widen our focus and consider what it takes to make people free across a lifetime of choices. This is the central aim of any liberal politics. So far, I have suggested a very broad and abstract way of thinking about it: a free person is a person who enjoys robust freedom, which means (1) the power to choose (2) among a broad range of desirable options, with (3) security in these choices across time. We can simplify this further by saying that freedom is the power to choose from a broad range of secure and desirable options.

This idea of freedom lies at the heart of radical liberalism. In fact, the rest of this book advances a fairly straightforward line of argument: if we take this commonsense idea of freedom seriously and acknowledge that everyone has an equal claim to it, we are led to fairly radical political conclusions. We can begin to understand what a free society would actually look like and how far we are from being there. We can also gain a better idea of which reforms to prioritize. But before we begin to unfold these political implications, we must first answer several more questions about freedom itself. The first is: why should we care so much about freedom in the first place?

The Value of Freedom

Liberals have explained the value of freedom in many ways—far too many to elaborate here. Instead, I will focus on the close connections between freedom and well-being. Simply put, liberals believe that freedom plays a crucial role in enabling us to live well: it helps us live in ways we are likely to recognize as good or worthwhile. I will develop this claim both by focusing on the hardships that freedom overcomes and by highlighting some of the unique benefits it confers.

Over the past two centuries, liberals have often dramatized the value of freedom by dwelling on its antitheses. The liberal impulse in the West was born of the European wars of religion and a widening perception of the immense suffering and anguish brought not just by war and instability, but also by religious persecution and intolerance.[9] By the late seventeenth century, Europe had suffered through 150 years of nearly constant warfare, which had been touched off by the Protestant Reformation. All across the continent, Catholics and Protestants had killed, brutalized, and oppressed each other over diverging interpretations of Christianity. The earliest liberals tried to defuse these conflicts and mitigate their horrors by achieving some separation between civil and religious authority and by institutionalizing religious tolerance. They believed that people should be freer to worship as they pleased.

A similar awareness of the human costs of unfreedom animated many of the subsequent liberal reform movements: the struggle to abolish slavery, to replace feudal status hierarchies with civic equality, to achieve and codify women's rights and civil rights, to widen people's economic opportunities, and to curb authoritarian political power. The most eloquent liberal advocates in these struggles—from Frederick Douglass and Elizabeth Cady Stanton to B. R. Ambedkar and Václav Havel—have always borne witness to the suffering inflicted on those who are controlled, dominated, or dehumanized by others. The impulse to shield human beings from such suffering forms the moral core of the human rights tradition, which remains the quintessential expression of liberalism in international politics.

Liberals have typically understood freedom as an escape, first of all, from oppression. Oppression is the cruel or arbitrary use of power over others, which damages their basic interests.[10] Liberals have long believed that oppression is tragically ubiquitous, partly because those who hold power, whether in public or private life, are commonly tempted to use it to serve their own pride, greed, or glory at the expense of others. Liberal politics therefore begins, as political theorist Judith Shklar once put it, as "damage control": it aims to protect people from mistreatment at the hands of the powerful.[11] It does this by trying to secure their freedom. When people hold the power to make important life choices for themselves—and when they enjoy security in these choices across time—they are shielded from comprehensive control or abuse at the hands of others.

Oppression stands out as one of freedom's antitheses, but it is hardly the only one. Deprivation is another. Deprivation is not just a lack of basic resources, but also a lack of opportunity to procure them reliably. When people lack access to food, clean water, warmth and secure housing, basic medical care, and other essentials, they suffer a level of deprivation that, like oppression, destroys their ability to live well. When Franklin Roosevelt addressed a group of farmers in Topeka, Kansas, in the midst of the Great Depression, he spoke of the crippling effects of rural poverty: the constant fear that basic needs would go unmet, the blasted hopes of attaining a better life, the desperate feeling of futility when plummeting grain prices wiped out a year of hard work and drove farmers into foreclosure. In Roosevelt's eyes and in the eyes of many other liberals of his generation, these farmers were unfree. Harsh economic conditions had eroded their power to make choices and pursue their goals. They lived in the "shadow of peasantry," he said, and lacked the resources even to "make decent living possible."[12] So he laid out a set of ambitious public measures designed to restore their ability to exert meaningful control over their lives. He famously recognized *freedom from want* as an essential component of a free life.

Although Roosevelt's policy agenda remains controversial in the United States, his basic insight about freedom is not. Liberals on both the political left and right acknowledge that people are freer when they are economically secure. When they have a decent income and money saved, people enjoy a range of options that would otherwise be out of reach: they can pay their bills and keep a roof over their heads; they can choose where to send their kids to school and what neighborhood to live in; they can take time off work to be with family or go on vacation; and a great deal more. Needless to say, these options improve people's lives immeasurably. To be free, then—to have the power to choose from a broad range of secure and desirable options—is to escape both oppression and deprivation, two of the most ubiquitous and intractable sources of suffering in human history. This is no trivial matter.

Still, this first defense of freedom may strike some readers as underwhelming. Doesn't freedom offer us more than just relief from oppression and deprivation? The answer, of course, is yes. A second powerful explanation of freedom's value centers on the importance of human agency. Liberals have long believed that our life goes better when we take an active role in shaping and defining it. We might say that liberals believe that people are far more likely to flourish when they exert control over their own lives—when they make their own plans and carry them out. If freedom describes the power to make choices, agency describes the reflective use of this power.

An agent, then, is something more than just a maker of choices. After all, animals routinely make choices, but we seldom count them as agents. A person exercises agency when she acts after weighing her alternatives and considering the *reasons* she has for selecting them. As you ponder what to do on a Saturday afternoon, for example, you might be swayed by different kinds of reasons. You might think about how long it has been since you last saw your friend and consider the importance of maintaining this friendship. You might think of the social pressure you feel—from your priest and other parishioners— to attend mass, and the gratification you feel when you meet their expectations. You might also feel a moral or civic obligation to join the protest, considering the recent behavior of your city councilors. Some of these reasons might pertain not just to the choice at hand but also to the kind of person you want to be: you might, for example, want to be the kind of person who makes time for their friends. When you make choices in this reflective way, you exercise agency.[13] Another way of putting it is that an agent is someone who can be held responsible for her choices.

There are different ways of explaining why agency matters, but the most fundamental rests on the ideal of human dignity. In exercising agency, we use and develop a set of powers that form an essential aspect of our humanity. We use our powers of reasoning, imagination, and judgment. We cultivate self-awareness as beings capable of giving deliberate shape to our lives. We also cultivate our capacity for moral reflection: we learn to think not only of what we want to do, but also what we ought to do. To imagine a person stripped of these capacities—or a person so thoroughly controlled by others that she rarely has occasion to exercise them—is to imagine someone who has been dehumanized, whose dignity has been deeply affronted.[14]

This idea of dehumanization brings to mind a minimal threshold of agency. It suggests that people must be shielded, above all, from the intrusive forms of interference that render decision-making all but impossible: from brutality or comprehensive control, for example. Liberal politics, of course, should always prioritize these most fundamental protections. But the liberal idea of agency is more expansive. Most liberals believe that human dignity is fully expressed when we make important life choices—about how to express ourselves, or what kinds of intimate relationships to pursue, or what kind of work to undertake. For example, when a gay man is forced to conceal his sexual identity and assimilate to the norms and expectations of the dominant heterosexual culture, his dignity is affronted. He is denied the opportunity to shape his own life in an area of profound significance to him. By contrast, those who are free to express their sexual identities without discrimination are protected from such affronts. In allowing people to pursue diverse ideas of the good life, freedom gives them broad scope to exercise agency and, in doing so, respects their dignity.

Both of these justifications of freedom rest on broad insights into the human condition. The first, as we have seen, is simply that human beings are vulnerable: we suffer when we are oppressed or deprived of essential resources. One of the key aims of liberal politics is to build shields around these vulnerabilities so that people can exert more control over their lives. The second insight concerns human diversity: in modern societies, people's values and goals vary widely. Individuals find satisfaction and meaning in different ways, and circumstances that are invigorating to some may be stultifying to others. Any effort to impose a single way of life or single system of belief is therefore likely to prove immensely destructive to human well-being. Coerced uniformity frustrates or destroys a great many people's projects, values, or identities. This insight clarifies the relationship between living freely and living well: the only way to protect people from such hardship is to give them broad latitude to shape their own lives.

Third and relatedly, liberal philosophers have often observed a deep human propensity for conflict. Although they place great hope in our capacity for sociability, empathy, and rationality, they see humans as imperfect creatures prone to selfishness and self-aggrandizement. They also recognize our tribal proclivities: we commonly find meaning by identifying intensely with in-groups—nations, ethnic or cultural groups, political parties, races, or castes—and mistrusting or vilifying outsiders. The conflicts that arise from these aspects of the human psyche give people motive to oppress others, deprive them of resources, and suppress their agency. These tendencies lend urgency to the liberal political project. They suggest that freedom is unlikely to flourish on its own, without robust institutional safeguards designed to soften the effects of human strife.

Basic Interests

Liberals have always believed that some options are more central to human well-being than others. Some—such as freedom of expression or freedom from arbitrary arrest and seizure—are so central that losing them is equivalent to suffering an acute injury. This idea of centrality reflects a distinctive view of human nature: liberals, whatever their disagreements, have tended to agree on a certain basic idea of what human beings need, at a minimum, to have a good chance of living well. To put it slightly differently, liberals believe that human beings share certain basic interests, no matter their particular projects or values. These basic interests are closely linked, in turn, to the two justifications of freedom outlined in the previous section. They describe areas of life in which deprivations of freedom are likely to bring suffering or affront personal dignity.

There are different ways of sketching a liberal account of basic human interests. What follows is not a definitive list, but it captures the essentials in five distinct categories:

—*Bodily integrity.* People must be secure, first of all, against assault and arbitrary detention or imprisonment. They must enjoy freedom of movement through space. Bodily integrity encompasses the right to choose what to ingest, the right to refuse medical treatment, and the right to control one's own sexuality. It also includes access to a reasonably clean environment: people who cannot escape toxic air or groundwater pollution, for example, are in effect forced to ingest toxins. The basic human interest in bodily integrity requires, in all of these ways and others, that the body be secured against unwanted manipulation and intrusion.

—*Thought and expression.* People must be free to think for themselves—to be free, in this sense, from indoctrination and thoroughgoing manipulation. They must also be free to express themselves without censorship or fear of punishment. Freedom of thought includes unhampered access to information, and it therefore requires, for example, a free press to disseminate such information, as well as the freedom to hold and express religious beliefs that others consider heretical or offensive.

—*Affiliation.* People must enjoy the freedom to join together with others for shared purposes, both public and private. This includes the freedom to form intimate relationships and families, including the right to marry and raise children. It also encompasses the freedom to create, belong to, and have access to formal and informal groups such as civic organizations, economic associations, religious groups, and clubs devoted to any number of private activities. This freedom, in turn, presupposes a measure of social status, so that people can appear in public without shame and not be subject to pervasive discrimination or contempt. Affiliation also requires that people enjoy the freedom to gather and associate in the many ways necessary for shared governance. The political community is itself a form of human association whose functioning is profoundly important to its members. Most fundamentally, affiliation rests on the insight that human beings are deeply social creatures who seldom thrive without a whole range of social and intimate relationships.

—*Work.* Work encompasses productive activity of all kinds. Freedom in this area means that people should be able, within reasonable constraints, to choose what kinds of work to engage in. It requires free access to different professions as well as freedom from discrimination and harassment in the workplace. More broadly, it requires meaningful economic opportunities.

—*Leisure.* People must be free to use their leisure time as they see fit. This includes pursuing diverse projects for personal enrichment or enjoyment, as well as creating and maintaining private spaces in which to relax and feel at home. Freedom in this area requires, moreover, that people have meaningful leisure time in the first place. If they have to spend virtually all of their waking hours working just to meet their basic needs, then this requirement is unmet.

I argued earlier that freedom requires access to a broad range of secure and desirable options. These five categories specify the idea of *breadth:* to count as suitably broad, the range of options must—at least—encompass all five of these categories and do so comprehensively. It is not enough, for example, to offer some elements from each category but not others (freedom from arbitrary arrest, say, but not freedom of movement). Radical liberalism should therefore aim to protect and facilitate freedom in each of these areas. More specifically, it should ensure, as much as possible, that people possess the power to choose among secure and desirable options as pertains to their basic interests.

This is a complicated task: each of these five categories is very broad, and liberals have disagreed about how to interpret them. The freedoms listed in each category also come into conflict with one another. My freedom to express myself as I please may conflict with your freedom to move through the world safely. My freedom to associate with others as I please may conflict with your freedom from discrimination. These conflicts typically require difficult balancing and compromise, and one of the aims of liberal theory is to explain how they should be negotiated. I will have plenty to say about this in later chapters.

Put together, these basic interests sketch the outlines of what philosophers sometimes call a *thin* theory of human flourishing. It is a theory of human flourishing because it describes the conditions under which human beings—in light of their particular capacities and needs—tend to thrive, to live well. It is thin because it is falls far short of a comprehensive vision of the good life. In fact, it is compatible with a wide range of ideas about what a good life looks like. This thinness arises directly from the liberal acknowledgment of human diversity: because people have different values, goals, and identities, no single ideal of the good life will suit everyone. The basic interests, then, describe the essential conditions that enable (most) people to pursue their own ideas of the good life, even as they live and work side by side and share social spaces and political institutions.[15]

There are limits, however, to the liberal appreciation for human diversity—and these limits, too, are essential to understanding the nature of radical liberalism. The first and most important limit arises from the norm of human equality. Radical liberalism holds that every individual human being possesses basic interests, and everyone has an equal claim to their protection and defense. Everyone has an equal claim, in other words, to freedom. This simple yet radical proposition rules out the vast majority of social arrangements that have structured human life since the Neolithic revolution, some twelve thousand years ago. It specifically forbids any way of life premised on the subordination of one group to another: of women to men, of the poor to the rich, of the low-born to the high-born, of one racial or ethnic or religious group to another. It also forbids individuals from making choices that injure others or endanger their basic interests, and thus rules out any heroic or aristocratic ethos that celebrates expansive personal freedom for the few at the expense of the many. Although this egalitarian norm will surely strike most readers today as simple and intuitive, it has never yet been fully realized in any human society.

The second key limit arises from the liberal emphasis on individual agency. For most of human history, people were regarded as creatures fit for submission and obedience, not expansive agency. If they were recognized as possessing moral worth, this worth was thought to derive from their membership in certain ethnic or cultural groups, from their playing certain social roles, or from their fealty to certain gods. Many of these attributions of moral worth were—and still are—perfectly compatible with compulsory patterns of social and political subordination. American men in the nineteenth century, for example, commonly argued that although women possessed equal moral worth, they lacked the capacity to live self-directed lives and should therefore be sheltered and controlled by their fathers and husbands. Any defensible version of liberalism rejects these hierarchical value systems and insists that we cannot respect others as equals without respecting them as *agents* who are entitled to direct their own lives. Radical liberals value and acknowledge human diversity, then, within the two constraints of equality and agency.

Liberal Rights

How does radical liberalism propose to protect people's basic interests? I explained earlier that liberals tend to deploy characteristic strategies, including checks and balances, constitutional guarantees, democratic accountability, independent judiciaries, economic markets, social welfare entitlements, and publicly funded educational systems. One of the leading liberal strategies is the codification of individual rights and the development of an institutional architecture for enforcing them.

We have already seen that robust freedom entails access to *secure* options—meaning options that persist through time and whose persistence is a matter of common knowledge and expectation. Rights speak to this dimension of freedom. They are not just entitlements to which people can lay claim *for now,* but entitlements that they can expect to persist into the future. Rights can and do change, of course, but they are understood to possess greater stability than ordinary law. In this sense, too, they fit well with the idea of freedom I am defending here.

Rights are also directly related to the basic interests outlined earlier: rights are best understood as entitlements designed to grant people the power to make choices in these critical areas of life. In this sense, the *content* of our rights is derived from our basic interests. The right of habeas corpus and the right to a fair and speedy trial, for example, derive straightforwardly from the interest in bodily integrity: because people share this basic interest, they are entitled not to be imprisoned and held without legitimate cause or recourse. The rights of free speech and free exercise of religion, along with the rights of the press, meanwhile, correspond straightforwardly to the basic interests of thought and expression.[16]

Other rights pertain to many or all of our basic interests. Liberals have long asserted, for example, the importance of private property rights. These rights pertain to work: they reflect the widely held conviction that people are entitled to the fruits of their own labor. But property rights also reflect an ideal of privacy that derives from both bodily integrity and thought and expression: ownership (of a house or a car, for example) grants people a measure of control over their immediate environment, which helps shield them from unwanted interference. Property rights also pertain to leisure, because many leisure activities in modern society are facilitated by the ownership of certain goods (such as a keyboard and amplifier, a PlayStation, or camping equipment). Of course, there is a flipside to this story: for those who do not own property and cannot afford it, private property rights seem like a catalog of exclusions.[17] When these exclusions affect people's basic interests, they can produce serious deprivation and loss of freedom: as the cost of housing rises, for example, more people find themselves unable to access it reliably, with dire consequences. I will have more to say about the proper scope and content of property rights later in the book; for now I simply want to note their complex relationship to several categories of freedom.

Rights are sometimes imagined in strictly negative terms, as immunities or protections against interference by others. But radical liberals reject this view. As we have seen, the power to make choices requires resources, both internal and external—and many rights reflect this reality by guaranteeing access to essential resources. The right to education at public expense, for example—which all liberal democracies recognize today—is designed to help cultivate the capacities people need to exercise agency. Welfare rights grant people access to some of the external resources without which it is nearly impossible to live freely. These "positive" rights have long been recognized in human rights discourse: we find them reflected, for example, in the 1948 Universal Declaration of Human Rights, which includes rights to food and shelter, medical care, education, and "social security" among other preconditions of human freedom. Such rights have an important place in the theory of radical liberalism.

Like the liberal approach to freedom itself, the liberal approach to rights should be empirically grounded. Radical liberals should ask which rights are needed, in any given time and place, to enable people to live freely. More precisely, they should ask which rights are necessary to empower people to make choices—and to enjoy access to secure and desirable options—as concerns their basic interests. The answer is subject to change. In a pre-modern agricultural society, for instance, the need for formal education was far less pressing. It was possible to enjoy the full range of freedoms associated with work, leisure, and affiliation without it. This is no longer true in the twenty-first century. Or consider a different example: the right to privacy takes on new meanings (and new legal requirements) in a world increasingly defined by large-scale data mining and invasive surveillance technologies. Part of the liberal project in the twenty-first century, then, is to uncover the obstacles that prevent people from achieving freedom in our particular time and place and to develop strategies for overcoming them. It is a project that needs continual updating: in this sense, liberalism is a dynamic and evolving political tradition.

Liberal Equality

Radical liberalism rests on the conviction that everyone counts as a moral equal, and more specifically that everyone has basic interests and an equal claim to their protection. It insists, in other words, that all individuals have equal *standing* in the political community. What exactly does this claim imply for the shape of liberal politics?

There are many ways to treat people as equals. They can be accorded equal rights, equal resources, equal social status, equal opportunities. The liberal theory I have outlined suggests that we should equalize *freedom* in particular. What this means, more specifically, is that the liberal society must "treat its citizens as equals in their claim to freedom."[18] This has three implications: people must enjoy equal recognition; they must have access to sufficient resources; and they must be shielded from domination. Radical liberalism aims to achieve these goals while also maintaining high levels of freedom for everyone.

Recognition. First, treating people as equal claimants to freedom means *recognizing* them as equals—and this means treating them, as political theorist Nancy Fraser puts it, as "full partners in social interaction."[19] Recognition has certain obvious formal components: citizens must enjoy equal protection under the law, for example, and equal rights. They must not face discrimination in their access to public goods or spaces. Their society's public institutions must acknowledge them as equals and treat them as such.

Yet the need for equal recognition extends beyond public institutions. People have a fundamental interest, for example, in being shielded from discrimination—in the workplace, in churches, in commercial spaces, and in civil society more broadly. Experience tells us that people can be subject to contempt and humiliation even if the letter of the law is egalitarian. In the aftermath of 9/11, for example, many American Muslims experienced pervasive bullying and harassment. Their children were shunned and belittled by their schoolmates; they endured vitriolic epithets when they were out in public; the walls of their apartment buildings were defaced by expressions of religious hatred; their colleagues began avoiding them or treating them with suspicion. Their lives changed profoundly as a result: many no longer felt free to live their lives or to express themselves as they had before.[20]

The idea of recognition is best captured in the commonsense notion that liberal society should not create—or tolerate the creation of—second-class citizens. No one should be subject to discrimination or pervasive contempt, or endure structural barriers that diminish their range of options, because of who they are or what they believe. Such hierarchies are plainly incompatible with the ideal of equal freedom. As always, liberals make exceptions for people whose identity or belief systems are premised on cruelty to others or the denial of human equality. White supremacists, for example, are not entitled to the full measure of recognition owed to other citizens. Liberal societies must accord such people equal treatment under the law, to be sure, but other, informal kinds of recognition can justifiably be withheld.

Access to Resources. Although recognition is vitally important, it is far from sufficient to guarantee equal freedom. To see why, we need only consider that equal recognition is compatible with crushing deprivation and lack of opportunity. A society marked by extreme economic inequality, widespread poverty, low levels of economic mobility, and anemic investment in public goods could still extend equal recognition to all. It could maintain equal treatment under the law and robust anti-discrimination measures, and its culture could be inclusive of different identity groups. Yet many people would languish in desperate poverty and lack the tools to escape.

We have already seen that freedom presupposes access to resources. In this context, equal freedom is best understood as both a threshold concept and an opportunity concept: it suggests that people must enjoy *sufficient* resources to attain a certain threshold of personal freedom, and also meaningful opportunities to accumulate more beyond that threshold. Where exactly the threshold lies will be a matter of continuing debate in liberal societies. But as we will explore later, millions of Americans fall well short of any plausible specification of it. There is no way to credibly maintain that the US economy today affords everyone an equal claim to freedom.

As we consider these questions, the widely embraced idea of equal opportunity can help guide us.[21] Equal opportunity may sound like a modest objective, but it offers a searing indictment of the American status quo and an argument for ambitious egalitarian reform. We now have ample evidence to suggest that equalizing opportunity in twenty-first century economies calls for robust investment in public goods.[22] To give poor children an opportunity to compete on fair terms with their affluent peers, for example, we need a level of investment that is manifestly absent in America today: well-funded schools, childcare and pre-K for working families, universal healthcare, affordable colleges and vocational schools, secure and affordable housing, and more.[23] As I will explore in Chapter 4, equal opportunity also requires aggressive measures to deconstruct racial hierarchies. Meanwhile, opening up meaningful opportunities for adults who have fallen on hard times—or whose job skills have been rendered obsolete by economic and technological change—requires a separate slate of investments, including a resource "floor" beneath which no one should be allowed to fall. Without such investments, people commonly find themselves deprived of the options they need to live freely.

These examples reveal another significant implication of equal freedom: equalizing opportunities often means granting different amounts of public resources to different people, depending on their needs. Schools that serve higher proportions of low-income children, for example, need more funding, smaller classes, and better counseling resources to enable these students to compete on fair terms with their more affluent peers. People with physical disabilities need extra accommodations and infrastructure to achieve the relevant threshold of freedom. So do people living in rural areas: extending infrastructure, postal services, and medical services to them, for example, is considerably more expensive (per capita) than delivering these services to city-dwellers. These differences are clearly required by the ideal of equal freedom: equal freedom does not mean equal *levels* of public investment, nor does it mean that everyone should have access to identical "bundles" of resources.

Protection from domination. Domination is about the distribution of power in society: a person *dominates* others when she holds so much power that she can damage their basic interests with relative impunity. We have already seen that the threat of political domination has preoccupied liberals for over two centuries. Many of the core liberal strategies are designed to prevent it.

Democracy itself is one of these strategies. Viewed from the liberal point of view, democracy is both a way of extending full recognition to all members of the political community and a strategy for neutralizing domination by dispersing power. It expresses the radical idea that everyone is entitled to an equal voice in collective decision-making, and furthermore that political leadership—and the power that comes with it—is no more than a conditional grant that the people can revoke at any time. Liberals have long believed that the freedoms of ordinary people are most secure under democratic institutions, where they have the power to stand up for themselves. By the same token, liberals have insisted on constitutional constraints to prevent democratic majorities from dominating and subordinating minority groups in society.

If taken seriously, the idea that power needs dispersing has fairly radical implications. It casts deep suspicion, for example, on huge inequalities of wealth. The logic here is obvious: tremendous accumulations of private wealth tend to create sharp imbalances of power, which in turn endanger freedom. It is well understood, for example, that big corporations in the United States (and their immensely wealthy owners and executives) have often achieved the power to write or rewrite the law, and to insulate themselves from legal challenge even when they behave egregiously—when they dump toxins into people's air and water, sell them exploitative loans, or lure them into drug addiction. In doing so, they have gained the power to shatter ordinary people's freedoms with relative impunity.

The disproportionate power of wealthy elites also extends, in obvious ways, to the workplace. Tens of millions of workers in the United States currently negotiate their employment contracts from a position of profound vulnerability: they are economically insecure and desperate; they lack access to the basic goods and services—including affordable housing and medical care—that they need to avoid severe hardship; and they lack the skills and training (and the organization) necessary to achieve even modest bargaining power with their employers. This vulnerability has given rise, predictably, to widespread economic exploitation. Workers are paid less than they need to cover necessities; they are subject to invasive surveillance and control while working; their schedules are subject to the whims of company algorithms; their legal protections are vitiated by arbitration clauses—and they have little recourse against such mistreatment. This pattern of domination undermines their freedom. The idea that freedom depends on an equitable distribution of power, both political and economic, will be an important theme throughout this book.

Many of our strategies for promoting greater social, political, and economic equality will reduce some people's freedom even as they expand it for others. If we impose substantial new taxes on wealth and inheritance to fund universal healthcare, for example, affluent people will have less money, and so a narrower range of options. I have already noted that in liberal societies, such tradeoffs are routine across a broad range of policy questions. Should we protect the freedom to own and carry guns, or the freedom to move through public spaces without fear of being shot? Should we protect people's freedom to refuse vaccination, or others' freedom to go to school without being exposed to serious, preventable diseases? In many of these controversies, there is no way to expand the range of options enjoyed by some people without contracting it for others. Any political theory that places freedom at its center must have something to say about these tradeoffs.

While I offer no precise formula for adjudicating these conflicts, the ideal of equal freedom defended here suggests two broad principles. First, the freedoms that lie closest to our basic interests deserve the highest priority, and those that lie furthest from our basic interests deserve lowest priority. Second, until we reach the three levels of equality spelled out earlier (recognition, access to resources, and protection from domination), we should prioritize policies that expand freedom for those who have the least of it. Often these principles will point in the same direction: taxing the wealthy to expand access to healthcare for everyone is justified both because healthcare protects very fundamental human interests and because it would expand freedom for those who have less than others.[24]

Together, these principles point toward a much more egalitarian society than ours—one without second-class citizens or durable status hierarchies, where everyone enjoys meaningful equality of opportunity. These principles also require that we eliminate, as best we can, relationships of domination and treat all concentrations of power—especially unaccountable power—with suspicion. And yet a society guided by these norms would still allow considerable inequalities: specifically, inequalities of wealth and esteem. Moreover, because both wealth and esteem enhance one's power to make choices, unequal distributions of both of these goods would yield unequal freedom. Why, then, should we not press for a more complete, more literal equalization of freedom?

From the liberal perspective, the answer lies in the meaning and implications of freedom itself. Any society that values individual freedom will, for this reason alone, give rise to social and economic inequalities. Many inequalities arise from the choices people make. Even if we imagine a world in which everyone started out with perfectly equal economic opportunities (the same amount of money, identical educations, good health, equal natural abilities, equal respect), inequalities would soon arise. Some people would choose, for example, to work longer hours or to pursue the highest possible salaries; others would pursue less materialistic priorities. Some people would save money while others would spend it freely. Over time, these diverging choices would create disparities in the distribution of wealth. Moreover, even among those who pursued the same paths, some would attract praise and recognition for their accomplishments and so begin to command higher incomes. Here too, inequality arises partly from choice: employers (or audiences, or clients) would be willing to pay more for their services.

To prevent such inequalities, many people's freedom would have to be severely curtailed. People with a penchant for saving money, for example, would have to be prevented from doing so. People with expensive tastes or a desire to work longer hours would have to be forbidden from acting on these preferences. Or private property itself would have to be heavily restricted, if not mostly eliminated. Some may value equality so highly that they are willing to bear these costs (and impose them on others). But liberals are not. Choices about how much to work and how to spend or save one's income are fundamental components of personal freedom that implicate virtually all of the basic interests listed above. From the liberal point of view, severely inhibiting these choices is akin to imposing a single religion on a diverse population: it fails to respect them as free people. Moreover, the pursuit of anything close to perfect equality requires intrusive public surveillance and oversight of private economic choices, which demand tremendous concentrations of power.[25] This too cuts against fundamental liberal priorities.

None of this should be read, however, as a defense of American levels of inequality or libertarian antipathy toward government. The previous two paragraphs are wholly compatible with a *far* more egalitarian society than our own. In 2017, CEOs of the 350 largest American firms made 278 times the salary of their average employees, a dramatic increase from the twenty-to-one disparity that existed in 1965. Such differences are morally grotesque and flatly incompatible with the pursuit of equal freedom. In fact, the logic of the previous two paragraphs could be fully upheld in a society that shrank the 1965 ratio even more. A fifteen-to-one ratio, for example, describes the disparity between an entry-level worker earning $40,000 a year and a CEO making $600,000—a massive difference, which would give the CEO a vastly different lifestyle and range of options. In such a society, people could still enjoy broad freedom to shape their economic lives in keeping with their values and priorities. When Americans are polled about the ideal pay gap between CEOs and employees, their answer is around seven-to-one.[26]

According to the dominant discourse of freedom in America today, a free society is one where we are left alone—where no one is telling us what to do or interfering in our lives. Such a society makes few demands of us: it asks mainly that we refrain from harming one another as we pursue our own private goals. I believe that this anemic ideal is deeply unappealing. People who are left alone can still lack the power to make choices. They can be poor and desperate; they can lack economic opportunity; they can lack education and skills; they can have so little social status that they are ashamed to appear in public; they can lack political voice; they can be living on the streets. In all these ways, they can lack the power to shape their own lives. If this is what freedom means, it should not rank highly among our political values. But if freedom means the power to choose from a broad range of secure and desirable options, and if we acknowledge that everyone has equal claim to such power, then the ideal of freedom can point toward a society that is more just, egalitarian, and humane. It can help us see the many ways in which our own society remains unfree and push us to seek deep reform. It can provide the foundation for a politics that is both liberal and radical.

Some critics might accept this expansive definition of freedom but deny that we have an obligation to provide it for others. They might deny, in particular, that we have an obligation, as a society, to provide one another with the resources and opportunities we all need to live freely. From this point of view, asking wealthier citizens to pay higher taxes so that others can enjoy universal healthcare, subsidized childcare, or good schools, is asking too much. It fails to respect our right to independence and to use our wealth and property as we please. I will address this objection in several ways later, but its most important flaw is simply that it fails to treat people as moral equals. Human societies are systems of cooperation that bring us into dense networks of mutual dependence. Their structure is, in large part, a matter of deliberate choice and design.[27] We cannot affirm that *all* members of society possess equal moral worth—that their hopes, their projects, their health and well-being are equally important—and then, in the same breath, defend social structures that consign millions to deprivation, domination, or second-class citizenship. To do so—especially in the most affluent society in the history of the human race—is to misunderstand the meaning and implications of moral equality.

It is worth reiterating, finally, that radical liberalism is not just a theory of government; it is a theory of human society. To say that equal freedom is the highest liberal objective is not to say that government—still less the federal government—is wholly responsible for delivering it. As far as we know, no free nation can exist in the modern world without a vibrant civil society, a thriving market economy, and citizens willing to accept and reinforce certain norms and to make sacrifices, large and small, to create the conditions under which freedom can flourish. Equal recognition, for example, cannot be achieved by government alone. Good policies, implemented at the federal, state, and local levels, are essential ingredients in this mix, but hardly the only ones.

This point suggests an obvious line of response to those conservative critics who have lately equated liberalism with limitless individual autonomy. Any version of liberalism genuinely committed to equal freedom requires certain forms of civic character: it requires empathy, generosity, and self-restraint. The best liberal societies ask their citizens not just to tolerate each other, not just to refrain from harming each other, but also to live and work together, share public spaces, jointly manage public institutions, and solve problems together. They demand that citizens learn to treat each other with dignity and respect—which in a diverse modern society is no small task. Nor is this just a theoretical commitment: anyone who has spent time around our elementary schools and playgrounds, sports leagues and union meetings, or community organizations and college campuses has met many people working tirelessly to teach and encourage these norms and to shape people's character in the ways that liberalism demands. Powerful forces are currently eroding the bonds of mutual trust and respect that bind liberal societies together, and there is much to be done to fight back. But those who deny that liberal societies have any response to these forces—or who pretend that the only active response emanates from our churches or from Christian morality—are guilty, at best, of willful blindness. In fact, liberal culture nurtures a potent set of moral values that point us toward cooperation, fairness, and mutual respect.[28]

2

Tyranny

Liberalism was born out of a centuries-long struggle against tyranny. When liberal ideas were first deployed in the seventeenth century to defend religious toleration, they were framed as bulwarks against tyrants, both political and ecclesiastical. Early liberals argued that people could not be free if they lived under governments (or churches) that claimed nearly unlimited power to impose religious orthodoxies and persecute dissenters. The idea that church and state should be separate, and that individuals possessed the right to worship, speak, and think as they pleased, were understood as shields against such power. Since then, liberals have come to see a wide range of institutions, including a government with checks and balances, an independent judiciary, and a free media, in a similar light.

Today, as despotic regimes consolidate their power throughout the world and authoritarian impulses are unleashed in our own society, these institutions are as important as ever. One of the great advantages of radical liberalism, compared to other radical traditions, is its principled commitment to preserving this inheritance. Radical liberals worry that concentrated power will be abused—no matter who wields it—and believe it needs to be carefully constrained and held accountable. They extend this concern to a wide range of actors: not just autocratic presidents, but also police forces, bureaucratic agencies, and powerful corporations. They understand that vulnerable minorities often have the most to lose when power slips its constraints.

If we want to achieve equal freedom in the twenty-first century, we have to come to grips with the main obstacles that stand in its way. Tyranny, in its many ramifying forms, is a good place to start.

Political Tyranny and the Assault on Liberal Institutions

Shortly after launching its invasion of Ukraine in February of 2022, the Russian government announced a wide-ranging campaign of repression against anyone who opposed the war or spread "false information" about it. Peaceful anti-war protesters were swept up by the police and arrested. A priest who spoke to a small group of congregants about the suffering of Ukrainians was taken into custody and fined. The owner of a computer repair shop was detained for displaying a link that read "No to War" on one of the store's computer screens. A former police officer whose father lived in Ukraine was arrested for expressing anti-war sentiments during a private phone conversation in his home.[1]

These people, and scores of others detained for similar offenses, stood in serious jeopardy. In March of 2022 the Russian parliament rubber-stamped a new law imposing a fifteen-year prison sentence on anyone found to have spread "fake news" about the war or criticized the Russian military. To control the media narrative about its floundering war effort, the government blocked access to internet sites that contradicted official propaganda, stepped up its surveillance of social media, and shuttered the country's few remaining independent media outlets. Police in Moscow began detaining passersby at random in popular commercial districts and demanding access to their text messages to screen them for "deviant" opinions.[2]

Such measures were not new to Russian citizens. Well before the invasion of Ukraine, the Russian government maintained a wide range of oppressive practices. Vague laws prohibiting extremism allowed public officials to crack down on any speech and association they found threatening or disruptive. In 2017, for example, Jehovah's Witnesses were declared an extremist organization, and according to Freedom House, their members were subjected to "a protracted campaign . . . marked by surveillance, property seizures, arrests, and torture."[3] The government also sanctioned—and still sanctions—pervasive discrimination against immigrants, many ethnic minorities, and LGBTQ people, and maintained tight control of any organizations involved in political or legal advocacy. Property is subject to arbitrary seizure, and businesses to arbitrary closure, to advance the interests of oligarchs connected to the state. And since the Russian judiciary is essentially an extension of the executive, citizens targeted by government and its allies have little hope of a fair hearing.[4]

Like billions of others today, Russians are subject to tyranny. Tyranny is what happens when oppressive power is institutionalized. We saw in Chapter 1 that oppression means the cruel or arbitrary exercise of power over others, which damages their basic interests. Under a tyrannical regime, the institutions of government are structured to facilitate and perpetuate such damage. Power is highly concentrated, and those who wield it use government—its bureaucracy, police, judiciary, and other institutions—in ways that consistently assail the interests of those over whom they rule.[5] Those afflicted by such power typically have little recourse. They stand at its mercy and can only hope that it will not crush them.

Tyranny often thrives in highly authoritarian regimes, where rulers are not subject to meaningful democratic oversight. In Russia, these rulers include not just Vladimir Putin himself but also an exclusive group of oligarchs who control whole swaths of the economy and rule the country like a mafia. Elections are a carefully orchestrated spectacle designed to buttress the legitimacy of Putin's political party, United

Russia, which does his bidding.[6] But tyranny can exist elsewhere too, in regimes that fall closer to the democratic end of the political spectrum. In the American South under Jim Crow, for example, white majorities enjoyed considerable political freedom and elections were often genuinely competitive.[7] But these southern states were deeply tyrannical regimes, in which Black citizens found their rights routinely denied and violated, their opportunities arbitrarily foreclosed, their access to public goods and spaces denied. Oppressive power was institutionalized in a system of caste hierarchy held in place by police, judges, legislators, businesses, and vigilante groups.

One of the most troubling political trends of the twenty-first century is the reemergence of tyranny through democratic channels. In Hungary, Poland, Venezuela, Turkey, India, the Philippines, and elsewhere, democratically elected leaders claiming a popular mandate have sharply curtailed their citizens' freedoms. In Turkey, for example, the Justice and Development Party (AKP) came to power in 2002 through elections that were widely considered free and fair. Since then, its populist leader, President Recep Tayyip Erdoğan, has gradually tightened his hold on power, consolidating control over the country's judiciary, media, and universities, harassing and detaining political rivals, purging or arresting thousands of civil servants who were not strictly loyal to him, and amending Turkey's constitution to further concentrate power in his own hands.

The AKP has used this power aggressively to undermine Turkish citizens' personal freedom. The government closely monitors millions of social media accounts and arrests critics at will. A wide range of groups—including not just political dissidents and opposition parties but also women's rights organizations and labor unions—are prevented from meeting, their leaders subject to police intimidation and sham trials. The judiciary is almost entirely controlled by the AKP, so Turks who run afoul of the ruling party have little recourse. Defendants are commonly held without trial for years and are subject to torture. Defense attorneys who dare to represent those accused of political crimes are sometimes arrested and detained.[8]

In Turkey and many other places, authoritarian leaders are eroding personal freedom by systematically dismantling liberal institutions. This should come as no surprise, because liberalism is the only political tradition that has reliably vanquished tyranny in the modern world. Find a place today where citizens are (largely) protected from tyrannical power, and you will find a liberal regime. Liberalism's strategies for taming tyranny are well known and widely emulated: they include the rule of law, the separation of powers, an effective slate of individual rights, a free and diverse media, democratic accountability for public officials, and an open civil society. It makes sense, therefore, that authoritarian populists such as Erdoğan would want to destroy these institutions. If we examine the political playbook used by these new authoritarians, we can isolate some of the particular ways that liberal institutions—when they are working well—protect people from tyranny.

Authoritarian populists first take aim at the checks and balances that disperse power among different branches of government. In recent decades, they have typically come to power through the executive branch, then worked tirelessly to discredit and undermine legislatures and judiciaries when these stood in their way. Independent judges have been dismissed or arrested and replaced with party hacks. Constitutional courts have been packed or disbanded. Legislatures have found their power gradually reduced and their authority bypassed on matters of vital interest to the emerging tyrant. Authoritarian leaders have also manipulated the electoral process to ensure that opposition parties are consigned to permanent minority status, gutting their ability to mount any meaningful resistance.[9]

Tyrants resent checks and balances because they enable judges, legislators, and other public officials to resist authoritarian power. These officials can delay or frustrate the tyrants' agendas, exercise formal oversight over them, and hold them accountable for abuses of office. Checks and balances are therefore essential in protecting equal freedom. They are especially crucial for anyone who incurs the ire of authoritarian leaders and their allies, including not only political activists and social reformers, but also private citizens overheard expressing the wrong opinions. They are essential, too, for minority groups whose identities stand at odds with the ruling party's idealized vision of the nation. Under successful liberal regimes, such people enjoy robust legal protections: they are protected by law and by a slate of individual rights, and when these are threatened, they enjoy due process, which gives them access to independent judges who have the power to punish their abusers. In liberal societies, these dissenters can also petition elected officials from opposition parties who, if they control other branches of government, can use their countervailing power to expose abuses and punish wrongdoers.

In liberal governments, checks also exist within the executive branch itself. This is one of the key roles of modern bureaucracy: to ensure that executive power remains lawful and that state benefits are distributed through impartial public procedures. Well-functioning bureaucracies are staffed by professionals who are hired and promoted on the basis of merit and ability, not their fealty to the ruling party. In countries with poorly institutionalized bureaucracies, state benefits—including access to healthcare, infrastructure, and police protection—are often doled out to political allies, to preferred ethnic or religious groups, or to "clients" in exchange for bribes. Such arrangements are obviously incompatible with equal freedom: they not only produce arbitrary and uneven distributions of public benefits, but also give governments tremendous discretionary leverage over their citizens. Authoritarian populists covet this power, and to get it they often purge bureaucracies of career civil servants and replace them with party hacks loyal to their leader.

Well-run bureaucracies and independent judiciaries are also critical for maintaining the rule of law, which imposes a host of meaningful constraints on those who hold power. The rule of law encompasses a complex set of requirements: it demands, for example, that public officials govern through a set of general rules, applicable to all and impartially administered. It demands that these rules be publicly proclaimed and accessible to those who live under their aegis. It demands that they apply only prospectively—that is, it prohibits government from punishing people for violations that occurred before the law was enacted. It also requires that laws be reasonably clear and non-contradictory.[10] By its nature, the rule of law requires a broad set of public officials—including judges, prosecutors, police officers, and regulators—who will adhere to standards of impartiality and professionalism.

Needless to say, the rule of law is indispensable to the protection of equal freedom in modern society. Without it, power can be exercised capriciously, and its subjects can never be sure when and where they will feel its sting. They can never be sure, in other words, which freedoms they actually possess, and whether these are robust or fragile. This is the condition of those living under those authoritarian regimes—populist or not—that have systematically undermined the rule of law and promoted in its place what political journalist Moisés Naím calls *pseudolaw*. Pseudolaw looks like law—it is ratified by legislatures and expressed as a set of general rules—but it is typically framed so broadly and vaguely that ruling elites and their henchmen have broad discretion to selectively target their opponents. Russia's expansive anti-extremism statutes, for example, allow the Kremlin to censor or arrest anyone it pleases. Pseudolaw is most devastating to those who are arrested under its authority, but its reach is far broader.

By combining murky legal standards with harsh punishments, it sows confusion and fear and gives rise to pervasive quiescence and self-censorship. Where "extremist" is a vague category applied to reformers and other regime critics, anyone who stands out has to worry that they could qualify as one.

A free and independent media is another core liberal strategy whose value has been proven by centuries of example. Liberals have long held that a media free from state censorship (and from monopolistic private control) is indispensable for holding public officials accountable to the public interest, and therefore in preserving individual freedoms. A free media exposes abuses of power—by government, by economic elites, or by dominant ethnic or religious groups. It draws attention to corruption and unfairness. These revelations then give leverage to the regime's critics and the political opposition. They also give the ruling party incentives to correct problems and deploy power in ways that serve its constituents' interests. If it refuses, revelations by independent media sap the regime's legitimacy and lay a foundation for political change. Like other checks and balances, a free media consists of centers of power—media outlets—that stand apart from the regime and can criticize it without fear of official repercussions. Its full realization also requires a culture of impartiality and professionalism among journalists and editors.

When authoritarian populists begin consolidating power, they move quickly to co-opt the free media. In Venezuela, for example, Hugo Chávez and his successor Nicolás Maduro used various strategies to assert control over it. They abruptly revoked the broadcast licenses of independent television stations, lavished government patronage on new media networks set up to spread government propaganda, and forced out the owners of prominent newspapers. In Turkey, Erdoğan employed even blunter tactics: many leading newspapers were simply shut down, their archives destroyed. Scores of journalists were arrested and imprisoned, along with other prominent critics of the regime, while government dollars flowed toward news outlets that bestowed favorable coverage on the AKP.[11]

Even as they take control of media outlets, authoritarian populists also undermine free media through a constant barrage of misinformation designed to sow confusion and uncertainty. They spread conspiracy theories, repeat flagrant falsehoods, and promote "alternative facts." They vilify experts—academics, scientists, public health officials, and others whose knowledge and expertise position them to challenge the government's lies. Those who contradict official propaganda are labeled "enemies of the people" and are accused of promoting "fake news" that serves the interests of some cabal of anti-democratic elites. In doing so, these rising tyrants reach for the very apogee of authoritarian power: control over the contours of reality itself. "I proclaimed it, and thus it was so." The more outrageous the proclamation, the more powerful the leader feels when subjects accept it—or at least feel compelled not to contradict it.

The destruction of free media and the erosion of the rule of law are related to another important aim of authoritarian leaders: to shrink civil society itself and bring it to heel. In liberal societies, media organizations exist alongside a wide range of other associations and advocacy groups serving various constituencies. These include civil rights groups, labor unions, churches and religious associations, political parties, and organizations working to promote the interests of different segments of the population. Such groups empower citizens by giving them places to congregate, share opinions and information, and build solidarity. They also give people voice and leadership, and a measure of collective power. Civil society organizations can and do serve many purposes, of course—both liberal and illiberal—but on balance they tend to make people's freedoms and fundamental interests more secure. Citizens who lack organization and are prevented from gathering openly with others who share their interests tend to be far more vulnerable to the encroachments of oppressive power.

Eventually, authoritarian populists take aim at democracy itself. Although they come to power through democratic means, they have no interest in being subject to democratic challenge. They insulate themselves by embracing a corrupt facsimile of democracy: declaring that they alone embody the true will of the people, they dismiss any evidence to the contrary as a vicious lie; they demonize opponents and critics as enemies of the sovereign *demos;* and they manipulate electoral outcomes to maintain the veneer of popular support. Over and over, they insist that any institutions that resist their authority are controlled by scheming elites out to thwart the true voice of the populace. These attacks on democracy are amplified by the erosion of liberal protections for dissenters. When the media is in government hands, when opposition parties are surveilled and harassed, and when critics of the regime are subject to arrest, there can be no free and fair elections.[12] Meanwhile, the eclipse of free elections compounds the threats to personal liberty and leaves citizens unable to protect themselves against abuses of power.

These embattled institutions constitute the lifeblood of liberalism. They are the core mechanisms through which liberal ideals are enacted. Yet the intellectuals who can be heard expressing disdain for liberalism—on both the left and the right—tend to focus their attention elsewhere. They take aim at the abstract ideals and attitudes that supposedly undergird these institutions: the dream of limitless personal autonomy, for example, or a strain of hubristic Enlightenment rationalism that supposedly courses through the veins of liberal reformers. Other critics denounce the materialism and selfishness ostensibly embedded in liberal assumptions and breezily conflate liberalism with (loosely regulated) corporate capitalism. It is easy to understand why they do this: it is far easier to criticize nihilistic materialism or corporate greed than checks and balances or the rule of law.

Consider Slavoj Žižek, one of the darlings of the Marxist academic left and a professor at the University of London who can often be found giving spirited talks to American college students. In his view, liberalism is little more than sophisticated camouflage for the ascendancy of global capitalism. In its place, he argues, we should create a politics of radical equality that explodes the status quo through communist revolution. But one searches his writings in vain for evidence of any concrete strategy that would prevent revolutionary violence from birthing new forms of tyranny. Instead, we find the old Marxist canard that the wretched of the earth are so profoundly oppressed and excluded that they have come to embody the raw essence of universal humanity itself, which will allow them to transcend all group antagonisms and, once in power, conjure up a free and equal society. Amid his ironic asides and jargon-ridden abstractions, we find Žižek praising Venezuelan strongman Hugo Chávez, the Yugoslav communist regime's willingness to subvert free elections in the 1940s, and a ninth-century militant Shiite movement that enforced its vision of egalitarian utopia by massacring dissidents.[13]

In an age of rising tyranny, we must resist such obfuscations. We should insist that liberalism's critics focus on its core institutions and explain which of them they propose to do away with. Would they forgo the rule of law? Free media and an open civil society? Or judicial independence and a professional civil service? Perhaps it is the idea of human rights that rankles them. If they do reject some of these, we should press them to explain what alternatives they propose and how they plan to forestall the tyrannical power we find ascendant in so many parts of the world—and we should insist on a better response than vague slogans or theoretical abstractions. If, however, we find them unwilling to forgo any of these institutions, we should call their bluff. In many intellectual circles—on the left and right alike—rejecting liberalism has become a badge of honor. It is a way for writers and scholars to establish that they are edgy and up to date. Much of this posturing is nonsense written by people who would always choose to live and raise their children under the protective shield of liberal institutions.

None of this is meant to suggest that liberal institutions are beyond reproach—far from it. The institutionalization of liberal principles in the United States has clearly been marred by pervasive failures and injustices. Some of these failures reflect the tremendous influence of corporations and their lobbies, which have worked tirelessly to erode the foundations of equal freedom for American workers. Some failures arise from the toxic polarization that has overtaken American politics and prevented commonsense problem-solving. Other failures reflect the hubris of planners and economists whose policies took little notice of the value and fragility of local cultures, neighborhoods, or ecosystems. Most insidious of all are the failures built into the very design of liberal institutions. The longstanding patterns of discrimination and neglect that have marginalized and impoverished Black and Native American communities, for example, originated in deliberate policy choices that were often made to conciliate racist constituencies. It bears repeating that the defense of liberalism I offer in this book is not a defense of the status quo or of American political history; radical liberalism calls instead for dramatic changes to our politics, economics, and society. For anyone pursuing such changes, however, liberal institutions remain indispensable: they have proven to be the only reliable means of containing tyrannical power in the modern world. Turning away from them is deeply self-destructive.

Yet as crucial as these core liberal institutions are in forestalling tyranny and defending equal freedom, they are not enough. As many philosophers and social scientists have pointed out, institutions are only as resilient, just, or impartial as the people who run and support them. Institutions are tools, and like any other tools, they work only so long as they are maintained and wielded in the right ways. Consider just one example: ample research has shown that if those tasked with implementing the law—such as police officers, prosecutors, and judges—hold patriarchal or misogynistic attitudes, then women's freedom will be compromised, no matter how egalitarian the letter of the law is. These officials invariably exercise discretion in responding to distress calls and deciding who to arrest and prosecute, how to instruct juries, and when to show leniency.[14] It follows that liberal institutions alone are no panacea. The fight against tyranny is a broader and more ambitious project than just writing a liberal constitution or designing liberal institutions.

Interlude: Power's Metastasis

If tyranny were a rare phenomenon, liberalism's elaborate institutional bulwarks against it might be unwarranted. The partisans of illiberal regimes on both the right and left have sometimes leveled some version of this accusation. They have argued that, once power is in the right hands—the hands of *the people,* or of enlightened party leadership—liberal institutions present unwanted obstacles to swift social and political change.

From the liberal perspective, such arguments seem extraordinarily naive, for they fly in the face of an ancient truism: power always seeks to grow and multiply. Liberal thinkers borrowed this insight from a much older, classical tradition that extends back to ancient Athens. One of its key insights is that great power—like great wealth—tends to throw the human character out of balance and inspire predatory behavior that, for most people, would otherwise be unthinkable. Plato, for example, reserved some of the most disquieting imagery in *The*

Republic to describe this transformation. Most tyrants, he wrote, rose to power by presenting themselves as "protector[s] of the people." But once they had gathered great power in their hands, they discovered an insatiable appetite for more:

> Having a mob entirely at his disposal, he is not restrained from shedding the blood of kinsmen; by the favourite method of false accusation he brings them into court and murders them, making the life of man to disappear, and with unholy tongue and lips tasting the blood of his fellow citizen; some he kills and others he banishes, at the same time hinting at the abolition of debts and partition of lands: and after this, what will be his destiny?[15]

Having thus tasted human blood, a man becomes another animal altogether: "a wolf—that is, a tyrant." Such a man would stop at nothing, Plato cautioned, to bring the entire political community under his thumb.

As Plato explored the psychological roots of this transformation, he emphasized the tyrant's fear of losing power and acclaim. The adulation and fealty of others were like a powerful drug, and those who tasted it craved more and began scheming immediately to preserve their supply. They quickly grew jealous of potential rivals, and in their efforts to destroy them, shattered limits and extended their domain.

Other writers have focused on the *arrogance* of power: people who grow accustomed to being venerated and obeyed come to regard themselves as a class apart. They grow intolerant of criticism; their capacity for empathy is short-circuited; they come to regard others mainly as instruments to serve their ambitions. They bridle at the limits that others would dare impose on them. Still others have emphasized the sheer pleasure of domination, or what Ralph Waldo Emerson called "the voluptuousness of having a human being in absolute control."[16] In his view, this gratification was so strong that it overpowered the restraints of reason and morality alike.

More than two thousand years after Plato wrote his reflections on tyranny, the liberal philosopher John Stuart Mill used the same insights as the psychological foundation of his seminal book *On Liberty*. Mill argued that power always threatens to overspill its boundaries, and that the central challenge of modern politics was to contain it and force it to serve the public interest. He laid out two key strategies: the recognition of individual rights and "the establishment of constitutional checks," including robust democratic oversight and accountability.[17] Mill insisted that these strategies were necessary even in democratic societies, because majorities and their leaders are not immune to the seductions of power. They too can feel intensely jealous of the rising power or status of minority groups; they too can move ruthlessly to preserve their prerogatives when their authority is challenged. In the pages of *On Liberty*, Mill chronicled the many ways in which majorities use their power to oppress, brutalize, and silence minorities.

Like many liberal thinkers since, Mill extended his logic beyond the formal institutions of government. Majorities could exercise tyrannical power informally by discriminating against minorities, ostracizing them, and treating them with contempt. In his view, tyranny could blossom in intimate relationships too, wherever some held substantial power over others. Mill's 1869 book *The Subjection of Women*— radical for its time—focused on the power that husbands held over their wives and daughters. The nearly unlimited control granted to husbands under Victorian marriage laws, he wrote, brought them immense psychological benefits: men treasured their status as petty lords of their domestic fiefdoms. It also made many of them arrogant, cruel, and fiercely defensive of their privileges. Those who suffered the effects of such corruption, of course, were the women who came under male control. Mill chronicled the many layers of harm they endured, including chronic abuse and infantilization, constant surveillance, and vastly diminished opportunities. He explored the way such domination was justified by a patriarchal ideology that taught women, at every turn, that they were irrational and incapable. Nothing less than strict gender equality, he argued, was compatible with liberal principles.

Liberal attitudes about power have sometimes been described as fundamentally pessimistic because they suggest a deep human proclivity to domination. But this is not quite accurate. Mill did not think such proclivities were unavoidable. His pessimism about the effects of concentrated power was balanced by his optimism about the human character when it unfolded under conditions of equality and mutual respect, subject to the rule of law. We might more accurately say, then, that thoughtful liberals have believed that the human character is fundamentally malleable. Under the wrong circumstances, people are capable of extraordinary callousness and cruelty. One of the organizing aims of liberal politics is to create conditions under which these pathologies are less likely to thrive, and in which better characteristics—such as empathy, cooperativeness, and responsibility—are more likely to take root. Attacking concentrations of power at all levels of government and society is fundamental to this project.

Finally, like so many other leading liberals, Mill left a decidedly mixed legacy. In many ways he was a radical reformer whose ideas are still useful and clarifying. He agitated for women's rights, for minority rights, and for economic democracy. But he also spent much of his career working for the East India Company, which oversaw the brutal British colonial occupation of India, and he defended some forms of colonialism because he believed not all societies were "ready" for self-government. He thought societies could be classified on a spectrum of less to more civilized, and that liberal democracy was suitable only for those on the "more civilized" end. His naive confidence in the good intentions of colonial officials also blinded him to its despotic realities.

Political Tyranny, American Style

In recent years, the danger of tyranny has often been invoked by the American right. Conservative activists and intellectuals commonly denounce government initiatives they dislike—from mask mandates and taxpayer-funded contraception to gun control and environmental regulations—as *tyrannical.* Most of these claims do not hold up to even casual scrutiny. The policies in question have been ratified through democratic processes, reviewed by courts, and vigorously contested during election cycles. They have met rigorous standards of non-discrimination (or they would have been struck down). And far from being arbitrary, they have almost always been tailored to balance personal liberty with other important public interests, such as health and safety. Such balancing, essential in any free society, has been a defining feature of American public policy since the founding. Lawmakers do not always get the balance right, but this is hardly evidence of tyranny.

There are, however, several real and dangerous forms of tyranny at work in American society. Ironically, they originate on the political right, where the song of individual liberty is sung most insistently. Three stand out as matters of urgent concern for anyone committed to protecting liberal principles. First, Donald Trump and his Republican acolytes have borrowed heavily from the authoritarian populist playbook and waged an increasingly brazen struggle against liberal institutions. Second, the power of large corporations has in many cases become so expansive and unchecked that it routinely tramples citizens' fundamental rights and interests. Finally, the violent deployment of police power against people of color—who have been detained, brutalized, and killed with relative impunity—is a fundamental affront to equal freedom.

The rise of illiberal populism in America has been exhaustively discussed by scholars on both the left and right.[18] There can be no doubt that Donald Trump's takeover of the Republican Party has introduced a dangerous strain of authoritarianism into the American mainstream. His strategies are familiar: contempt for checks and balances and the rule of law, vilification of the media and embrace of flagrant falsehoods and conspiracy theories, brazen attempts to manipulate the electoral process, disdain for a professional civil service (maligned as an anti-democratic "deep state" that must be destroyed), and a persistent rhetoric of catastrophe—often directed at immigrants and vulnerable minorities—which is used to justify a call for extraordinary political measures. Trump's 2024 presidential campaign encapsulated this authoritarian drift: he repeatedly promised to weaponize the justice department against his critics should he win office again. He also intensified his reliance on overtly fascist tropes—calling his opponents "the enemy within" and likening them to "vermin"—even as party leaders continued to issue full-throated endorsements of his candidacy.[19]

Since taking office in January 2025, Trump has sharpened his attack on liberal institutions. He has usurped legislative authority by taking an axe to federal agencies—from the Department of Education to the Consumer Financial Protection Bureau—that were authorized and funded by Congress. He has tried to bully and silence judges by defying court orders, claiming the right to ignore judicially imposed Constitutional limits, and issuing impeachment threats. He has begun detaining, deporting, and imprisoning people without due process. He has tried to gut our professional civil service through illegal mass firings. He has issued unconstitutional decrees targeting law firms that represent his political opponents. And he has continued his efforts to intimidate his critics in the press by suing media organizations, berating journalists, and turning the Federal Communications Commission into an instrument of personal and partisan revenge.[20]

None of this could have happened without the active complicity of the Republican Party. Republicans control both houses of Congress and hold the power to impose limits on the executive, but as I finish writing this book, they have refused to do so. Some are evidently afraid—not just for their political careers, but for their families' safety. Those who stand up to Trump in this political climate have often become targets for harassment and death threats.[21] Other Republicans have simply decided that their political objectives are more important than liberal democracy. These are profoundly dangerous trends. When Richard Nixon used the FBI to persecute his critics, he inspired widespread revulsion across both parties. When the House Judiciary Committee voted to adopt articles of impeachment in July 1974, seven Republican members (out of 17) voted with the Democratic majority.[22]

The authoritarian rot at the heart of the Republican Party has been spreading for some time. After the assault on the US Capitol on January 6, 2021, Republican leaders had an opportunity to discredit Trump permanently and decisively. By then, they knew how dangerous Trump was, and they seemed ready to denounce him and his allies for their unprecedented efforts to overturn the results of a presidential election, their flagrantly dishonest attacks on the integrity of the democratic process, and their incitement of deadly mob violence. Instead, after a brief period of indecision, party leaders blocked the formation of an independent commission to investigate the events of January 6, and worked actively and openly to impede the House investigation. The few Republicans who participated in that investigation were officially censured by their party.

The GOP then sought to capitalize on Trump's "big lie" by launching a wide-ranging assault on the American electoral process. Despite having no credible evidence of election fraud, Republicans in statehouses across the country introduced hundreds of "election integrity" bills designed to limit access to the ballot. They made it more difficult to vote by mail, banned drop boxes, restricted early voting, enacted strict voter-identification laws, and moved to criminalize small infractions.[23]

A number of Republican-led legislatures also moved to put Trump loyalists in charge of elections, or to facilitate the removal and even the criminal prosecution of nonpartisan election officials.[24] Meanwhile, prominent Republican pundits and politicians openly praised Hungary's prime minister, Viktor Orbán, who has repeatedly used state power to subvert democratic processes.[25] Put together, these facts form a clear pattern: scholars who study the integrity of democratic procedures have observed a strong correlation between democratic "backsliding" in American state governments and Republican control. They have also found an erosion of support for liberal democracy among Republican voters.[26]

Republicans loyal to Trump bristle at the suggestion that they have become authoritarian. They loudly proclaim their allegiance to democracy and imagine that they are defending fair elections and protecting the constitutional rights and "legitimate political discourse" of peaceful protesters. But partisans of authoritarian populism elsewhere make the same claims. They too have convinced themselves that they alone speak on *the people's* behalf. They too claim—with little credible evidence—that they and their allies are the real victims of shadowy conspiracies. They too close ranks and refuse to investigate their own side's most flagrant abuses of power, claiming that any accusations are politically motivated. Such rhetoric is a flimsy rationale for unbridled assertions of power. The simple truth is this: a political party that refuses to sharply condemn clear attacks on the electoral process and root out gross violations of the law within its ranks is tilting in a dangerously authoritarian direction. It is, in effect, declaring its right to rule by any means necessary.

When authoritarian parties come to power in liberal societies, they seldom achieve total control right away. Usually, there is a gradual erosion of liberal safeguards alongside a gradual subversion of democracy. If these parties are able to hold onto power through several election cycles, the threat becomes especially dire. Over time, by appointing loyalists and purging moderates and career civil servants, authoritarians corrupt liberal institutions from within and turn them into partisan instruments. And once liberal safeguards are weakened, party leaders feel emboldened to entrench themselves in power, silence critics and intimidate opponents, and suspend or break constitutional limits. They move to normalize these transgressions by escalating the rhetoric of emergency and painting even moderate opponents as traitors whose ascendancy would imperil the nation. When they succeed, the result is political tyranny.[27]

Such developments are by no means a foregone conclusion in the United States. Trump's efforts to consolidate power in his own hands, weaponize the federal bureaucracy, and intimidate his opponents may fail. His recklessness, cruelty, and corruption may lead to decisive electoral setbacks and course corrections. Our Constitutional guardrails might hold up just long enough. But liberal democracy in the United States is entering a period of heightened peril. The Supreme Court's extraordinary decision in 2024 to grant presidents broad immunity from criminal prosecution only heightens the danger, and scores of political scientists, legal scholars, and nonpartisan watchdogs have sounded the alarm. Trump's success virtually guarantees, moreover, that his style of authoritarian politics will continue to resurface long after he has left the stage. There is simply no way to defend equal freedom in the

United States without defeating it and marginalizing its practitioners. As we have seen, equal freedom depends on the very institutions that authoritarian populists everywhere have set out to dismantle.

Although it is by far the most important threat, authoritarian populism is not the only source of tyrannical power in American government. Such power can accumulate, in principle, in any public institution, including bureaucratic agencies. The FBI's surveillance and intimidation of civil rights leaders and other political dissidents under J. Edgar Hoover is one infamous example, but there are many others. In the 1950s, for example, the US Department of Agriculture (USDA) was asked to address the spread of fire ants—an invasive species—in southern states. Responding partly to alarmist reports from southern farmers who worried that their crops and livestock were in danger, the USDA began an aggressive campaign to eradicate the insect by spraying highly toxic chemicals (dieldrin and heptachlor) over millions of acres of southern land, including both public and private property— often without the property owners' consent. After rolling out the program without adequate research into its damaging health effects and without meaningful consultation with affected communities, it then ignored dissenting scientists and lied repeatedly about the chemicals' toxicity. The result was widespread extermination of wildlife, with toxic residues seeping into twenty million acres of land.[28] The USDA's fire ant campaign is widely seen as an example of arrogant and unaccountable bureaucratic power. It was not full-blown tyranny because the agency was ultimately accountable to elected officials, who began to demand explanations—but it was a close relative.

Corporate Tyranny in America

There is nothing especially radical about the political agenda I have outlined so far. Liberals have been fighting political tyranny for centuries, and their arguments and strategies are well established. Still, we can draw surprising implications if we apply these arguments to other forms of concentrated power, notably the business corporation. Corporations are extraordinarily powerful agents that can (and often do) damage people's basic interests with relative impunity. Their oppressive power is deeply institutionalized in American law and political practice, and has grown considerably stronger in the past several decades. This power afflicts millions of Americans each year and many more worldwide. It is manifest in several ways.

First, many large corporations violate the law—egregiously and repeatedly—without suffering serious consequences. In doing so, they routinely upend people's lives and destroy their freedoms with little consequence. In many parts of the United States, for example—especially in low-income communities—Americans are exposed to toxic chemicals and pollutants that bring sickness, long-term disability, and premature death. These toxins are in the air they breathe, in the water they drink, and in the foods they consume. Many people are exposed to levels of toxicity far above legal thresholds. Consider air pollution alone: a detailed 2021 report by ProPublica suggests that as many as 250,000 Americans are living in "toxic hot spots" in which the levels of carcinogens released into the air by nearby industrial plants are dangerous to their health.[29] Many of these people are unaware of this danger, and most of the polluters responsible do not face aggressive enforcement actions. In Calvert City, Kentucky—to cite just one example—a company named Westlake Chemical has been releasing extraordinary amounts of carcinogens into the air for decades, exposing thousands of residents to levels of pollution as much as seventeen times what the Environmental Protection Agency (EPA) deems safe. Westlake Chemical has been fined several times for its violations, but the fines have been too small to persuade the company to change its behavior.[30] How could this be?

The answer lies in a culture of corporate immunity that has grown more pronounced over the past two decades, extending not just to pollution but also to dangerous negligence in the workplace, financial fraud, and other white-collar crimes. The scholars and journalists who have documented this culture find that it has many sources. One is the chronic underfunding of regulatory agencies tasked with implementing legal rules. Regulators have been starved of funds for decades, largely because of the intense deregulatory zeal of Republican lawmakers. The 9/11 attacks intensified this problem by shifting federal resources away from corporate crime and toward terrorism. Since January 2025, the Trump administration's indiscriminate attacks on the federal bureaucracy have only added fuel to the fire. Regulatory agencies now lack the inspectors and auditors to monitor compliance with tax law, labor law, environmental law, and more; they also lack the resources to conduct thorough testing, even of chemicals that appear routinely in consumer products. And the intense politicization of the rulemaking process has slowed it significantly, preventing regulators from keeping up with new threats to public health and safety.[31]

These are not the only barriers to enforcement. At the state level, deep-pocketed corporations wield tremendous influence over legislators and governors, making many officials hesitant to enforce the law. At the federal level, meanwhile, the internal dynamics in the Department of Justice have also played a part. Its staffing and resources pale in comparison to those of large corporate defendants, and prudent managers in the department have become wary of long trials that drain public funds. After a handful of embarrassing setbacks in the early 2000s, federal prosecutors adopted risk-averse strategies that result in fewer prosecutions: they now commonly pursue "deferred prosecution agreements," which require that corporate offenders show progress toward greater compliance to stave off criminal action. But legal scholars have shown that these agreements are often toothless:

monitoring is weak, and even repeat offenders often avoid serious consequences. Having gotten away with the initial crime, offenders have little incentive to make the institutional changes necessary to protect the public.[32] Even in successful prosecutions, the corporate managers whose decisions caused the harm almost never see jail time.

The biggest corporate criminals enjoy a further layer of protection: prosecutors and their elected bosses worry about the economic consequences of imposing serious penalties on corporations that employ tens of thousands of workers, because these penalties could affect stock markets and the entire domestic economy. Scholars and journalists alike have cited this worry to explain the federal government's leniency toward big banks in the wake of the 2008 financial crisis. Attorney General Eric Holder made this astonishing admission to the Senate Judiciary Committee in March 2013: in deciding whether to prosecute big banks, he worried aloud that some were "so large" that prosecuting them might "have a negative effect on the national economy, perhaps even the world economy."[33] In other words: these corporations' sheer size conferred extraordinary privileges and immunities on them, which they exploited to inflict tremendous suffering and loss on millions of people. They were not only *too big to fail;* they were also *too big to jail.* As legal scholars have made clear, this phenomenon is hardly confined to banks: it extends to other sectors of the economy that are dominated by a few big companies.[34]

If government tyranny subverts the rule of law through pseudolaw, corporate tyranny does so partly through *hollow law.* Hollow law consists of legal rules that are on the books, partly to create the appearance that the public good is being protected, but are not consistently or adequately enforced. When laws that protect people's fundamental interests are hollowed out in this way, the effect resembles that of pseudolaw: citizens stand at the mercy of powerful actors who can damage their health, their property, even their lives, at will. They may find their life savings wiped out by the criminal misbehavior of banking executives. They may find their children suffering from aggravated asthma—or worse—or their groundwater and livestock poisoned by chemicals leaking from industrial facilities. Or they may find their homes, their health, or their livelihoods destroyed by industrial accidents that result from the extraordinary negligence of corporate managers. Those who suffer these effects commonly report a feeling of utter powerlessness: they feel that they have little recourse against the overwhelming power of corporate leviathans.

Corporate crime—and corporations' immunity—are just the tip of the iceberg. Much of the oppressive power exercised by big business unfolds *within* the law. It is no secret that the economic power wielded by large corporations wins them many political allies. They continually petition these allies to modify the law in their favor, or to carve out exceptions that serve their financial interests. While some of these exceptions are relatively benign, others are catastrophic for those who suffer their effects. Consider the US meatpacking industry's extraordinary efforts, at the height of the COVID-19 pandemic, to secure exemptions from public health measures that would have protected its employees. By successfully lobbying the Trump administration and its allies at the USDA, and by threatening meat shortages if they didn't get their way, the powerful companies that dominate this industry secured permission to continue operating manifestly unsafe plants while receiving immunity from potential lawsuits. Some 59,000 employees of the five biggest meatpacking companies contracted COVID-19 in the first year of the pandemic, and meatpacking plants became epicenters of disease transmission. One academic study estimates that the meatpacking industry was responsible for 18,000 COVID-related deaths.[35] A subsequent Congressional investigation found that these companies showed flagrant disregard for their workers' health and safety.[36]

Pick up a reputable newspaper on any day of the week and you are likely to find an article about some comparable form of perfectly legal corporate misbehavior. You might read about energy companies securing immunity from prosecution for the use of toxic "forever chemicals" in their drilling operations, even as these chemicals sicken and kill people living nearby. Or mining companies exploiting legal loopholes in bankruptcy law to avoid the costs of toxic cleanups, shifting huge financial and health burdens onto poor communities. Or you might find powerful drug companies blocking the sale of generic alternatives to their life-saving drugs, in effect condemning some underinsured patients to death, even when the economic rationale for such blocks is tenuous at best. Or perhaps gun manufacturers lobbying to defeat even the most moderate gun-control legislation even as their products are used to massacre people in American streets, schools, and churches. All of these examples feature powerful corporations exerting control over political processes in order to facilitate destructive behavior—behavior that tramples people's basic interests.

What explains this pervasive warping of the law to enable corporate destruction of citizens' health and freedom? Here too, the story has many layers. It begins with the vast expansion of corporate lobbying over the past four decades. Corporations and trade associations now pour billions of dollars each year into highly sophisticated lobbying operations that dwarf the efforts of unions and public interest advocates. For every dollar spent by these other groups, business interests spend thirty-four dollars.[37] As corporate lobbying has grown more lucrative, it has also absorbed many skilled staffers and ex-politicians, speeding up the revolving door that links Capitol Hill with K Street. Scholars and journalists who interview legislators, legislative aides, and lobbyists themselves describe an environment awash in corporate money and influence, in which lawmakers increasingly rely on the knowledge and policy expertise of corporate lobbying teams. These lobbyists are especially adept at exploiting the many "veto points" in American government to block legislative changes that would damage their clients' interests.[38]

The next layer is the influence of money in American elections. This influence has mushroomed since the infamous 2010 Supreme Court ruling in *Citizens United v. FEC* struck down longstanding limits on corporate political spending. Many close elections today are inundated with money from Super PACs—secretive groups, often with undisclosed donor lists, that can spend without limit to influence the outcome. These groups are overwhelmingly financed by wealthy individuals and business groups.[39] Meanwhile, the amount of money a candidate must raise to finance a successful campaign keeps rising, forcing lawmakers to spend more and more time on the phone with wealthy donors, many of whom manage or own successful companies. "Increasingly, the main qualification for the job," writes political scientist Lee Drutman, "is having a unique personality trait that allows one to withstand several hours a day of begging rich people for money."[40] It would be extraordinarily naive to imagine that lawmakers' dependence on wealthy donors doesn't shape public policy.

Corporations and their owners also flex their muscle by waging systematic, well-funded public relations campaigns designed to shape the views of voters, jurors, and lawmakers in ways that protect corporate interests. They buy media outlets, fund think tanks and policy centers, bankroll lavish junkets and training sessions for judges and policymakers, subsidize favorable academic research, and engineer fake grassroots movements to sway public opinion.[41] Scholars have also documented the lengths to which major American companies have gone to cover up, deny, and obfuscate their products' harmful health effects. With the help of public relations firms that recruit scientists-for-hire to produce false or misleading analyses, these companies mount all-out attacks on scientific findings that threaten their bottom lines.

Their aim is to manufacture enough uncertainty to forestall regulation and defeat expensive lawsuits so that they can keep making money as long as possible. To be clear: these are not erroneous attempts to reach for the truth. They are lies, cynically told and systematically spread to advance a corporation's financial interest.[42]

A final source of corporate influence arises from the mobility of capital itself. In the twenty-first century, companies are more mobile than ever. They commonly move their production facilities and even their headquarters from one country to another, chasing lower taxes and labor costs as well as less burdensome regulations. The same dynamic operates within the United States: companies commonly search for the most profitable labor and regulatory environments and invest their resources there. Such mobility further enhances their political power. The prospect of new jobs and tax revenues—or of *lost* jobs and tax revenues—puts pressure on state and local officials to shower powerful corporations with favors, and to out-compete rival cities and states by creating a business-friendly environment tailored to these companies' needs. Some of this competition can be beneficial to citizens—for example, it can lead to valuable investments in infrastructure. But it can also lead to weaker environmental and public health protections coupled with lax enforcement, lavish giveaways of tax revenue, or anti-union policies that depress workers' wages and benefits. Although scholars disagree about the magnitude of this political "race to the bottom," there is considerable evidence of its effects in the United States.[43]

When we put these disparate sources of power together, they paint a disquieting portrait of both tremendous concentrations of power and its chronic, reckless abuse. The most devastating example can be found in the politics of climate change. It is now well known that fossil fuel companies have waged a decades-long campaign to undermine climate science, block climate legislation and regulation, weaken public support for clean energy, and turn climate denialism into a partisan issue.[44] They did this even as their own scientists warned of the dangers of climate change. And they have been remarkably successful, especially in the United States. If mainstream scientific projections are accurate, the cost of our collective failure to control global warming will be almost incalculable: Billions of people will be harmed. Hundreds of millions will face food or water shortages. Hundreds of millions will be displaced by rising seas, causing unimaginable personal and social disruption as they seek new places to live. Mass extinctions of plant and animal species will accelerate, with unknown, cascading effects.[45] And the corporations that profited immensely from this destruction and then went to great lengths to block reasonable political responses—along with their enablers in the world's capitals—will bear much of the blame.

The fossil fuel industry is not commonly recognized as a *tyrant*. Part of this reticence lies in our association of tyranny with armed force and sovereign power. Governments exercise tyranny through violence or the credible threat of it: they use armies, police forces, prison systems, and secret police to compel their subjects' submission and obedience. But violence operates in other ways, too: if I poison your well water or set fire to your farm—or if I intentionally cause one of these things to happen—that too is an act of violence. If I terrorize a community by committing such acts regularly, I exercise oppressive power. And if this power is institutionalized—if I have rewritten or hollowed out legal rules to facilitate such acts of aggression—then I have become a tyrant. This is the form of power wielded today by massive corporations in the United States. Needless to say, such power is inimical to the ideal of equal freedom: if my basic interests stand at the mercy of powerful and unaccountable actors, I am not a free person.

For well over a century, apologists for corporate power have tried to deflect such criticisms by insisting that the corporation is fundamentally benign. The financial interests of big corporations, they argue, are closely aligned with citizens' own interests: when corporations thrive, they buoy the economy, create jobs, and deliver innovations that raise standards of living. Consumers benefit from cheaper and better products, and retirement funds grow as corporate stock prices rise. Defenders of corporate power reject the idea of corporate tyranny, in other words, by denying that corporate power is cruel or arbitrary. Because it is constrained by the market, they claim, it is fundamentally unlike political power.

In the mid-twentieth century, these claims had a certain plausibility: the economic success of major American corporations did seem to correlate with widely shared economic gains and a rising standard of living for workers. The prevailing management theories at the time, moreover, held that prudent corporations should attend to the long-term interests of a broad range of stakeholders—including workers, communities, and society at large.[46] Circumstances today are different. For the past three decades, record corporate profits have not generated meaningful economic gains for most wage earners. The vast majority of the new wealth generated in this new economy—including investment income—is flowing to the wealthy. As I will show in Chapter 3, American corporations have aggressively pioneered new forms of labor exploitation and used them to impoverish and dominate American workers. Moreover, the relentless pressure to deliver short-term returns to investors, along with weakening public oversight, has created a widening divergence between corporate incentives and the long-term interests of virtually everyone, including those very investors—who also need clean air and water, fertile topsoils, a physical environment uncontaminated by carcinogens, and a political community undistorted by extreme partisan polarization and mistrust.[47]

The point is not that all or even most corporations are evildoers—they are not. Nor is there any sense in denying that successful companies deliver valuable benefits to consumers and employees—they do. A vibrant economy led by efficient and innovative private firms is indispensable to any free society. None of this is in dispute. The point is that in our present regulatory and political environment, the interests of large corporations and their owners often diverge widely and predictably from the interests of workers, communities, and the public at large. Scholars and journalists who study corporate misbehavior have found that it has deep structural causes. Corporate managers are under intense pressure to deliver short-term profits for investors, and this often leads to reckless risk-taking, chronic lawbreaking, underinvestment in safety precautions, and resentment of anyone trying to get in the way. The top echelons of corporate leadership commonly embrace an aggressively antiregulatory ideology that treats auditors and inspectors, lawmakers, and community activists as hostile agents. Meanwhile, responsibility within corporate hierarchies is often too widely diffused, and individual managers too deeply insulated from criminal liability. Corporate misbehavior is not a story of a few bad apples; it is a systemic crisis.[48]

Corporations are not people, so their characters cannot be *unbalanced* by a surfeit of power. In this limited sense, the apologists for corporate power are right. But by the same token, there is no reason to expect the corporate "character" to be balanced in the first place. Corporations today are best understood as finely calibrated profit-making engines that will seek to override all other values and constraints when it serves their leading objective. Their characters are thoroughly unbalanced, in other words, by design—and this is what makes them so efficient. In publicly traded companies, managers are under pressure to focus single-mindedly on boosting profitability.[49] There is therefore every reason for liberals to approach these giants the way they would approach any person or institution that holds massive, concentrated power: with a firm resolve to impose strict limits and develop effective countermeasures.

Although corporations themselves are not vulnerable to the seductions of power, their owners and executives surely are: many have displayed extraordinary hubris, egomania, lust for power, resentment of those who assert authority over them, and callous disregard for those who bear the costs of their recklessness. These vices have flourished unchecked among many Silicon Valley executives, Wall Street moguls, fossil fuel billionaires, and other corporate titans who have persuaded themselves that they are entitled, as a matter of private right, to damage the basic interests of millions of people.

The liberal response to corporate tyranny originated in the late nineteenth century, in the political struggle to tame the new power of industrial corporations. This was a period of rampant violence and exploitation in the workplace, of growing industrial pollution and corporate crime, and of tremendous economic inequality and runaway corruption in American politics.[50] Many of the theorists, politicians, and policymakers who sought to curb these new dangers—from the Progressive Era through the Nixon administration—understood themselves to be carrying out a fundamentally liberal agenda, centered on protecting personal liberty and opportunity and making them more widely and fully available.

To advance this agenda, they employed recognizably liberal strategies: They sought to disperse corporate power while also hemming it in with checks and accountability mechanisms, which included robust anti-trust laws and a strong regulatory regime supported by aggressive enforcement. They implemented measures to contain the political spending of big business and insulate regulators from industry influence. They also encouraged strong labor unions as a counterweight to the power of corporate boardrooms, along with diverse traditions of community activism to stand up to corporate abuses. The role of organized labor in particular is chronically misunderstood in American political culture. It is, among other things, a seminal anti-tyranny mechanism that reflects the fundamental liberal commitment to checks and balances.

This expanding liberal agenda came under sustained and successful assault starting in the 1980s, with the rise of the Reagan coalition and its new emphasis on the power of free enterprise to solve social and economic problems. Reagan and his allies, determined to emancipate business from tax and regulatory burdens, immediately began to block new regulations, appoint former industry lobbyists and insiders to key regulatory posts, and slash the budgets of federal regulatory agencies. Environmental limits were attacked with special gusto: the EPA's budget contracted sharply, and Reagan famously declared his fealty to the oil industry by removing the solar panels that Jimmy Carter had installed on the White House roof and gutting the Department of Energy's renewable energy research program. Reagan and his advisers also encouraged the privatization of public services, which would eventually expand the discretionary power of private business in many areas of American public life, including prisons, the military, education, and student lending.[51] Perhaps most significantly, his administration played a key role in weakening antitrust enforcement. In an effort to bolster US businesses' global competitiveness, it lifted restraints on both horizontal and vertical mergers, paving the way for massive consolidations of corporate power. These tendencies were further deepened and entrenched under Bill Clinton in the 1990s as the Democratic Party rushed to court Wall Street and Silicon Valley.[52]

For the past four decades, these changes in American policy and governance have been aggressively justified by neoliberal—or market fundamentalist—rhetoric and ideas. Their advocates in the business community, in business-funded think tanks, in law schools, and in economics departments have sung the praises of loosely regulated markets and warned of the failures and excesses of government regulation. Largely heedless of the dangers of concentrated private power, they have approached corporations through a narrowly economic lens, asking only whether they were economically efficient and how they could be made more so. From their perspective, unions, minimum wage laws, worker safety laws, and most other regulations function mainly as drags on innovation and economic performance. Worse, neoliberals have worked hard to recast freedom itself as the absence of government interference in economic relationships, and they have used this anemic ideal to systematically unwind liberal buffers against corporate tyranny.

One of the most insidious claims repeated by market fundamentalists is that government regulation of big business is counterproductive and therefore worse than futile. Beginning in the 1970s, conservative economists began arguing that regulatory agencies, in particular, would quickly be "captured" by the industries they were intended to regulate and then repurposed to serve company interests. The only solution, these economists held, was deregulation: markets would almost always serve the public interest more faithfully than regulators. From the beginning, the evidence supporting these claims was weak—gleaned from abstract economic models rather than empirical study. More responsible scholarship has recently shown that this whole vein of analysis is largely specious. There can be no doubt that big business often succeeds in thwarting and weakening regulation, or that its influence penetrates government at many levels. But none of this means that we should give up the fight. Sound regulation works, and there exist well-understood strategies for limiting industry influence over regulators.[53] Market fundamentalists' antipathy toward regulation has nonetheless enjoyed credibility among lawmakers for decades and has greatly facilitated the expansion of tyrannical power in the United States.

Liberal Experiments

Critics of liberalism never tire of arguing that it is out of ideas— that it has become a stale and sclerotic system lacking the imagination and flexibility to meet new challenges. The truth is quite different: liberal governments, large and small, are continually experimenting and evolving. As new expressions of tyranny manifest themselves, so too do new strategies for taming and destroying them. While some liberal polities are gridlocked, others are adjusting to meet new challenges. Some of their experiments are top-down initiatives that strengthen the government's capacity to protect and expand freedom, while others are bottom-up solutions designed to hold power accountable. Both are crucial to any forward-looking liberal agenda.

Since the liberal fight against political tyranny is centuries old, we would expect to find considerable variety and experimentation in this area. And we do: different liberal societies have embraced a range of strategies to insulate their political institutions from attack by would-be tyrants. They have created anti-corruption watchdogs or ombudsmen, with the powers to investigate and report on public malfeasance in other branches of government. They have strengthened judicial review as a way of protecting liberal constitutions from attack, and created non-partisan commissions to insulate judiciaries, bureaucracies, and electoral processes from partisan control. They have also incorporated key elements of international and human rights law into their domestic legal architectures, thereby further strengthening liberal freedoms.[54]

To fight tyranny in the United States, we need to limit the immense, concentrated power of the American presidency. Over the past century, Congress has steadily ceded its own prerogatives to the executive, throwing our constitutional system out of balance. Today, presidents hold the power to declare (and renew) broad states of emergency and use them to curtail basic rights and liberties. They can wield tariffs unilaterally to wreak economic havoc and commandeer the Department of Justice to persecute political opponents. Meanwhile, antiquated laws—such as the Insurrection Act of 1807—leave room for an unscrupulous commander in chief to deploy troops against American civilians. When Donald Trump leaves office, we need a serious reckoning: Congress should claw back and constrain the president's emergency powers and severely limit the use of military force domestically. Congress should also challenge the Supreme Court by narrowing the scope of presidential immunity, and empower truly independent prosecutors who can investigate abuses of power without being fired by the president. (Such prosecutors existed after Watergate but were phased out in 1999.) Political scientists have shown that "executive aggrandizement" is the single leading threat to democratic constitutions in our time; we should heed their warnings.[55]

While these bulwarks can succeed temporarily in containing authoritarian leaders once they are in office, it is even more important to defeat them at the polls. In the United States, this can be accomplished only if our democratic institutions remain strong. As we have seen, the Republican Party's authoritarian tilt has coincided with a sustained attempt to make voting more difficult and to corrupt the electoral process. When Democrats win power again, they should move aggressively to protect and expand voting rights. Congress should require automatic or same-day voter registration nationwide, mandate significant early voting and mail-in voting periods, and make Election Day a national holiday. Given the racial disparities in our criminal legal system, no one should lose their right to vote over a criminal conviction—or if they do, these rights should be restored automatically, without fees or cumbersome application processes, upon release from prison. We should also recognize partisan gerrymandering for what it is: an attempt to undermine democracy by insulating incumbent parties from political challenge. A number of states—including Michigan and Colorado—have empowered commissions that remove the process of redistricting from partisan control and create more competitive districts. All of these changes would bring the United States into closer alignment with most other advanced democracies.[56]

Of course, none of these measures will prevent authoritarian populists from sweeping to power with majority support, as Donald Trump did in 2024. Ultimately, the answer lies in defusing the MAGA movement's energies—and this requires solutions that reach well beyond electoral reform. Although the roots of authoritarian populism are hotly debated, many leading scholars agree that it is driven partly by rising economic inequality and insecurity, which have fueled popular resentment.[57] I will consider these trends in more detail in Chapter 3. For now, it is worth emphasizing the Democratic Party's complicity in the growth of economic inequality since the 1980s, which has coincided with a marked atrophy of the party's capacity to reach working-class voters.[58] Simply put: many of these voters no longer believe that Democrats have their economic interest at heart. Too few Democratic leaders are drawn from the working class; too few are able to connect with people without a college degree. Over the past four decades, the party has also abandoned rural voters and become ever more beholden to affluent city-dwellers. The long-term decline of organized labor has reinforced both of these problems: it has undermined the economic prospects and political influence of blue-collar Americans while also facilitating the gentrification of the Democratic Party.[59]

Until these trends are reversed, right-wing populists will continue to make deep inroads among the working class. But none will be reversed unless we counteract the huge, lavishly funded right-wing media network whose influence and reach have grown tremendously since Trump first rose to power in 2016. This network now encompasses not only Fox and its parent company, News Corp., but also Newsmax, One America News Network, Sinclair (whose radio stations, TV stations, and newspapers reach into countless local markets), iHeart Media, Bott Radio Network, the social media platform X, a wide range of popular conservative podcasts, and more. These are not just partisan news outlets. Since 2016, they have gleefully amplified Trump's attacks on American democracy and spread baseless conspiracy theories designed to discredit public institutions. Their coordinated propaganda campaigns increasingly drive the news cycle and distort voters' perceptions of reality, making it difficult for them to assess their government's performance and hold leaders accountable.

Patrician news organizations catering to highly educated audiences, such as the *New York Times* and MSNBC, stand virtually no chance against this sustained onslaught. We desperately need a counter-network of talk radio and television stations, newspapers, podcasts, and social media networks dedicated to exposing the MAGA movement's lies and corruption, its pandering to corporate barons, and its brazenly authoritarian proclivities. All of this can be done in the plainspoken, irreverent tones that have found such success on the right, but without abandoning fact and evidence or jettisoning journalistic integrity. If left-leaning donors do not awaken soon to the existential threat posed by the right-wing propaganda machine, liberal democracy in America may not survive.[60]

The liberal struggle against corporate tyranny is also evolving—but not fast enough. Given the magnitude of the problem, we need to think beyond the usual regulatory strategies and embrace more ambitious goals. Radical liberals should strive, ultimately, to contain corporate power by embracing far-reaching anti-trust reforms, re-thinking corporate governance, and promoting organizational structures that are more accountable to the interests of workers and citizens. These objectives rest on a fundamental insight about the corporate form itself: it is a privilege granted by government, which confers extremely valuable legal advantages—including limited liability and asset shielding—without which the modern corporation could not function as it does.[61] These advantages were originally designed to empower private groups to serve some important public interest. But these origins have been carefully obscured by corporations and their libertarian apologists, who have worked tirelessly to redescribe the corporation either as a "natural person" entitled to Constitutional rights or, more recently, as a "nexus" of private contracts over which government has very limited authority.[62] In an era of widespread corporate domination, we have every reason to reject these mystifications and rethink the corporation's legal and political status.

The idea of "stakeholder" capitalism has recently become a trendy topic, not just among scholars and activists but also among executives and business gurus. Broadly speaking, it claims that private companies should not be fixated on boosting the short-term value of their stock; they should focus instead on creating long-term value, not just for shareholders but also for workers, consumers, and the communities affected by their business practices. Stakeholder capitalism comes in many different forms: at one end of the spectrum lie the relatively toothless versions that depend on business leaders' voluntary cooperation. Given the deep structural problems identified in this chapter, these versions hold little promise. At the other end of the spectrum, however, we find serious efforts to reimagine the corporate form. In 2019, for example, the British Academy called for changes to corporate law that would explicitly recognize the claims of diverse stakeholders; regulatory changes that would reclassify a broader range of businesses as "public benefit companies" and subject them to much stricter oversight; revisions to the tax code designed to unlock long-term financing and encourage corporate managers to build value over longer horizons; and other significant reforms.[63]

Corporate boards are a key leverage point. As part of her 2018 Accountable Capitalism Act, for example, Senator Elizabeth Warren proposed that 40 percent of corporate board members should be elected by workers, and that any political spending or lobbying should require the approval of those worker-elected board members, so that corporate coffers are not vectors for oligarchic power.[64] Progressive legal scholars have made similar recommendations. Some have argued, for example, that corporate boards should include representatives elected not just by workers, but also by communities where the company employs large numbers of people.[65] These proposals would shift the balance of power within boardrooms, and they are fiercely opposed by corporate power-brokers. They do have compelling precedents, however: for decades, German law—under a system of "co-determination"—has given workers a right to substantial representation on corporate boards.[66]

We should also consider reforms designed to render managers and investors more accountable for the harms created by corporate recklessness and illegality. Expanding managers' legal and financial liability for any misconduct under their watch is one place to start.[67] In the wake of the financial crisis, some legal scholars proposed revisions to the idea of limited liability itself, so that shareholders in financial firms would face larger risks if their companies went bankrupt. Following the French example, we could also tighten corporations' liability for legal and human rights violations committed by their subcontractors. There are many options to consider.[68] Meanwhile, a reinvigorated antitrust movement could begin to reverse the consolidation of the economy, break up corporate giants, and rediscover antitrust policy's original meaning as an antidote to concentrated power rather than merely an effort to keep consumer prices low.[69] Crucially, citizens and liberal intellectuals alike must recognize that these are central questions in liberal politics and theory—as central as tyranny itself—and not strictly economic matters properly delegated to economists and management experts. The business corporation, like government itself, is a vector for tremendous power, and we must therefore consider its design in political terms.[70]

Alongside these more ambitious reforms, we should also adopt some commonsense measures that have already found success in other liberal societies. For example, other countries employ a range of strategies to limit the influence of corporate money in politics. These include public financing of elections, aggressive regulation of corporate political speech, and heightened standards of transparency for political spending. While scholars remain uncertain about the long-term effects of these policies, it is clear that since *Citizens United,* the United States has moved in the opposite direction from most other liberal democracies.[71] The "balanced mix of regulatory policies" that appears to be working in other societies has been short-circuited by a Supreme Court that is increasingly oblivious to the political power of big money.[72] The Court has also adopted an extremely narrow view of political corruption that excludes most of the influence peddling that currently envelops American politics—including the Court itself.[73] Future appointments to the Court must be made with an eye to reversing these precedents.

Europe has also taken a more aggressive approach to regulating big companies, as shown by its 2018 General Data Protection Regulation and its 2022 Digital Services Act, which subject big tech companies to a raft of rules designed to protect the public interest. These include robust protections for user privacy and rules that allow public officials to review company algorithms. To motivate compliance, they are backed by fines far bigger than what US regulators impose. More generally, regulatory agencies in many countries have pioneered a number of strategies for limiting corrupt industry influence. These include a division of power across agencies, the formal empowerment of citizen groups in the regulatory process, the creation of academic review panels, the codification of robust administrative procedures, and more.[74] Simply funding our regulatory agencies adequately, so that they could hire enough auditors and inspectors to track and investigate corporate malfeasance, would go a long way. Effective regulation, like so many of the other approaches canvassed in this chapter, is a way of curtailing unchecked power and thus serves a crucial role in the fight for equal freedom.

I want to re-emphasize two key points in closing. First, tyranny in any form poses a mortal danger to human freedom. To live under cruel or arbitrary power that is deeply institutionalized and hostile to one's interests is to suffer a grievous loss of liberty. Shielding people from such power must therefore be a focal point for liberals everywhere. Second, the project of containing tyranny is far broader than just developing the right institutional checks, no matter how ingeniously these are designed. Liberal institutions will thrive only if citizens believe in them and have the time, the willingness, and the resources to maintain them. And this, in turn, depends on an economy that creates widely shared opportunity and financial security.

3

Exploitation

For the past four decades, the American economy has grown at an enviable pace and produced prodigious amounts of new wealth. This growth has been driven, in part, by a 60 percent increase in worker productivity. Yet as Americans are increasingly aware, most of the economic gains over this period have been captured by the wealthy. Wages for most American workers have grown very slowly, and benefits have eroded even as living expenses have soared. Meanwhile, the fortunes of the "super rich" have ballooned. As a result, the American economy is now more unequal than at any time since the infamous Gilded Age of the late nineteenth century.[1] As of 2022, the top 10 percent of American families owned 74 percent of the nation's wealth, whereas the bottom 50 percent of families owned just 2 percent.[2] Although their earnings have grown slightly since the COVID-19 pandemic, low-wage earners in the United States still earn substantially less than their counterparts in nearly all other wealthy industrialized nations.[3]

Inequality is only part of the problem. Our economy also leaves far too many people impoverished and deprived of opportunity. At the heart of the issue lies the widespread exploitation of workers. In the United States alone, millions of people have little choice but to accept unfairly low compensation for grueling and demoralizing labor. To make things worse, their vulnerability is not just an accidental byproduct of global economic forces. Over the past half century, it has been exacerbated by a series of policy choices backed by business interests and their ideological allies. Economic elites have spent a great deal of their innovative energy devising ingenious new ways to exploit workers at home and abroad, and removing or blocking legal obstacles that might interfere.

This pervasive exploitation damages the personal freedom of millions upon millions of people. Its corrosive effects are felt in many ways: in the impoverishment of the American working class, in the capricious authority of corporate bosses over their employees, in inhumane hours and working conditions, and in the escalating toll on workers' physical and psychological health. All of these effects undermine workers' power to choose and restrict their access to desirable options. The widespread exploitation of American workers therefore stands out, from radical liberalism's point of view, as an egregious political failure. And yet today, as in the previous Gilded Age, exploiters have deployed recognizably liberal arguments—centered on property rights, freedom of contract, and individual freedom more broadly—to justify their actions.

Markets and Freedom: A Brief (American) History

The idea that tens of millions of Americans are exploited and unfree may seem implausible, largely because the relationships that structure our economy have been thoroughly normalized. But we need not invoke any exotic theories to justify this view of the US economy; we need only appeal to a set of economic ideas that were widely held in the generations after the nation's founding. When free-market ideas were first popularized in the 1830s and 1840s, they were commonly associated with both fairness and economic parity. Over and over, Americans made it clear that they did not expect markets to create huge disparities of wealth—certainly not among the white men who

were allowed to participate fully. This was largely because they expected *economic power* to remain decentralized and evenly distributed.
By "economic power" (which I will also call bargaining power or bargaining leverage), I mean the power to set the terms of a market exchange. Most Americans believed that gross inequalities in the distribution of this power would strip workers of their economic freedom
and corrode the very foundations of the republic. Revisiting their
economic assumptions can help us think our way out of the ideological straitjacket that encases so much of our economic conversation
today.

I should note that anyone attempting to reclaim economic ideas
from this period must proceed with caution. Economic freedoms belonged almost exclusively to white men, most of whom imagined that
they alone were entitled to them. This was a time of extraordinary
cruelty and oppression visited by white Americans on people of color,
including Black Americans, both free and enslaved, and Native Americans. It was also a time of profound gender inequality, when women's
opportunities to participate in economic life were severely constrained.
The ideals of the period are worthless to us unless they can be carefully disentangled from these forms of subjugation.

During the first half of the nineteenth century, the United States
experienced explosive economic growth driven partly by a revolution
in transportation. Local and regional economies were linked together
by an expanding network of canals and railroads, and by newly designed steamboats plying the country's waterways. In the northern
states, more and more small farmers produced surpluses to sell in distant markets and calibrated their decisions to the market's price sig-
nals. They sold goods for cash, which they could then use to buy the
consumer products—from fabrics and hats to furniture and musical
instruments—that flooded into the American inland on canal barges,
steamboats, and rail cars. Their economic lives became less governed

by the interpersonal bonds that had anchored local economies for generations and increasingly structured by impersonal competition and contract.

Most white Americans at the time celebrated these changes. Like Americans today, they believed that the expanding market economy brought them greater freedom. Markets not only delivered more income for small farmers, but also provided access to cheaper and better consumer goods and wider opportunities. These benefits, in turn, gave people the power to make more choices: to buy clothes rather than make them at home, to build more comfortable houses, to invest in and expand their farms and businesses. At first glance, their attitudes toward the market seem similar to those held by Americans today. But if we look more closely, we notice some striking differences. These are evident, for example, in the sprawling controversy over "wage labor" that extended throughout much of the nineteenth century. Working for wages is, of course, entirely uncontroversial in our time, so it may come as a surprise that many Americans in the early nineteenth century saw wage work as a threat to personal freedom. In fact, people who worked for wages were often compared to serfs or slaves.

Wage labor was growing in the 1830s and 1840s as entrepreneurs began implementing early forms of mass production. Goods that had once been handcrafted by master artisans in small shops—including shoes, clothes, furniture, books, and more—were now being standardized and produced in bulk in new "manufactories." Instead of making goods from start to finish, workers were assigned routinized, specialized tasks. Their jobs were less skilled and less varied, and they were paid less. Crucially, whereas successful artisans could look forward to owning and running their own shop, these new wage workers felt that their economic prospects had dimmed.[4] They complained that wages were too low to provide a comfortable subsistence, let alone get ahead, and that they could be fired at a moment's notice. Critics of wage labor argued that this vulnerability left workers ripe for exploitation and control. Because they had little economic cushion, and because there were many other desperate jobseekers in their situation, wage workers had little bargaining power relative to their employers. Their supposed freedom to negotiate the terms of their employment seemed illusory: in practice, the terms were dictated by their bosses, who held all the cards.

Most critics of wage labor believed in free markets, but they envisioned these as markets for goods and services sold by small proprietors who owned their own farms or businesses. Since America was an overwhelmingly rural country, small farmers in particular were seen as the archetypes of market freedom. When they brought their products to market, they sold their goods, not just their labor. Unlike wage workers, they retained control over their own work lives: they chose what to plant, what hours to keep, what livestock to raise, what agricultural methods to use. They were their own bosses. Markets constrained their decisions, to be sure: farmers who chose inefficient strategies would lose money compared to their neighbors. But they still enjoyed a great deal of choice and control in their everyday work lives. Crucially, many farmers negotiated with their buyers from a position of relative security. They could feed themselves and their families—and supply their basic needs—from their own farms. Failure to find a profitable market for their produce would be a setback, but it would not throw the family into destitution. For these reasons, small farmers were celebrated as paragons of economic independence, which was widely seen as a precondition for personal freedom. Because the farmer bargained with others from a position of relative security, he did not stand in their power. He could look them in the eye as a social and civic equal.[5]

This idea of economic independence was deeply embedded in

American culture and politics throughout the nineteenth century, and politicians of all persuasions made sure to align themselves with it. To be accused of undermining the independence of American workers was to be accused of betraying American freedom. Those who defended mass production and wage labor therefore had to be very careful to show that these economic innovations posed no threat to workers' independence. They did this by insisting that wages in America were uniquely high. In their eyes, the American economy was exceptional: the workforce was educated, the economy was booming and demand for labor was robust, and marketable skills could be readily acquired through brief and informal apprenticeships. All of this, in their view, meant that no one was trapped: workers could save enough, in short order, to start their own farms or businesses. Abraham Lincoln famously expounded this view of the American economy when he observed, while speaking to the Wisconsin State Agricultural Society in 1859, that "the prudent, penniless beginner in the world, labors for wages awhile, saves a surplus with which to buy tools or land, for himself; then labors on his own account another while, and at length hires another new beginner to help him." Surveying his audience, he guessed that "many independent men, in this assembly, doubtless a few years ago were hired laborers."[6]

Those who held Lincoln's view often contrasted the free and prosperous white worker in America with his benighted English counterpart. In fact, the English wage worker—poor, undereducated, packed into a factory, living under the thumb of his industrial boss, and therefore deeply unfree—was a common fixture in nineteenth-century American political rhetoric. From the American vantage point, the English worker lacked economic power: without skills and education, crowded into cities teeming with other desperate job seekers, he negotiated from a position of extreme vulnerability. He was easily exploited, and the free market offered him little relief. Those who defended wage work in the United States took pains to show that American workers were far less vulnerable. Calvin Colton, for example, summed it up this way: "American labor, therefore, does not *accept* a price imposed, but *commands* its own price. At least, it is always an *independent* party in the compact. It is made *freely*, and can be as freely dissolved, without incurring the doom of starvation or distressing want."[7] This last phrase is crucial. American wage workers, Colton argued, were like independent farmers in that they negotiated from a position of security and therefore strength. They had abundant well-paying opportunities at their fingertips and probably savings to fall back on. This bargaining power, he believed, was the very source of their freedom.[8]

Although they disagreed about wage work, Americans on both sides of this controversy shared certain key beliefs. They believed that markets would enhance freedom by expanding individuals' power to make choices and direct their own lives. But this belief rested on several assumptions about what market relations should be like. First, they assumed an economy of small producers: no buyer or seller should control more than a minuscule share of any market, and there should be no huge asymmetries between any two parties. Second and crucially, they assumed that markets would deliver freedom only if workers bargained from a position of relative strength and security.[9]

In the dominant culture of the time, white men alone were entitled to this freedom. During these years, many women were drawn into the labor force, but they earned only a fraction of men's wages, and married women's income belonged legally to their husbands. Meanwhile the thirst for land, the foundation of the small farmer's independence, drove a relentless quest for territorial expansion and motivated countless acts of theft, fraud, and genocidal violence against Native Americans. Free Blacks faced systematic discrimination and terrorism, and most were denied all but the most menial jobs in the burgeoning market economy. In the South, millions of Black slaves were held as commodities and bought, sold, and brutally exploited in the rush to capitalize on the global cotton boom that drove the earliest phase of industrialization. The abstract language of individual independence and freedom, so widely used at the time, masked these harsh exclusions.

It would be a mistake, however, to see this language merely as an ideology of oppression. In fact, those pressing for greater equality and inclusion frequently used it for their own purposes. These included not just the white working class, but also women and people of color. Women's rights activists, for example, often condemned patriarchal marriage because it reduced wives to a condition of abject dependence living under the thumb of an arbitrary and capricious master. They asserted their right to own property and participate in the economy as free and independent persons. Freedmen, meanwhile, embraced the ideal of independence as the foundation of their vision of a free South after the Civil War. Without access to their own land, they insisted, free Blacks would remain slaves by another name, working for low wages at the beck and call of their former masters. Real freedom meant controlling the conditions of their own work and bargaining from a position of security, and this in turn meant owning their own plot of land. They therefore fought for the elusive promise of "forty acres and a mule."[10] The Knights of Labor, which led the first racially integrated labor movement in American history in the 1870s and 1880s, also drew heavily on these ideas.[11] Americans of all backgrounds tended to view widespread economic independence—and the bargaining power it conferred—as a precondition for any free society.

As the economy lurched into its industrial phase in the closing decades of the nineteenth century, it profoundly unsettled this way of thinking. When Americans looked around them, they saw indebted farmers who had lost all bargaining leverage against big banks and railroads, on whose whims they now depended for their livelihoods. They saw urban slums filled with poor immigrants who looked just like English laborers: poor, insecure, and trapped. They saw new corporate behemoths dominating the American economy and using their economic power to impoverish and silence workers, prevent them from organizing, and break their spirits. They saw their politics corrupted by big money, which ruptured the bonds of democratic accountability that bound public officials to their constituents' interests. Millions came to believe that the economic foundations of their freedom were eroding.

The growing inequality and social unrest that mushroomed in the Gilded Age (1870–1900) unleashed tremendous intellectual and political ferment and experimentation, much of it focused on trying to restore the bargaining power—and thus the freedom—of American farmers and wage workers. Some of these experiments were top-down efforts to regulate and break up monopolies and trusts, or to create entitlements that would reduce workers' vulnerability; some were bottom-up efforts to enable farmers and workers to exert countervailing power through unions and cooperatives, and restore collectively what they once had possessed individually: meaningful control over their own work. The Populist movement that swept across rural counties in the late nineteenth century called for a raft of reforms, including expansive public control over railroads and banks, and underwrote a broad network of farmers' cooperatives designed to wrest control from corporate middlemen. Progressive reformers in the early twentieth century pushed for aggressive antitrust enforcement, worker safety and minimum wage laws, worker ownership of businesses, and many other measures. Labor unions grew more powerful and assertive.

These movements, which remain key sources of inspiration for radical liberals today, crested during the New Deal and its aftermath, which brought a profound realignment of the American economy. By the middle decades of the twentieth century, economic inequality had plummeted in the United States and opportunities had expanded for working people, especially the white working class, which benefited most from New Deal investments. But the New Deal consensus unraveled in the 1980s and 1990s, and by the early twenty-first century, its demise had brought the United States back to a period of staggering inequality and unaccountable corporate power. Like the first Gilded Age, this one is also marked by a profound imbalance in bargaining power between capital and labor. Many Americans of the 1830s would recoil if they could see our current economy. To their eyes, it would look fundamentally unfree.

What Exploitation Means, and What It Looks Like

In the broadest terms, exploitation means taking unfair advantage of another person's vulnerability. Let us begin with a made-up example. You hire a highly skilled landscaper to manage the substantial grounds of your country estate. At some point, you learn that this landscaper is supporting and caring for her ailing mother who lives just down the road. Because she has to rush back during her breaks to attend to her mother's needs, she needs a job very close to home. Yours is the only estate close enough to make this possible. After looking into it for a while, you realize that her only alternative (other than working for you) is intermittent gardening work for low pay. Seeing an opportunity to cut costs, you lower her wage to a fraction of what it was before. She bitterly resents this but, having no better option, keeps working for you.

Two key features of this example are worth pointing out. First, even after her wage is driven down, your landscaper continues working for you voluntarily—she is not forced. Exploitation often occurs in relationships that are strictly voluntary. Second, even at the lower wage, the job on your estate still *benefits* her: it leaves her better off than she would be without it. Of the options available to her, yours is the best one, which is why she chooses to stay. Of course, the job is considerably less beneficial than it was, and the terms of her employment are now unfair. But this unfairness does not erase the job's benefits altogether. This is a key point: employers often try to deflect the charge of exploitation by insisting that their jobs benefit workers. But the example of the landscaper shows why this response misses the mark.[12] Labor contracts can be simultaneously beneficial and exploitative.

The moral centerpiece of exploitation is the idea of fairness. To exploit someone is to leverage their vulnerability to produce an outcome that is unfair to them—often deeply so. To establish that any relationship is exploitative, we must therefore contrast it to some fair baseline. What makes an agreement fair? Fortunately, the free-market thinking of the early nineteenth century suggests a place to start. Fair contracts are contracts that would be agreed to under certain conditions: between parties who regard one another as social and civic equals, who negotiate from positions of relative security, and who have other reasonable options.[13] In these circumstances, economic power is evenly distributed. The further a bargaining situation falls from this baseline, the more danger that the result will be exploitative.

We need not reach back two centuries to find examples of fair negotiations: many small business owners find themselves in more or less this situation today. Consider an acquaintance of mine who works as a contractor in Burlington, Vermont. He has many small clients and plenty of demand for his labor. His work is varied and skilled, and he can choose what jobs he takes on and what hours he keeps. He earns a good income—good enough to afford a mortgage and save for his kids' college tuition (though healthcare costs remain a struggle). He employs a few workers, who work alongside him—doing the same range of tasks—and hone valuable skills on the job. His clients, meanwhile, have access to plenty of competitors whose prices and materials they can compare. None of these parties are desperate, or deprived of the information they need to weigh their options rationally. When he is bidding for a new contract, our contractor bargains with his clients as a social equal. In all of these ways, his situation corresponds fairly well to the free-market ideal of the nineteenth century.[14]

Anyone with even a passing familiarity with the American economy today knows that a great deal of wage work looks nothing like this. Millions of workers lack the skills to command a decent salary and lack the resources to obtain those skills. They negotiate with giant companies whose massive wealth and resources yield systematic advantages at the bargaining table. Workers are subject to constant surveillance and invasive control by their bosses. They work long hours, often doing work that is both repetitive and intensely stressful, and they enjoy little if any paid time off or family leave. Their schedules, often dictated by company algorithms, can change from week to week, which makes planning difficult. Meanwhile, the remedies that other advanced democracies have developed to enhance workers' bargaining power have been either blocked or deliberately dismantled. Unionization is rare and difficult, and labor laws are under-enforced. A weakened and porous social safety net leaves workers economically insecure and often desperate for work on just about any terms. Insufficient government investment in public goods—including child and elder care, health care, and education—saddles them with expenses that they can ill afford and narrows their children's opportunities, while regressive tax codes cater to the well-to-do. Even workers' access to legal remedies for flagrant mistreatment has been rolled back.

Let us review these features of today's wage work in more detail, starting with the question of skill. My Vermont contractor is highly skilled: his work is admired and respected, his reputation spreads by word of mouth, and his services are in demand. Clients are willing to pay him well. Low-skilled workers face a very different bargaining situation. Most do not possess skills that are highly valued by employers, which means they face greater competition for jobs. This combination undercuts their bargaining power and depresses their wages. Simply put, employers can afford to let them go because they can usually find a comparable replacement. If not, they can either move their factories someplace where labor is cheaper and more abundant, or they can automate. Together, these factors heighten low-skilled workers' vulnerability and prevent them from commanding a decent price for their labor.

For much of American history, the response to this kind of vulnerability has been Lincoln's: this situation is unenviable, but in America it is temporary. If you simply work hard and save, you will soon ascend from the ranks of the laboring poor. This was always an exaggeration: even in times of high mobility, a great many people who worked extremely hard (and saved, and persevered) never ascended the economic scale. In our own day, Lincoln's rosy picture is simply false: the economic conditions that underwrote it are mostly gone. Unskilled workers do not earn uniquely high wages compared to their European counterparts—in fact, their wages are far lower than they are in Germany, Australia, Canada, the United Kingdom, and many other advanced economies.[15] Although the post-pandemic economy has brought some improvement, millions of Americans still work for poverty-level wages. They are barely able to cover monthly expenses, let alone save enough money to start their own businesses. Without savings, many cannot afford to quit their jobs and look for new ones. A missed paycheck can mean failure to pay rent or put food on the table. Nor are marketable skills easy to acquire: public education in the United States is underfunded and underperforming, especially in less affluent school districts, and declining public investment in higher education (including trade and professional schools) has left that option out of reach for millions of American families. It should come as little surprise that economic mobility in the United States is now lower than in many other advanced democracies.[16]

These economic hardships leave low-wage workers primed for exploitation, and with Silicon Valley's help, big business has taken advantage. Pick up a first-hand description of entry-level wage work at a big American company—a major fast-food chain, a call center, a slaughterhouse owned by a major meat producer, a leading box store, a shipping warehouse—and you will probably find yourself reading a bracing account of workplace misery. Many workers are subject to minute-by-minute surveillance, their speech and movements are scripted, and their bathroom breaks are monitored or timed. Conversations with co-workers and other small diversions that humanize the workday for more affluent people are considered "time theft" and strictly policed. This comprehensive control is deployed in the name of corporate efficiency so that workers' labor can be sped up as much as possible. And it is enforced through fear: workers face ambitious daily targets for routinized tasks and are fired if they fail to meet them. Because flexibility is another key managerial objective, workers face uncertain hours and ever-changing schedules; they are also expected to be on call at any time even when working part-time, which makes it difficult for them to hold down other jobs. Thus even when their hourly wages look decent ($17.50 an hour at Walmart, for example), their monthly take-home pay is not. They usually have little if any paid time off—not even paid maternity leave or sick leave. Opportunities for meaningful promotion are few.[17]

This invasive control is moving into new sectors of the American economy, driven by the push for efficiency and profits demanded by Wall Street investors and corporate consulting firms. Consider agriculture, once seen as the bastion of independence and freedom in America. Today, many farmers are mere cogs in a vast corporate machine, subject to escalating surveillance and control from managers. A key part of the story here is corporate monopolies: meat production, for example, is now dominated by a handful of companies that have consolidated control over the entire supply chain—including feed production, slaughterhouses, and trucking lines.[18]

These few large agricultural companies have also carved the country up into geographic fiefdoms within which they dominate the market. If you farm chickens in Arkansas, for example, you have little choice but to sell them to Tyson Foods. But Tyson drives a hard bargain: its farmers must raise chickens exactly as the company dictates. They must use Tyson's feed and feeding schedules, Tyson's medicines, Tyson's advisers. They must build expensive facilities (funded by debt) precisely to Tyson's specifications and give Tyson ownership of the farms' key asset, the chickens themselves.[19] Farmers are subject to abrupt termination if they violate Tyson's conditions, and they are forbidden to talk to each other about the price that Tyson pays them per chicken. They must agree to let Tyson harvest extensive data from their farms and use it to micro-manage their work, but in return they get no access to Tyson's technical knowledge or decision-making rationales. Their work is thus tightly controlled and deskilled. Tyson's market power, meanwhile, allows it to set prices. It should come as no surprise that the company makes billions while its farmers live on the very edge of solvency.[20]

As we have seen, the sheer scale and wealth of big companies also gives them access to tremendous political power, which they use to shore up their control over workers and find new ways of tightening it. One especially flagrant example is the arbitration agreements that many workers (and farmers) have to sign as conditions of employment. These agreements block workers, if they are mistreated, from seeking legal remedies in the US court system; instead they have to present their case to arbitrators, whose salaries come from the repeat business of corporate clients. Studies show that employees fare significantly worse with private arbitrators than they do in court.[21] The viral spread of arbitration agreements confronts us with the truly remarkable spectacle of millions of American workers (and consumers) who lack access to the courts to protect their basic rights, including the right to work without enduring sexual harassment, discrimination, or wage theft. As of 2018, over half of private-sector workers who were not unionized had signed away their right to go to court. Low-wage workers were most affected.[22]

Work is not the only locus of American exploitation. As sociologist Matthew Desmond has shown in his book *Poverty, by America*, poor people are also exploited as consumers. Landlords in high-poverty neighborhoods tend to make more money than landlords in high- and middle-income areas, largely because many poorer residents are trapped. Moving is expensive, and property owners often reject applicants with bad credit, prior evictions, or criminal records. Landlords in high-poverty areas commonly take advantage of this immobility by driving up rents while underinvesting in their dilapidated properties.[23] Trailer parks offer an especially egregious illustration of this pattern. In recent years, private equity firms and other large investors have been buying these parks and then jacking up rents and fees, generating substantial revenue streams. Because "mobile" homes are actually difficult and expensive to move (or resell without a loss), and because their owners have often invested their life savings in them, these low-income residents are primed for exploitation: they can't just pick up and leave.[24]

Banks and payday lenders have also contrived a wide variety of strategies for extracting money from the poor, including overdraft fees, fees for cashing paychecks, fees for failing to maintain minimum balances, and exorbitant interest rates for short-term loans. Basic financial services are a necessity, and with few other options, the poor often find themselves at the mercy of corporate predators. As researchers have made clear, these predatory practices are driven not by the need to cover costs, but by an aggressive push to maximize profits. In 2019 alone, the largest banks in the United States charged $11.68 billion in overdraft fees, which were overwhelmingly paid by poorer customers.[25]

Let us pause to take stock of the argument so far. We began with our fair baseline, represented by the skilled contractor in Vermont who commands a good wage and controls his own working conditions and hours. His contracts with his clients embody the fairness that nineteenth-century Americans expected of free-market interactions. We then saw that profound imbalances in bargaining power have left millions of today's workers light years from this baseline. They lack the skills to command a good salary as well as the means to acquire those skills. Many live paycheck to paycheck and can barely afford to take sick days, let alone time away to get a degree or to receive skills training—or even to conduct a comprehensive job search. They have no financial cushion and find it difficult to save. They work for corporate behemoths that have perfected sophisticated and patently inhumane techniques of surveillance and control. No impartial observer would describe this as a fair negotiating situation. One writer, detailing her own harrowing experiences as a low-wage employee, sums it up this way:

> So let's break this down: you're poor, so you desperately need whatever crappy job you can find, and the nature of that crappy job is that you can be fired at any time. Meanwhile your hours can be cut

with no notice, and there's no obligation on the part of your employer to provide severance regardless of why, how, or when they let you go. And we wonder why the poor get poorer?[26]

In short, workers commonly find themselves in a position of radical vulnerability, with virtually no economic power. They are thus ripe for exploitation. To Americans living during the first several generations after the country's founding, it would have been painfully obvious that such workers are unfree.

We often think of exploitation as something perpetrated by a particular actor who bears sole responsibility for it. This is clearly true in the example of the landscaper with the ailing mother: you, her hypothetical employer, are responsible for taking unfair advantage of her vulnerability. No one else shares the blame. But when exploitation is widespread, the answer is more complicated. In a competitive economy in which the rules reward exploitative employers, all employers feel pressure to follow suit. Those who try to compensate their workers fairly risk being driven out of business. Many American businesses have been hearing this message from management consultants for decades: unless they drive down their labor costs by taking ruthless advantage of their employees' vulnerability, they will not survive. Under these conditions, workers suffer from *structural exploitation*. Structural exploitation does not render employers blameless, but it weakens their responsibility by limiting their range of options.

The most effective response to structural exploitation is to reform the rules themselves, so that exploitative behavior no longer brings the perpetrators any financial advantage. Steps must also be taken to insulate the rules from manipulation by wealthy donors and lobbyists, so that businesses have less incentive to spend their money and energy creating new forms of profitable exploitation. In other words, structural exploitation is not mainly a question of business ethics; it is a political question that demands political solutions. Such solutions are absolutely central to the pursuit of equal freedom in liberal societies.

Interlude I: Free Market Myths

To understand how exploitation became so thoroughly normalized in the United States, we must take a brief detour into the realm of ideology. The unraveling of the New Deal economy since the 1980s coincided with the rise of an aggressive form of free-market thinking that some have labeled market fundamentalism. One of its purposes, it turns out, is to conceal economic exploitation. It does this by propagating a heavily idealized picture of economic markets from which power has been banished. Competitive markets are imagined as domains of free and fair exchange with a profusion of options, where no one is compelled to accept any deal they don't like.[27] Once we adopt this picture, the idea that a market economy could be marked by widespread exploitation seems deeply implausible.

The idea that the market is inherently both free and fair forms part of an elaborate mythology that has long shaped free-market thinking in the United States.[28] When Americans speak reverently about the free market, they often picture a harmonious system of rules and natural laws that stands separate from government and directs the flow of economic activity impartially and efficiently. They imagine that this system rewards people who work hard and show discipline and skill, even as it punishes those who are lazy or negligent. It thus allows people to control their own fate and rewards those who make good choices. Government, meanwhile, is imagined as an intrusive threat that subverts the market's meritocratic logic by forcibly reallocating resources to the undeserving. This mythologized background picture encourages many Americans to believe that freedom can be obtained simply by withdrawing the hand of government from economic life.

To see this mythology in action, let us come back to the hypothetical case of the landscaper with the ailing mother. I argued that she was being exploited, and that we could see this by comparing her labor contract to a fair baseline in which she enjoyed (roughly) the same bargaining power as her employer. Market fundamentalism teaches, instead, that the market itself can provide our fair baseline. What makes our landscaper's situation unfair, from this point of view, is simply that she is deprived of the market rate for her services. I suspect that many readers feel drawn to this perspective—why should anyone be entitled to more than the market rate?

But this view is mistaken. As we have seen, the market rate for labor is heavily influenced by the relative bargaining power of employers and employees. And this, in turn, is deeply shaped by a host of political questions. Do workers have access to affordable, high-quality education and skills training? Do their country's trade agreements build in labor standards for foreign competition, or do they force workers to compete with child labor and slave labor? What are the alternatives to employment—are workers able to collect unemployment insurance, for example, or other welfare benefits? What is the minimum hourly wage that employers can legally offer, and is it enforced? How widespread are "non-compete clauses," which stipulate that employees cannot quit to take a job with a competing firm?[29] In countries like the United States, where the answers to these kinds of questions are heavily influenced by business interests, the market rate for many kinds of labor is likely to be comparatively low. There is also little reason to expect that it will be fair: these are the places where structural exploitation flourishes.

To put the point more broadly, markets are political creations. They are structured by political rules—including the laws that regulate property and contracts, monopolies, bankruptcies, and inheritance—that are written and enforced by government. "Government intervenes in the market," writes political scientist Vanessa Williamson, "in the same way your skeleton intervenes in your body; it is the organizing structure, not an external force."[30] Except that with markets, this structure has no natural or independent configuration. It reflects moral and political choices grounded in competing interests and values, and it invariably confers advantages on some competitors over others. To present markets as domains of free choice unmarked by power is to falsify reality.[31]

If this seems too abstract, consider another example: intellectual property law. How long should the inventor of a certain idea—a prescription drug formula, for example, or a bit of software code—enjoy the exclusive right to monetize it? Without political "intervention" in economic life, inventors would own no intellectual property rights at all, and new ideas would immediately be copied and monetized by others, who would have no obligation to compensate the inventor in any way. Most people would consider this unfair, not to mention inefficient (because it would weaken incentives for innovation and for bringing new products to market).

In a world in which government "intervenes" in economic life to create and enforce intellectual property rights, these interventions invariably shape the market. These property rights—in the form of patents—grant temporary monopolies to their owners, and this allows them to charge more money for their inventions. The market rate for these inventions goes up, as does the reward that inventors reap. In the United States, for example, drug prices are very high partly because drug companies' patents have very long lives—largely due to relentless lobbying from pharmaceutical companies—and these companies are therefore able to block the introduction of generic versions of their drugs for a very long time.[32] Drug companies are also allowed to pay generic drug makers to delay the release of their products.[33] In countries with different approaches to intellectual property, drug prices are lower. The key point is that these are political choices: we cannot turn to the market itself to resolve them. How fairly markets operate will depend largely on how these political questions are resolved—how these basic rules are framed—not on the inherent properties of markets themselves.

Markets, in other words, are indelibly marked by power. First, their fundamental rules embody political choices that typically reflect the underlying power relations in society. Second, these rules shape the different parties' bargaining power as they negotiate with one another. When this second form of power is severely maldistributed, the market economy becomes a site of exploitation and unfreedom. Though their agreements are still technically voluntary, those who lack bargaining leverage have little choice but to accept patently unfair terms. They are like the English factory workers whose condition was so widely denounced in nineteenth-century America. When governments move to correct this maldistribution of power, they are not "interfering" in the free market; they are reconfiguring it to make it freer for workers.[34] This is one of the fundamental responsibilities of government in any society committed to equal freedom. In the United States, however, our government has often done the opposite: it has stripped away workers' economic power and rewritten the rules to favor the rich and powerful.

Undermining Workers' Economic Power

The widespread vulnerability of American workers in the twenty-first century is especially galling because in many respects we have been here before, and we already know a great deal about how to alleviate the problem.[35] After similar patterns of exploitation emerged in the Gilded Age and early twentieth century, liberal societies developed countermeasures designed to enhance workers' economic power and protect their freedom. These included collective bargaining rights, minimum wages and overtime pay, antitrust enforcement, regulations designed to shorten the workday and improve working conditions, welfare provisions to protect people from desperate poverty, and universal healthcare.

These strategies were always imperfect, and they have been better designed and institutionalized in some places than in others. In the United States, for example, they were deeply marred by a pattern of racial exclusion that benefited whites at the expense of people of color. But they also achieved an unprecedented rebalancing of the economy, and for those workers who benefited fully, they expanded opportunities and created a pathway to middle-class stability.[36] The industrial economy did not create such stability on its own, nor did wealth and opportunity "trickle down" as an inevitable byproduct of economic growth. The advent of the "good industrial job" in the twentieth century, writes labor historian Louis Hyman, was a deliberate product of "state power allied with worker organization."[37] As the global economy grew more integrated and competitive in the second half of the twentieth century, liberal societies had to update their strategies and shore up workers' bargaining power in new ways—and many did.

But the United States did not. Not only have the older rebalancing strategies not been updated to reflect new economic realities; they have been systematically unwound by deliberate policy choices backed by powerful business interests. These interests spent a great deal of time, money, and energy heightening the vulnerability of American workers, and then moved to exploit these vulnerabilities in immensely profitable ways. They were assisted by political leaders in both parties—but especially by Republicans—who have long sought to ingratiate themselves to big business and reap their deep-pocketed political support. Together, they justified their actions by appealing to a rogue version of liberalism centered on market fundamentalism. Their tireless and ultimately successful efforts are among the main reasons so many American workers are now less free than their peers in other advanced democracies.

Reviewing these recent assaults on economic freedom can help clarify its legal and institutional foundations. Take labor unions. Throughout the industrialized world, unions have been a leading response to worker vulnerability. Collective bargaining rights are an important way of leveling the playing field: they force companies to negotiate with an organized body of workers that has clear leadership, resources at its disposal, and negotiating expertise. Unionized workers tend to command better salaries, better benefits, and better working conditions than nonunionized workers. When President Roosevelt signed the Wagner Act into law in 1935, he established the right to unionize (and bargain collectively) as a fundamental feature of the new economic compact between workers and employers. By 1960, 30 percent of American workers were unionized. Since the 1970s, however, business leaders and their allies have mounted a full-scale offensive against this right, erecting barriers to unionization and weakening labor laws and enforcement. Business-funded "right to work" campaigns have undermined unions' ability to collect dues. And they have largely won: as of 2023, only 10 percent of American workers were unionized, which is one of the lowest rates among advanced democracies today (the rate in Canada, for example, is around 30 percent). Just 6 percent of private-sector workers are union members.[38] Meanwhile, American companies routinely violate the law by punishing and harassing employees who try to unionize their peers—and they get away with it.[39] The decline of organized labor in the United States has brought a massive erosion of workers' economic power; the loss of organization and leadership has also weakened the political clout of working-class constituents, which has tilted the balance of power even more. These trends are likely to intensify under a second Trump administration packed with apologists for corporate privilege and power.

Welfare benefits are another key strategy for thwarting exploitation: in setting an economic floor beneath workers (and would-be workers), welfare keeps them from having to negotiate from a position of utter desperation. Workers with nothing to fall back on can be compelled to take even the most inhumane jobs, for the most miserable salaries. Here again we confront a widespread misunderstanding, spread by employers who profit from it. Those who deride welfare programs as "handouts for the undeserving" fail to acknowledge the key role these programs play in creating conditions under which free and fair bargaining can take place. And contrary to conservative mythology, Americans have long turned to government for precisely this kind of support. The independence of small farmers in the nineteenth century, for example, was partly enabled by generous federal subsidies and grants: settlers were guaranteed access to public lands at rates far below market value; and after the Homestead Act of 1862, generous plots of land were given for free to families as long as they lived on them. Some 270 million acres were handed out in this way to white settlers, laying a broad foundation for their economic freedom. At the time, some did try to present these land grants as illegitimate giveaways to the undeserving, but they lost the argument decisively.

In the twentieth century and beyond, however, the American welfare state has been weaker and more porous than its equivalent in other leading Western economies. Benefits are stingier and harder to access, and in many areas they have been eroding. It is well known, for example, that the United States stands alone among affluent democracies in failing to provide universal healthcare for its citizens. Even after the Affordable Care Act expanded eligibility in 2010, roughly thirty million Americans (including nine million children) still lack health insurance, and many more are underinsured, leaving them with high medical bills and uneven access to care. Even those with relatively good, employer-subsidized plans have seen their premiums and deductibles creep up as employers slash their expenses. Services that are free in other countries, such as the brief hospital stay associated with an uncomplicated childbirth, often cost Americans many thousands of dollars.[40] Health expenses remain key drivers of personal bankruptcy in America and leading sources of economic insecurity. Meanwhile, lack of access to basic medical care inflicts unnecessary sickness and pain on poorer families, and the urgent need for money to pay for such access renders their bargaining position that much more desperate.

Or consider unemployment benefits, which keep people out of poverty and enable them to bargain with prospective employers from a position of relative security at a time when jobs have become less and less stable. These benefits have weakened steadily over the past half-century as states struggle to finance them. Eligibility rules have tightened, and benefit levels have fallen. As of 2013, only 27 percent of the unemployed were receiving benefits. Rates were especially low among low-wage workers who needed them the most.[41] This contraction has largely been accomplished through deliberate policy moves, notably the political choice—backed consistently by business interests—to steadily reduce the state taxes that employers pay to fund unemployment insurance in the first place. As this tax base has fallen, these programs have been gradually starved of funds.[42]

Other government interventions that can ward off exploitation include the minimum wage, which should in principle make employers pay their workers enough to live on. In the United States, however, it is plainly inadequate: in most areas, the minimum wage is set far below the living wage. The value of the federal minimum wage has also eroded steadily, losing almost a quarter of its value between 1968 and 2014 because it was never indexed to inflation. Deliberate policy choices have also left fewer Americans eligible for overtime pay, stripping away another protection against exploitative overwork. This erosion is compounded by weakening enforcement: between 1980 and 2007, the workforce increased by over 50 percent while the number of federal minimum wage and overtime inspectors fell by 31 percent. As the government's capacity to enforce minimum wage rules has contracted, wage theft by employers has grown. Some estimates place it at nearly $50 billion per year—a staggering number, especially from the viewpoint of low-wage workers who are already under financial duress.[43]

In some cases, the problem lies less with the erosion of safeguards than with their failure to keep up. One of the major structural changes reshaping the American economy in recent decades has been the rise of the "fissured" workplace. Large firms used to employ their own workforces, which consisted of full-time employees who qualified for benefits and pensions and whose wages tended to grow when the company prospered. Recently, however, firms have increasingly outsourced jobs to subcontractors and temp agencies, reclassified employees as independent contractors, and replaced steady full-time jobs with part-time positions whose hours vary from week to week. Since part-timers and independent contractors are not entitled to benefits—including healthcare, retirement benefits, worker's compensation, and paid time off—employers can reduce labor costs by hiring armies of them. Uber is only the most visible example of this trend, which stretches across the service industry to companies such as Walmart, Starbucks, and Target. Worker protections that were designed when stable, full-time jobs were the norm have not evolved to meet these new threats. As a result, workers have had to accept lower wages, fewer benefits, less control over work hours, and increasing financial insecurity. When lawmakers have tried to rewrite laws to extend benefits to part-time and temporary employees, powerful business interests have blocked them.[44]

The rise of "gig work" epitomizes these long-term shifts. The gig economy is a useful touchstone for our analysis of exploitation because it bills itself as a source of economic independence—the very independence so widely celebrated by nineteenth-century Americans. The companies that populate this landscape—from Uber and Lyft to DoorDash and TaskRabbit—frequently pitch their platforms as a way for workers to become their own bosses, to control their own work lives, and to find the flexibility that suits their needs and desires. And for some, this is true: if you are fortunate enough to have capital or highly valued skills (or both), you can make a good, flexible living. In other words, if you have the economic power to set the terms of market exchanges, the gig economy can work well for you. But those who lack such power tend to be worse off—and less free—than they would be with a steady blue-collar job paying a decent wage with benefits and security. For them, the ideal of economic self-governance is often illusory: they find themselves governed instead by opaque company algorithms and tethered to corporate platforms that demand a willingness to be constantly on call. Low wages and unpredictable schedules also leave gig workers scrambling to find enough work to cover their basic expenses.[45]

Most vulnerable of all are the millions of undocumented workers who perform vitally important tasks in the US economy, but labor under extraordinarily difficult and precarious conditions. A 2020 report by the Center for Migration Studies estimates that 5.5 million undocumented persons are working in "essential critical infrastructure," in areas like agriculture and meat packing, food service, construction, and manufacturing.[46] For these workers, the threat of arrest and deportation typically vitiates any bargaining power they might otherwise have used to secure better working conditions or stop abuses. Undocumented workers are subject to pervasive wage theft, denied overtime pay, made to perform dangerous tasks without adequate safety equipment, fired at will for minor infractions, and subject to racist invectives. Many receive less than the minimum wage.[47] Writing about the trials of undocumented day laborers in New York, Karla Cornejo Villavicencio explains that they

> often do not get protective equipment, meal breaks, or even bathroom breaks. They have all experienced racist abuse and wage theft at the hands of their employers, are all owed thousands of dollars by white men who made them work for days, promised payment, then simply disappeared. Some days laborers are dropped off at remote locations to do work, then left there without a ride back, unpaid and helpless. . . . Workers absorb exceptional emotional and physical stress every day and, because they are undocumented, they're on their own, with no workplace protections, no regulations, and no collective bargaining.[48]

These conditions are, again, an artifact of US policy. Congress's repeated failure to pass a comprehensive immigration reform bill has perpetuated a broken system that leaves millions vulnerable to exploitation. Many American employers, meanwhile, continue to benefit from having a vulnerable workforce with virtually no legal protection, one that can be exploited and discarded at will.

The Effects of Exploitation

To most readers, the harms of exploitation probably seem obvious enough. It may therefore come as a surprise that many market fundamentalists dismiss them as morally insignificant. Their argument goes something like this: "So what if labor contracts seem unfair, and so what if they generate tremendous inequality? Fairness is subjective and equality is overrated. What matters is economic efficiency and growth, which benefit everyone. American workers today are better off than they were a generation ago because they have access to a wider range of goods and services: air conditioners and washing machines are cheaper, medical treatments are more effective, and most have internet connections, cell phones, and flat-screen TVs. Moreover, since workers are not *forced* into labor contracts, there is no reason to see these contracts as a threat to freedom. What you call exploitation is not only voluntary but also hugely beneficial: it has boosted worker productivity, made businesses more flexible and dynamic, and expanded everyone's power to make choices." Seen from this point of view, American workers should celebrate their extraordinary prosperity and join the Koch Brothers in calling for further deregulation of the economy and contraction of the social safety net (which is what many market fundamentalists advise).[49]

I have no interest in disputing the transformative power of market economies. Over the past two centuries, market-driven growth has lifted billions of people out of destitution and brought immeasurable expansions of human freedom. In this sense, market economies have proven to be essential tools in the liberal toolkit. The question is *how* these economies should be configured, and whether our present configuration is unfair and unduly harmful to workers on the lower end of the income scale. When they consider this question, market fundamentalists tend to brush aside the mountain of evidence, carefully compiled by social scientists, journalists, social workers, and civil society professionals, showing that working-class Americans are suffering in today's economy. They may have cellphones and cheap air conditioners, but lower-income Americans are also reeling from the harsh pressures of an economic system reshaped by three decades of neoliberal enthusiasm.

I have already laid out considerable evidence in support of this claim, but I want to devote more attention now to exploitation's effects on freedom. As their bargaining leverage has eroded, many workers have found it difficult to obtain livable wages and decent benefits. OECD data show that a significantly greater share of full-time American workers earn "low pay" compared to their counterparts in other affluent countries (24 percent of full-time wage-earners in the United States, but just 8 percent in France).[50] This has obvious implications for these workers' freedom. According to a study published by the Urban Institute in 2018, 38 percent of Americans have difficulty meeting their basic needs, which the authors defined only as "housing, food, utilities, and health care." They did not include such essentials as transportation or childcare.[51] This level of privation forces people to make agonizing choices—between paying rent and paying utilities, between paying for food and paying for medicine, between taking on extra jobs and being around to take care of their kids.

Working or not, the thirty-five million people who actually live in poverty in the United States commonly suffer forms of deprivation that are usually associated with developing economies. According to a 2022 study, one in ten American families has trouble covering their water bill.[52] Nearly half a million households lack proper plumbing, and many more have polluted water running from their taps.[53] Food insecurity is also widespread: in 2015, for example, almost sixteen million households (more than one in ten) "had difficulty at some time during the year providing enough food for all their members due to a lack of resources."[54] Millions have trouble paying their electricity bills; millions lack basic healthcare, and many of these millions suffer from untreated chronic illnesses and injuries; millions lack access to affordable transportation and therefore have trouble finding and holding down a job.[55] As I explained in Chapter 1, freedom means the power to choose from a broad range of secure and desirable options, especially in areas that pertain to one's basic interests. For people living in poverty in the United States today, such options are highly constrained; their lives are therefore substantially unfree.

The epidemic of homelessness sweeping the country offers further evidence of this widespread lack of freedom. On any given night, over 770,000 Americans are homeless, with 2024 marking the highest number of homeless Americans on record.[56] Homelessness has many causes, including our inadequate mental health services and the opioid epidemic. But another key cause is the combination of stagnating wages and soaring housing costs: housing has simply become unaffordable—or barely affordable—for millions of American families. Millions are evicted every year because they cannot afford to pay their rent. These people often have no place to go. Their belongings are dumped out on the sidewalk and they are forced to rely on friends and relatives who might have a spare couch, or seek refuge in homeless shelters. Meanwhile, a shortage of shelter beds leaves millions sleeping under bridges and in makeshift tents. Such is the yawning void that stretches beneath low-skilled workers in the richest country in the world.[57]

Even for those who are not in or near poverty, rising economic insecurity poses another potent threat to freedom. Studies have shown that American families now face far greater economic volatility than they did two generations ago. This can be measured in the rising number of bankruptcy filings and mortgage foreclosures each year, in the rising number of evictions, in the rising likelihood of losing one's job in a corporate "downsizing," and in the growing instability of family incomes from one year to the next and even one month to the next. Instability is especially difficult for the growing number of Americans living close to insolvency: a nationwide poll in 2021 showed that over 60 percent of Americans had less than a thousand dollars in savings; in 2013, 55 percent reported that they did not have enough money saved to replace a single month of income.[58] With such a small cushion, unexpected setbacks—the loss of a job, unexpected medical expenses, an expensive car repair—can be hard to overcome. Freedom means having access to options that are relatively secure. Living in fear of economic ruin, with little to no cushion to soften a temporary fall, is deeply constraining.[59] In fact, researchers have shown conclusively that poverty, and the stress it produces, significantly degrade people's health and cognitive capacity, leaving them at a serious disadvantage in the struggle to find firmer economic footing.[60]

Having enough income to cover basic needs and save for emergencies is a fundamental economic prerequisite of freedom, but it is hardly the only one. The tightening surveillance and control to which workers are now routinely exposed also reduces their freedom significantly. Here again, the nineteenth-century perspective is instructive. Control over one's own workday is an important dimension of personal freedom. Americans spend a huge slice of their lives working—more than people do in any other affluent society (except for South Korea). Workers who are subject to constant surveillance and control on the job have lost a great deal of their power to shape their daily lives. The widespread erosion of stable and predictable work hours only heightens workers' powerlessness and causes significant anxiety and unhappiness.[61] Meanwhile, the stress of workplace environments that have been engineered to speed up workers to the breaking point exacts a significant toll on their mental and physical health.[62] Workers who suffer from depression and anxiety are less free, in obvious ways: the entire range of options available to them is worsened.

In these circumstances, work and work stress spill over, chronically and inevitably, into other areas of life. As workers take on extra jobs to pay their bills, or find themselves unable to afford vacations or family leaves or even sick days—or as they scramble to find and keep and commute to enough temporary work to pay the bills—they find less and less time for family, for hobbies, for learning, or just for relaxing. At the turn of the millennium, Americans worked *five weeks* more each year, on average, than they did in 1973 (including "non market" work such as housework); they also work far more than their counterparts in Western Europe, who enjoy abundant paid vacation time.[63] For labor activists in the nineteenth and early twentieth centuries, limiting the workday and preserving space in human life for leisure and for family were essential goals. Meaningful leisure time is an essential aspect of any free life. In this area too, the American economy is out of sync with the aspiration to equal freedom.[64] People who *want* their work to consume almost all their time should be free to make this choice—but in the most affluent society in the history of the world, this option should not be compulsory or driven by economic desperation.

As we saw in Chapter 1, the idea of equal freedom requires that people have access to sufficient resources to grant them equal opportunity—or close to it—to chart their course in life. American society is not remotely close to this threshold. Researchers have shown, for example, that children's long-term economic prospects are deeply shaped by the neighborhood in which they grow up. Access to a good education throughout childhood, which is also highly correlated with economic opportunity, is highly uneven: poorer children are far more likely to end up in underperforming schools and to lack access to an affordable college education. Racial disparities in opportunities are also strong, with Black and Native American children suffering sharp disadvantages. More broadly, rising inequality, paired with anemic investment in public goods, has eroded economic mobility for poorer Americans and left more and more trapped in or near poverty. It has also accelerated the downward mobility of middle-class families.[65]

Finally, the ideal of equal freedom requires that everyone have enough resources to participate in social life. To those who study poverty and its social effects, it is abundantly clear that the poor are commonly treated as second-class citizens.[66] For Americans who are homeless, who lack access to health and dental care and bear visible marks of this disadvantage, or who attend failing schools and never achieve basic competencies, the opportunity to participate in society as a social and civic equal often remains out of reach. Such exclusion is corrosive of personal freedom: it eliminates a wide field of options that more affluent people take for granted.

In Chapter 2, I explained that equal freedom depends on a host of strategies whose core function is to check and restrain power, beginning with the power of government. These strategies include, among other things, constitutions and individual rights, the rule of law overseen by an independent judiciary, free media, and open civil society. They also include democratic accountability, which allows citizens to remove public officials who pose a threat to their basic interests. Unfortunately, governments are not the only threat to freedom: in capitalist economies, powerful private actors continually seek ways of profiting from the oppression and exploitation of others. The work of protecting freedom in the twenty-first century depends on the muscular deployment of government power *against* these private actors. In industrial and post-industrial economies dominated by large firms, where most workers do not own any land or capital goods (such as buildings or machinery), governments must move decisively to shore up workers' bargaining leverage so that they can negotiate fair labor contracts and earn a decent living. Without such interventions, workers fall prey, routinely and predictably, to exploitation.

Liberal societies have flourished since World War II, not just because they have successfully constrained government power, but also because they have built and channeled it within those constraints. Liberal states in this era have been *strong* states, capable of taming giant corporations, forcing rich people to pay their taxes, uprooting Jim

Crow, and making large investments in infrastructure, education, health and welfare services, regulatory oversight, and military capacity. This too is part of the essential architecture of human freedom.[67]

Interlude II: Taxes and Freedom

Why are so many Americans still drawn to the view that freedom calls for *less* government support for workers, and for economic policies that interfere as little as possible with the agenda of big business? There are two main reasons. One, as we have seen, is a heavily fictionalized view of the market economy, which imagines that markets are naturally fair, that they grant people control over their own lives as long as they are willing to work hard, and that they exist largely independent of government. The other reason is the popular anti-tax, anti-government narrative that celebrates the sanctity of property rights. This narrative taps the widely held intuition that there's something wrong with taking the money that people have earned through hard work and perseverance, and using it to confer benefits on others.

Some version of this intuition is inseparable from liberalism itself. Liberals believe in property rights partly because they believe, broadly speaking, that people are entitled to fair compensation for their work. The ability to work and earn a decent income gives people an important lever for asserting control over their lives. When people are able to earn their own income, they are less dependent on others and less subject to unwanted control, and they can use their income to organize their lives according to their values. All of this depends, in part, on their earning a decent wage. It also depends on property rights: for this story to work, people must *own* their incomes and the goods they purchase with it. If property rights are absent or insecure, working and earning are no longer reliable levers. Where the fruits of one's labor can be summarily taken away by others, work itself can change from a source of freedom to a form of bondage.

The problem arises when these sensible ideas linking property and freedom are hijacked for entirely unreasonable ends. They go off the rails, for instance, when people start believing that their *pre-tax income* embodies fair compensation for their work, and that they are therefore entitled to all (or almost all) of it. This intuition, which is widespread in the United States, gives rise to some predictable cognitive dissonance: Americans know that taxes are needed to fund such essentials as infrastructure, public education, and national defense, and they tend to support such spending.[68] But many view taxation itself with suspicion, because it feels like they are being forced to part with their own money. Taxation seems to bear a family resemblance to theft or extortion: government officials are reaching into taxpayers' pockets and taking money from them to pursue goals that these taxpayers may or may not wish to fund. And when people refuse to comply, they get punished.

This view is fundamentally mistaken. When tax rates are set at fair levels, earners possess property rights to their after-tax incomes, not their pre-tax incomes. To take part of someone's after-tax income is theft. But pre-tax and after-tax income are not morally the same. Society has every right to claim a portion of pre-tax income and use the money to advance socially useful goals. There are several reasons to embrace this view, one of which we have already explored: if the market rate for labor at a given time reflects a set of rules and power relationships that are unfairly tilted in favor of some groups and against others, then this unfairness will be baked into people's pre-tax incomes. In today's economy, as we have seen, workers receive considerably less than they would under fair bargaining conditions, and powerful corporate employers receive considerably more. Taxes levied on wealthier citizens are one way of correcting these distortions and rebalancing the economic scales. Such rebalancing is fully consistent with the liberal rationale for property rights: it is a way of trying to ensure that people receive fair compensation for their work.

Second and more fundamentally, the high levels of productivity for which people get paid are made possible by a wide range of public goods. These include not just a legal system and a stable currency, not just a market economy, not just basic infrastructure and public safety, but also public health measures and public schools (which lay the foundation for a healthy and skilled labor force), public investments in research and innovation, and a great deal more. Among other things, this public architecture creates stable pathways of cultural transmission that allow knowledge and technology to be passed on from one generation to the next and to grow cumulatively, vastly enhancing each person's productive power. Anyone curious to know what their individual labor is worth, unmixed with any of these societal resources, need only try to survive alone, off the grid and beyond the law, in some remote corner of the Amazonian jungle or the Siberian steppe.[69] The meager subsistence these rugged individualists might scrabble out of nature would indeed be theirs alone. No one would have any right to tax it.

Some libertarians have argued that we could maintain high productivity, freedom, and intergenerational transmission under a minimal state, with low tax rates, that offers very few public goods—no health or welfare services, for example, no public schools, and no child labor or worker safety laws.[70] Like much else in libertarian theory, this is an entirely speculative claim. No minimal state has ever existed for any length of time in the modern world. It seems far more likely, given the empirical evidence at our disposal, that a minimal state would quickly collapse under the weight of its inequality and cruelty: it would leave huge numbers of people poor and desperate and foment serious political unrest, which would be quelled either through increasingly authoritarian measures or by granting substantial concessions to those in need. Either choice would end the minimal state.

In functional modern societies, the question of taxation—who to tax, how much to tax them, and how to spend the revenue—has always been a legitimate and essential topic for political debate. This debate cannot be settled by appealing to property rights—because, again, people do not possess property rights to their pre-tax income. One of the key questions that needs answering in this debate is *how much of our pre-tax income are we entitled to own in the first place?*[71] In liberal societies, this evolving conversation should be guided by the fundamental value of equal freedom. There are good reasons not to take too much pre-tax income, especially from people who are not affluent. High taxes can deprive people of fair compensation for their labor, and it leaves them with fewer private resources (and so diminishes the range of choices they can make with them). High taxes can also weaken private investment and spending in ways that harm society as a whole. But setting taxes too low can also exact serious costs. Failure to invest enough in shielding workers from exploitation can undermine their prospects for equal freedom. Failure to invest enough in infrastructure, research, training programs, and other measures designed to widen opportunities can also leave people trapped and deprived.

The evidence from the middle decades of the twentieth century—not just in the United States but also in Europe and Japan—suggests that setting high marginal tax rates on the wealthy and using that money to expand opportunities for everyone else yields highly beneficial social and economic effects. Most Americans today are shocked to learn that between 1932 and 1980, the highest earners paid a marginal tax rate that reached, on average, *81 percent.* The revenue generated through steeply progressive taxation brought greater equality, wider opportunity, and more inclusive freedom, all without seriously dampening innovation or productivity.[72]

Liberal Experiments

The key to solving the scourge of labor exploitation lies in boosting workers' economic power so they can negotiate fair labor contracts. Given the scale of the assault on workers' economic power, this is a huge, multi-faceted task. We must build workers' power by enhancing collective bargaining rights, worker ownership, and co-determination, and by offering affordable skills training and retraining. We must also provide all citizens with reliable access to a range of essential resources, so that they won't have to bargain from a position of desperation. Radical liberals should remain open to the widest range of experiments in both of these areas and pursue the strategies that deliver the best results.

As part of this multifaceted effort, US labor law clearly needs to be overhauled. Rebuilding the power of organized labor is perhaps the most important step toward reducing labor exploitation and creating the countervailing power needed to fight exploitation. Unionization should be made easier for employees, and companies should face stiff penalties when they intimidate and punish workers who try to organize (this behavior is pervasive, and the existing penalties are meager).[73] "Right-to-work" statutes, which are designed to weaken unions, should be repealed or overridden by federal law. Workers not covered by existing labor laws—including domestic workers, agricultural workers, and independent contractors—must also be granted the right to organize.[74] More fundamentally, the right of representation should be deepened and reimagined so that workers can organize sector-wide unions, as they do in most European countries. If fast food workers, for example, could organize a national (or even statewide) union, it would enhance their bargaining power substantially. California has taken steps in this direction by creating a state labor council with the power to set minimum standards—including minimum wages—across the fast food industry.

Unions should also be empowered to engage in a broader range of activities, including picketing and boycotting companies that they do not work for directly and striking in solidarity with other workers in their employer's supply chain. Like our welfare system, our labor laws are out of step with economic reality: in a world of multi-billion-dollar corporations with sprawling global supply chains, American workers simply lack the legal tools they need to get a fair deal. There is much to learn from other advanced democracies, such as Germany, where workers exercise considerably more bargaining power than they have in the United States—and enjoy better wages, benefits, job security, and economic mobility.

These changes should be paired with other policies designed to improve salaries and working conditions. These include not just a higher minimum wage but also broader efforts to promote "broad-based capitalism"—that is, a capitalism with a broad and inclusive ownership class. Studies have consistently shown that firms with profit-sharing or worker-ownership schemes are better places to work: salaries and benefits are better, there are more opportunities for training and advancement, and working conditions overall are healthier. These firms also tend to perform well economically.[75] A great deal can be done to promote these models. Government can create financial incentives to encourage small business owners, for example, to sell their businesses to employees when they retire—and it can expand access to credit on favorable terms to help employees become co-owners. Corporate tax rates can be structured to provide strong incentives for firms to offer profit-sharing programs for employees, and procurement policies could be structured to give worker-owned companies—and those with substantial profit-sharing initiatives—preference in competing for government contracts. Financial institutions could be given incentives to invest a substantial share of their capital in worker-owned companies and cooperatives. Profit-sharing and worker ownership have long histories in the United States—including at huge firms such as Procter & Gamble and Southwest Airlines, and successful niche companies such as Dansko and Bob's Red Mill.[76] But shifting the economy decisively in this direction has yet to become a national priority. The goal should not be to replace shareholder-owned businesses entirely, but to promote a far more diversified economy in which workers can realistically choose to work in more democratic workplaces.

The deepening exploitation of American labor has been partly driven by the extraordinary power that Wall Street investors have amassed since the 1980s. Giant firms such as BlackRock, Vanguard, and State Street have accumulated substantial ownership stakes in American businesses across all sectors of the economy and have used this leverage to insist that corporate managers focus single-mindedly on maximizing stock value. In so doing, they have significantly worsened the misalignment between the interests of executives and those of their workers. Companies like Walmart and Costco have been punished, for example, for raising wages or investing in their workforces.[77] Wall Street also pushes companies to thwart unionization and, more generally, to treat most workers as disposable assets. Meanwhile, the worst offenders of all—private equity firms—have perfected the art of buying up successful companies, selling off their assets and loading them with debt, and driving them into bankruptcy while they reap hundreds of millions in profits.[78] In all of these ways, Wall Street aggressively transfers wealth from workers and communities to investors and shareholders (the vast majority of whom are rich: the wealthiest 10 percent of Americans own 89 percent of all US stocks).[79]

Scholars have proposed a range of solutions to this problem. Weakening shareholder power by diversifying corporate boards is one obvious solution. So is breaking up massive investment firms or capping the amount that any one firm can own in a given industry or corporation.[80] The Stop Wall Street Looting Act, introduced by progressive lawmakers in 2022, would give workers stronger claims in bankruptcy proceedings and curb some of private equity's worst excesses. We should also outlaw stock buybacks, which encourage corporate executives to inflate their company's stock price at the expense of investments in their workforces or in research and development. (These were illegal before the Reagan administration.) None of this will come easily: finance routinely spends more to lobby Congress than any other industry.

Alongside finance, no sector of the American economy is more in need of a thorough overhaul than agriculture. Our food production is dominated by ecologically destructive, chemical-intensive monoculture farming, which produces huge quantities of cheap food, but immiserates workers while enriching a handful of mega-corporations and their investors. Extending equal freedom to those who actually work the land and grow our food should be an urgent priority. From a policy perspective, this means withdrawing government support for industrial agribusiness and instead encouraging the growth of local, sustainable food systems that will support decent rural livelihoods. This would also require that we rebuild the local infrastructures—including financing and retail infrastructures—needed to help small farmers bring their goods to market, and support farmers' cooperatives and other participatory organizations devoted to improving rural livelihoods.[81] Strong measures are also needed to combat the exploitation of migrant farmworkers. Allowing these workers to unionize would be an important first step.

In this time of immense national wealth, everyone living in the

United States should also enjoy guaranteed access to certain essential resources and a modicum of economic security. To accomplish this, we must expand and update the welfare state so that it can meet the challenges of the twenty-first-century economy. The American welfare state was designed in the mid-twentieth century, amid very different economic conditions. At a time when jobs tended to be stable and long-term, it made sense to funnel public benefits like healthcare and paid family leave through employers. Today, as the average US job tenure has dropped sharply, as more Americans are cobbling together part-time and temporary work, and as automation and machine intelligence have begun to eliminate more and more jobs altogether, this model no longer makes sense. Virtually all other advanced democracies now recognize both healthcare and paid family leave as fundamental rights that expand people's range of options. Americans should emulate their successes. We should also widen access to secure, affordable housing, strengthen unemployment benefits, and provide access to free bank accounts and publicly subsidized microloans to preempt the financial exploitation of the poor.[82] Postal banking, or the provision of basic financial services through post office outlets, has been a highly successful model historically, and it could bring substantial benefits today.[83]

As globalization and technological change displace more and more workers and eliminate well-paying jobs, there is tremendous need for public investment in training and education programs designed to help workers acquire the skills to shift careers. Public funding for such programs has declined in recent decades even as the problem has intensified, and private firms are often loath to make such investments themselves because retrained workers can easily take their skills elsewhere. (Other affluent democracies spend, on average, five times more money per capita on "active labor market" programs than the United States does).[84] A 2020 study by the MIT Task Force on the

Work of the Future, for example, calls for robust public investment in community colleges, apprenticeship programs, and retraining programs as part of a fundamental social contract to help workers share in the benefits of economic growth and technological change. The report points to successful models from Boston to Florida to South Carolina that feature close regional partnerships between private firms and educational institutions. When these partners work closely together to design training and certificate programs that qualify workers for existing job openings, and when community colleges maintain state-of-of-the-art facilities and offer adequate financial support for trainees, they help restore workers' economic power by widening their access to good jobs and making them more valuable to employers.[85] To fulfill the promise of equal opportunity, these programs must be accessible to all: community colleges should be free for anyone with a high-school diploma (or its equivalent).

As automation and artificial intelligence (AI) displace more and more workers, we will likely need a more ambitious renegotiation of our basic social contract. In the past few years alone, powerful new forms of AI have emerged that threaten to replace not just truck drivers and Uber drivers, but also graphic designers, editors, and a range of other workers. Without fundamental changes to our economic entitlements and expectations, it seems likely that these changes will only deepen the harsh, exploitative tendencies in today's economy: they will deliver cheaper consumer goods, but at the price of greater poverty and economic insecurity for millions. More and more workers who make costly long-term investments in developing their skills will wake up to find that these skills are now obsolete—and they will be thrown into competition for low-wage and temporary work. Widening poverty and insecurity, in turn, will only intensify the cresting political backlash that is destabilizing American politics and society. This dystopian future has already been anticipated by some Silicon

Valley entrepreneurs working at the cusp of technological change, leading them to call for significant economic reforms.[86]

What alternatives can we imagine? More specifically, what would it mean to try to harness these new technologies in the service of equal freedom? If AI is used to enable everyone to work less—by shortening the work week substantially—and if reduced work hours are paired with a universal basic income (UBI), we might remember the first half of the twenty-first century as a period of profound expansion in human freedom. A UBI is a monthly cash payment made to all adult citizens without exception. It could be set at a relatively modest level—say, $1,000 a month—and indexed to inflation. In establishing a financial floor underneath all Americans, a basic income would substantially increase workers' bargaining power. The millions who currently feel compelled by economic desperation to take demeaning or harrowing low-wage jobs would be able to hold out for better wages and working conditions. They could also afford to spend more time looking for better work—or raising their children, caring for elderly family members, or pursuing hobbies or civic projects. Dozens of pilot programs are already experimenting with basic income schemes across the United States (and around the world), and the returns have been positive.[87] Among other benefits, they infuse cash into depressed local economies and help build financial independence for women, who still shoulder a disproportionate share of household and child-rearing work. UBI also treats recipients like free persons: they can spend the money as they see fit, they are not stigmatized (since everyone receives a UBI), and they are not subject to paternalistic oversight by federal bureaucracies. Other reformers, using successful New Deal programs as their model, have suggested a universal jobs guarantee (at a livable wage) as an alternative to a universal basic income.[88] This too would promise to dramatically improve workers' bargaining leverage.

These spending initiatives will inevitably be met with skepticism: where will the money come from? Aren't we already running big budget deficits? There are thorny questions to be answered here, to be sure. But in the wealthiest society in human history, there are plenty of potential answers. Some economists are calling for a dramatic overhaul of American tax policies to make corporations and the wealthy pay their fair share, curtail capital flight, and lay the fiscal foundation for equal freedom. This would mean, for example, restoring high tax rates on large incomes, raising capital gains taxes to bring them in line with income taxes, raising estate taxes, closing the many loopholes that rich people use to game the system, cracking down on offshore tax shelters, regulating and fining the consulting firms that make their fortunes helping rich people dodge taxes, sanctioning countries that maintain tax havens, imposing wealth taxes on billionaires, and taxing financial transactions.[89] Those who balk at these suggestions should remember that the United States once maintained the most progressive tax system in the world and used it to fund a broad slate of public investments that widened opportunities and raised the standard of living among the working class.

One of the most resilient tenets of market fundamentalist ideology is that higher taxes on the rich reduce investment and innovation, dampen economic growth, and ultimately hurt everyone. We now have considerable evidence to the contrary, painstakingly assembled by economists Thomas Piketty and Emmanuel Saez: trickle-down economics is bad policy. It allows the rich to capture an ever larger slice of the economic pie and augments their political and economic power while under-delivering for everyone else.[90] It is an economic program calibrated to produce oligarchy and exploitation, not freedom.

All of these ambitious policy goals may seem remote in our current political landscape. Many of the policy experiments that shielded workers from exploitation in the mid-twentieth century have been weakened and rolled back by forty-five years of concerted activism by business elites. In Donald Trump, they have found a president committed to carrying this pro-corporate project to ruthless new extremes. But the ideological ground is shifting beneath their feet: the neoliberal consensus that has long justified their assault on American workers has splintered. Since 2016, elements of the Republican Party have begun to pivot—albeit haltingly and unevenly—away from market fundamentalism. As the GOP seeks to tailor its appeal to white working-class voters in post-industrial areas, its message has become inflected with economic populism. At the same time, the Democratic Party under Joe Biden mostly rejected Clinton-era deregulation, which was still residually influential during the Obama administration, and embraced a more egalitarian economic agenda.

Public opinion surveys suggest that voters want a lot more. During the 2024 election cycle, an overwhelming majority of American voters—on both the left and right—declared that our economic system "unfairly favors powerful interests." Younger Trump supporters were far more likely to express this view than older ones. At the start of the COVID-19 pandemic, moreover, 45 percent of respondents in the United States, including around 40 percent of lower-income Republican voters, said they would favor a universal basic income of a thousand dollars a month.[91] This incipient realignment has created opportunities for substantial policy shifts, and the American left should capitalize on them wherever possible. Still, it will take time—and hard work—to lay the ideological groundwork for these changes and to channel working-class anger toward progressive economic goals. It took decades of activism and ideological struggle to create the political climate that, in an unprecedented economic depression, allowed the Roosevelt administration to push through the New Deal.

4

Racial Hierarchy

Status hierarchies are among the oldest and most resilient enemies of human freedom. Throughout human history, whole groups have been deprived of status because of traits over which they have little control, such as their race, ethnicity, gender, caste, or sexual identity. Those who belong to these disadvantaged groups have often suffered status deprivations so severe that their basic interests are irreparably damaged. They have been subject to arbitrary violence and abuse, denied legal protection, shut out of economic opportunities, consigned to ghettos, and singled out for public humiliation and contempt. In the most egregious cases, these hierarchies give rise to tyranny. But even when they fall short of this, they tend to produce deep, durable inequalities that are inimical to equal freedom.

There are many forms of status hierarchy in American society, and no two are alike. Gender identity and sexual orientation, for example, can produce several overlapping layers of unequal status—man over woman, straight over gay, cisgender over transgender—each with a distinctive history. Rather than generalize about all our hierarchies, I will focus on racial hierarchy and the experience of Black Americans in particular, which casts an especially harsh light on this country's liberal aspirations. Since the nation's founding, critics of the American political experiment have continually singled out race relations as the leading evidence of its hypocrisy and moral failure.

Liberals are sometimes accused of pursuing superficial reforms that ignore or downplay structural barriers to freedom. They are accused, specifically, of ignoring the institutions and power imbalances that hold racial hierarchies in place. While this is true of some versions of liberal thought, it is not true of radical liberalism. Radical liberals believe that freedom means the power to make choices. Because structural barriers tend to destroy this power, radical liberalism compels us to identify and dismantle them.

The Broken Promise of Racial Equality

At the close of the Civil Rights Era almost sixty years ago, there was reason to be hopeful. Jim Crow had finally been dismantled, and it seemed possible that the end of legal discrimination would mark the beginning of a steady march toward racial equality. This hope has proven hollow: much as it was in the late 1960s, American society today is deeply scarred by racial inequality, caused by both historical injustice and ongoing discrimination.

The persistence of racial hierarchy can be documented in many ways. Let me begin with some of the most obvious indicators. As of 2021, the median wealth of white households was $250,400, compared to $27,100 for Black households—a nine-to-one ratio. Fully 24 percent of Black families had no wealth at all or negative wealth, meaning that their debts exceeded their assets (compared to 9 percent of white families).[1] The Black unemployment rate is roughly double the white unemployment rate (although the gap has narrowed in the past decade).[2] Health indicators show that African Americans consistently suffer higher rates of poor health and disease—including life-threatening ailments, from COVID-19 to cervical cancer—and worse access to medical care.[3] Meanwhile, broad disparities persist in education: our public schools are highly segregated, and schools with a large proportion of Black students tend to be underfunded and overcrowded. Facilities are degraded, discipline is harsher, teachers are paid less. Overall, educational outcomes are considerably worse for Black children than for white children.[4] In this area, racial disparities have actually worsened in recent decades.

Wealth, health, and educational disparities reflect racialized differences in America's neighborhoods. African Americans are far more likely to live and grow up in neighborhoods blighted by poverty and unemployment, high crime rates, and environmental pollution, with few economic opportunities and poor access to essential economic services (including banks, doctors, and grocery stores that sell fresh food). The numbers are striking: of children born between 1985 and 2000, two-thirds of Black children were raised in neighborhoods with poverty rates of at least 20 percent, compared to just 6 percent of white children.[5] Sociologists have shown conclusively that children growing up amid such poverty are far more likely to experience permanent disadvantages in wealth, educational attainment, health, and other areas, and to pass these on to their own children.[6]

These inequalities are further aggravated by racial disparities in our criminal legal system. People of color—and Black people in particular—are more likely to be pulled over by police, more likely to be arrested, more likely to be wrongfully convicted, more likely to be imprisoned, more likely to receive harsh sentences, and more likely to end up in solitary confinement. Black Americans are put in state prisons at roughly five times the rate of white Americans. They are also more likely to suffer grievous violence at the hands of both police officers and vigilantes.[7] The effects of these disparities are magnified by the extraordinary harshness of the US criminal legal system, which is vast, brutal, and punitive compared to those in other affluent democracies. All of this has wreaked havoc on Black lives and communities. Among other things, those enmeshed in the criminal legal system suffer significant economic losses, diminished opportunities, and higher rates of poverty and homelessness.[8] These losses are then transmitted to the next generation as children grow up deprived of their parents and the economic resources and stability their parents might have provided. Our criminal legal system thus intensifies racial inequality. Donald Trump's promise to scuttle federal oversight of local police departments will only exacerbate this trend.[9]

The story of racial hierarchy in America cannot be told, however, simply through a snapshot of current conditions; it must include the nearly four centuries of racial injustice that have brought us to this point. For two of those centuries, Black Americans were enslaved and systematically dehumanized—treated as personal property, not as human beings. With every passing decade, it seems, historians discover more about the appalling brutality of Southern slavery, especially at the height of the cotton boom, when white plantation owners competed to find more efficient and ingenious ways of exploiting Black bodies.[10] After emancipation and a brief experiment in trying to build a racially egalitarian society in the South (1867–1877), Black communities were subjected to another eighty years of Jim Crow, during which they were demeaned, terrorized, denied equal treatment under the law, deprived of economic and educational opportunities, and consigned to the bottom rung of a harsh racial hierarchy.

The story hardly ends there: in recent decades, historians have emphasized the complicity of northern cities and states—and the federal government—in creating and maintaining racial hierarchy throughout the country. The twentieth century was a period of extraordinary wealth creation for white families, who in the wake of the New Deal benefited from a host of government policies designed to expand economic opportunity and strengthen the middle class. At almost every step of the way, these policies were deliberately crafted to exclude Black workers and families. New Deal laws guaranteeing a minimum wage, social security, and unemployment insurance excluded the sectors of the economy where African Americans tended to work—including agriculture and domestic service. When labor unions achieved legal recognition under the 1935 Wagner Act, they were allowed to discriminate by race; so too were the local officials who administered new anti-poverty programs (Aid to Dependent Children in particular). After World War II, when the GI bill expanded economic opportunities for white veterans, millions of their Black counterparts were denied access to its benefits.[11]

Housing policy has been especially significant in reproducing racial inequality, because homeownership is such an important vehicle for wealth creation. In the middle decades of the twentieth century, the federal government embarked on a sustained effort to expand homeownership as a way of building wealth and financial security—and it helped millions of white families. With the government insuring mortgage loans to reduce the risk to lenders, interest rates came way down, mortgages were suddenly affordable, and white families rushed to take advantage. Again, Black families were systematically excluded: government agencies refused to insure loans in neighborhoods that were predominantly Black (a practice known as "redlining"). Black buyers had to contend instead with predatory contract loans, in which a single missed payment could mean not just losing the home, but also forfeiting all of the buyer's accumulated equity. Black families were also prevented—sometimes by official government policies—from buying in predominantly white neighborhoods. The Federal Housing Administration, for example, financed the construction of entire suburban neighborhoods on the explicit condition that the homes be sold only to white buyers.[12] In doing so, it facilitated white flight from urban centers even as it prevented Black families from following. These exclusionary patterns were reinforced by a host of local practices, including restrictive covenants among homeowners (forbidding sale to Black buyers), discriminatory zoning laws, and when all else failed, intimidation and violence, which was sanctioned or ignored by local police forces.[13]

Racial exclusion in the housing market not only denied Black families a vital source of wealth and economic mobility, it also contributed to the creation of urban ghettos and their ramifying harms. Beginning in the 1960s, the US economy experienced a precipitous "deindustrialization" as manufacturing jobs were moved offshore. Urban areas, and the Black workers concentrated there, were especially hard-hit by job losses and unemployment. How did our governments respond? Instead of reviving urban centers, most took a different path: they encouraged white out-migration by investing heavily in white suburbs and the highway systems that linked them to commercial centers, while moving to isolate Black urban populations and disinvest from their neighborhoods. Suburban school districts were split off from urban districts and given a disproportionate share of public funding, contributing to disastrous declines in the quality of urban schools. Public housing projects were concentrated in Black neighborhoods and allowed to deteriorate, and industrial pollutants were disproportionately concentrated there. Meanwhile, the ghetto was increasingly treated as a problem to be contained through aggressive policing, surveillance, and control. Although these patterns unfolded unevenly across different cities and states, the overall trajectory is unmistakable.[14]

Black communities have not been passive victims; instead, many proved immensely resilient in the face of these continual affronts. From the abolitionist movement and Reconstruction to the Civil Rights and Black Power movements to the Movement for Black Lives, they mobilized to resist discrimination and overcome racist obstacles. Through church and community organizations, networks of thriving Black-owned businesses, historically Black colleges and universities, and other educational initiatives, they created vibrant neighborhoods and opened up paths to the middle class.[15] Millions of Black workers and home-buyers redoubled their efforts to make ends meet and get ahead. But with every step, they faced far steeper obstacles than their white counterparts, and success often proved fragile. Black-owned homes have a greater risk of depreciation, partly because white flight from neighborhoods with growing numbers of Black residents can undermine local housing markets.[16] Moreover, structural disadvantages affecting the entire Black population mean that Black workers tend to have less access to family help when they suffer setbacks. There are fewer obstacles to downward mobility.[17]

Recently, numerous studies have documented the persistence of racial discrimination in twenty-first-century America. Scholars have repeatedly demonstrated the power of implicit bias in many different contexts, with grave implications for Black people in particular.[18] Studies have shown that racial bias exists in the criminal legal system, from police and prosecutors' behavior to judges' sentencing decisions.[19] Other studies reveal patterns of discrimination in the housing market: in the behavior of realtors, for example, and in white residents' continued aversion to having Black neighbors. In the years leading up to the subprime mortgage crisis, Black homebuyers were more likely to be offered subprime mortgage loans than white buyers with similar economic profiles, and they therefore suffered disproportionately.[20] Similar patterns can be found in the job market: a much-cited 2004 study showed, for example, that resumés listing identical qualifications received substantially less interest when the applicant had a Black-sounding name (a number of experimental studies have since confirmed this result).[21] Black and Latino workers also earn lower wages than white workers with comparable educational backgrounds.[22] It is impossible to measure the cumulative effects—psychological and economic—of these continuing forms of discrimination, but they clearly inflict serious harm on Black Americans.

It is important to underscore that the oppression and marginalization of Black Americans form part of a broader pattern of racial injustice that also afflicts other groups, including Hispanic and Native American people. Native Americans, for instance, suffer from acute disadvantages that are directly linked to the historical injustices they have suffered. In 2018, a quarter of Native Americans lived in poverty—and the rate was substantially higher for those living in tribal areas.[23] Schools on tribal lands have never been adequately funded, and the federal allotment per student continues to decline. There are few Native American teachers, and little effort is made to design curricula that will educate students about their own culture and language. Meanwhile, access to basic infrastructure is significantly worse on tribal lands. In short, Native American communities continue to endure chronic public neglect and underinvestment, which result in significantly diminished opportunities.[24]

By any reasonable moral standard, these patterns of racial inequality and injustice are inexcusable. Our willingness, as a nation, to continue heaping insult and disadvantage on groups that have already suffered centuries of abuse stands as a profound indictment of American politics and society. Radical liberalism can help bring these injustices into clearer focus; it can also guide a just and appropriate response.

The Denial of Equal Freedom

In Chapter 1, I argued that the *equal* in equal freedom expresses three interlocking goals: equal opportunity, equal protection from domination, and equal recognition. The racial inequality in America today violates all three of these standards. It produces deeply unequal opportunities; it exposes Black citizens to domination at the hands of white majorities and their proxies; and it fails to grant them equal recognition. It therefore stands fundamentally at odds with the project of realizing equal freedom in the United States.

The denial of equal opportunity is perhaps our most obvious failure. Black youth in America—Black boys most of all—have significantly fewer economic opportunities than their white counterparts. This is especially true for Black youth growing up in high-poverty neighborhoods—which, as we have seen, is the norm in the United States. Schools are much worse, jobs far scarcer, violence more endemic, and family wealth harder to accumulate.[25] But neighborhood effects do not tell the whole story: studies of economic mobility show that a substantial Black-white gap exists even for children growing up in "good" neighborhoods.[26] Meanwhile, the harshness of our economic system only magnifies the effects of unequal opportunity: Black workers are overrepresented in low-earning jobs, where they enjoy few workplace benefits and little job flexibility, and where work hours are unstable and unpredictable.[27] Combined with Black families' far lower median wealth, these disadvantages eviscerate Black workers' bargaining power and leave them, as a group, highly vulnerable to economic exploitation.

The failure to shield Black citizens from domination is also glaring. Recall that dominating another means holding the power to damage their basic interests with relative impunity. Nowhere is this more apparent in America today than in the criminal legal system. It has become agonizingly clear in recent years that police officers exercise vast discretionary power to brutalize and kill Black citizens, and that they often escape punishment. Prosecutors also exercise extraordinary discretion in their sentencing decisions and in extracting plea deals from vulnerable defendants, often with life-altering consequences.

In the War on Drugs, which has targeted Black communities disproportionately, aggressive prosecutors have used this discretion to upend
countless lives—guilty and innocent alike—and indeed whole communities.[28] Meanwhile, the Supreme Court has made it almost impossible to successfully challenge racial bias in the criminal legal system. In *McCleskey v. Kemp* (1987), a 5–4 majority ruled that anyone
alleging racial bias in criminal sentencing had to show specific evidence of discriminatory *intent*—a very difficult threshold to meet. It
was not enough to demonstrate a disparate impact on racial minorities, no matter how severe. A series of subsequent decisions, from
United States v. Armstrong (1996) through *Alexander v. Sandoval* (2001),
raised further barriers to successful litigation. These decisions have
allowed police and prosecutors to proceed with near impunity unless
(in the case of police) they happen to be caught on camera or (in the
case of prosecutors) they operate in districts with substantial minority
voting power and determined grassroots mobilization.[29]

The criminal legal system is hardly the only site of racial domination. In recent years, Americans have witnessed the extraordinary
spectacle of cities with majority Black populations falling into such
profound disrepair that the most essential services—including the
flow of clean water—begin to fail. From Flint, Michigan, to Jackson,
Mississippi, Black residents have found themselves living in conditions more typical of poor developing countries because the infrastructure that serves them has been neglected for so long. The causes
of these crises are complex, but they clearly originate with the creation of urban ghettos through white flight and disinvestment, which
collapsed municipal tax bases and left cities unable to maintain basic
infrastructure. The problem was then aggravated by state legislatures'
refusal, decade after decade, to allocate the funds necessary to avoid
catastrophic degradation. White-dominated state governments (and

their constituents) essentially said: *We will let your communities literally fall apart and ignore your repeated pleas for help, and we will do so with impunity.*[30]

This brings us to the question of recognition, the most complicated of our three egalitarian goals. Since equal recognition is a less intuitive standard than the other two, it is worth exploring in more detail. Equal recognition, as I explained in Chapter 1, means being accorded "the status of full partners in social interaction" and not being treated as a second-class citizen. Its first requirements are equality under the law and equal political rights, but that is not the end of it. Even people who enjoy equal rights can be denied equal recognition. This can happen, according to political theorist Nancy Fraser, when "institutionalized patterns of cultural value" consistently portray them as "inferior, excluded, wholly other, or simply invisible."[31] Such portrayals have the cumulative effect of eroding their social status and making it difficult to participate on equal terms in many kinds of social interaction. Earlier, I cited the experience of American Muslims in the wake of 9/11 as an illustration.

The history of discrimination against LGBTQ people in the United States offers another example. Heterosexual bigotry clearly was enshrined in law, from the criminalization of sodomy to the many exclusions that shaped family law. It was encoded in diverse areas of public policy, including, for example, immigration and asylum policy. But it also took other insidious forms. It shaped professional practices in medicine and psychotherapy. It was expressed in demeaning stereotypes that circulated widely in popular culture. It found expression in harassment, shaming, and bullying, as well as discrimination in employment. LGBTQ people commonly felt that social inclusion could be achieved only by concealing or suppressing their sexual identity, which imposed heavy psychological burdens. Together, these overlapping forms of discrimination and contempt denied them equal recognition and severely diminished their freedom. This loss of freedom cannot be fully appreciated unless we look beyond the law itself to the "institutionalized patterns of cultural value" that shape everyday life.[32]

How is any of this relevant to the problem of racial justice in America? It is obvious that Black Americans have long suffered from discrimination and contempt that reach far beyond the law and affect many aspects of social and economic life. But I want to make a narrower point about the enduring cultural significance of historical injustice. When a group is singled out for horrific abuse; when this abuse creates deep, heritable patterns of disadvantage; and when these disadvantages are allowed to persist and fester in the midst of spectacular affluence and economic growth—these facts alone convey a profound *disrespect* for the affected group. Its members are in effect being told: *We cannot be bothered to heal the wounds that our government and society have inflicted on you, because your lives do not matter enough; we do not count you as our equals.* This country's failure, since the close of the Civil Rights Era, to make significant progress toward acknowledging and remedying the effects of historical injustice amounts to a deep failure of recognition. This failure has only been aggravated by many white Americans' tendency, throughout this period, to blame African Americans for their own persistent disadvantage.

Countless Black writers have borne witness to this third dimension of inequality. Consider, for example, the words that Ta-Nehisi Coates wrote in an open letter to his son in 2015. He begins by reflecting on the pervasive violence and fear he experienced growing up in West Baltimore and his awareness of the chasm that separated his own world from the white, suburban neighborhoods that he saw on television, "where children did not regularly fear for their bodies." To his young eyes, these distant places seemed almost unfathomably alien—they were "organized around pot roasts, blueberry pies, fire-works, ice-cream sundaes, immaculate bathrooms, and small toy trucks that were loosed in wooded backyards with streams and end-less lawns." He writes of his own obsession with this divide:

> I knew that my portion of the American galaxy, where bodies were enslaved by a tenacious gravity, was black and that the other, liber-ated portion was not. I knew that some inscrutable energy pre-served the breach. I felt, but did not yet understand, the relation between that other world and me. And I felt in this a cosmic in-justice, a profound cruelty, which infused an abiding, irrepressible desire to unshackle my body and achieve the velocity of escape.

Coates then responds to the killing of Eric Garner, in broad daylight, by police on a Staten Island sidewalk:

> It is not necessary that you believe that the officer who choked Eric Garner set out that day to destroy a body. All you need to under-stand is that the officer carries with him the power of the American state and the weight of an American legacy, and they necessitate that of the bodies destroyed every year, some wild and dispropor-tionate number of them will be black. Here is what I would like for you to know: In America, it is traditional to destroy the black body—*it is heritage*. . . . you are a black boy, and you must be re-sponsible for your body in a way that other boys cannot know. Indeed, you must be responsible for the worst actions of other black bodies, which, somehow, will always be assigned to you. And you must be responsible for the bodies of the powerful—the police-man who cracks you with a nightstick will quickly find his excuse in your furtive movements.[33]

These passages convey a great deal. Tremendous economic inequality, whose origins lie in the most brutal forms of racial exploitation. A vast, racialized power to dominate and destroy with impunity, of which young Black men must always be aware. But also a powerful status hierarchy, conveyed by the accumulated wrongs of American history, which have been allowed to persist and scar the lives of generation after generation of Black citizens. A society that allows these patterns to persist, writes Coates, is not a society that recognizes Black people as equals. This is the essential point I want to make about equal recognition.[34]

For African Americans, of course, unequal recognition is deeply entangled with both unequal opportunity and domination. Coates makes this clear: the persistence of these other forms of inequality, against the background of this country's history of racism, is a key component in the denial of equal recognition to Black Americans. It is important to see, however, that unequal recognition is not simply reducible to these other dimensions of inequality. We can imagine a group of recent Ukrainian immigrants who, arriving in this country with nothing but the clothes on their backs, experience severe economic inequality and feel powerless when dealing with unfamiliar institutions (and public officials), but do not experience a lack of recognition. Failures of recognition have to do with the cultural meanings that attach to these other forms of inequality. Many Black Americans feel, justifiably, that the tangible economic and legal inequalities imposed on them have a particular meaning in this country: they reflect a continuing tendency to treat Black people, in particular, as unworthy of equal respect. The slogan Black Lives Matter captures this feeling precisely.

The Role of Liberal Individualism

If racial hierarchy presents such a serious threat to human freedom, dismantling it should be a matter of urgent priority for liberals. Yet liberalism stands accused, by some critics on the left, of ignoring or even perpetuating racial inequality. This criticism often centers on inequality's structural causes: liberalism is too *individualistic,* critics claim, to successfully diagnose or attack structural inequalities, and it therefore tends to protect existing patterns of power and privilege. Although some versions of these criticisms depend on caricatures of the liberal position, others expose real weaknesses in the liberal outlook. Evaluating them will help us take stock of these deficiencies and consider how to correct them.

As we evaluate these criticisms, I want to keep in mind the difference between two questions: first, *can* liberal ideas be used to justify, excuse, or tacitly conceal racial hierarchy? And second, are even the best versions of liberalism susceptible to these tendencies? The answer to the first question is undoubtedly yes. Like any broad, complex family of political ideas, liberalism can be appropriated for a wide variety of purposes. Its principles can be (and often have been) distorted, cherry-picked, or selectively used to justify oppressive inequalities. It is also true that some influential versions of liberalism— including those that tend toward market fundamentalism—are still deployed to buttress longstanding status hierarchies in the United States.[35] Although it is very important to explore and document these tendencies, none of them shows that liberalism is incapable of seeing or responding to racial injustice. As we consider the merits of radical liberalism, we should therefore remain focused on the second question: does liberalism, in its most defensible formulations, tend to excuse or conceal racial injustice?[36]

The argument that liberalism is too individualistic to recognize racial injustice comes in several forms. The first takes aim at what we might call *colorblind liberalism,* or what Eduardo Bonilla-Silva has called "abstract liberalism."[37] This view holds that the appropriate response to racial injustice is to cease granting preferential treatment to any and all racial groups: the only way to promote equal freedom is to embrace a colorblind attitude that treats people simply as individuals. Chief Justice John Roberts famously endorsed this idea when he wrote, in a 2007 decision, that "the way to stop discrimination on the basis of race is to stop discriminating on the basis of race."[38] From this perspective, affirmative action programs in college admissions, for example, look like "reverse racism": instead of evaluating candidates strictly on their merits, colleges treat people differently according to their racial identity. Superficially, this view seems to draw support from liberal principles: it demands equal treatment under the law, and it condemns racial bias of all kinds as a threat to individual liberty and opportunity. Its implications also reach well beyond affirmative action: when conservative groups sued the Biden administration in 2021 to block its efforts to earmark debt relief for Black farmers (who, as a group, had suffered overt discrimination at the hands of the USDA for decades), they too proclaimed their adherence to the liberal ideals of nondiscrimination and equal opportunity.[39] The Trump administration has used the same rhetoric as it dismantles programs designed to widen opportunities for racial minorities. These programs include diversity, equity, and inclusion (DEI) initiatives across the public and private sectors, and entire federal agencies such as the Minority Business Development Agency.

It does not take much to see that this form of colorblindness, as deployed in America today, is morally perverse. First the dominant majority brutalizes, demeans, and constrains a racial minority, producing deep patterns of heritable inequality and hierarchy. Then members of the same majority group insist that any policies specifically designed to alleviate the effects of historical injustice amount to illegitimate discrimination. In this context, colorblindness functions as a way of perpetuating unjust inequalities. It is manifestly incompatible with the goal of realizing equal opportunity—or equal freedom more broadly.[40]

There is an important distinction to be drawn here. When we try to envision what a perfectly just society would look like, colorblindness has an important role to play. We should aspire to live in a society in which people's racial identity does not shape their life chances or the way they are treated by police. This aspiration embodies some of the core principles of liberal philosophy. But the struggle to promote equal freedom *here and now,* against a historical background marred by profound injustice, demands different norms and strategies: it requires that we acknowledge and make amends (as best we can) for past injustices and work hard to eliminate their continuing effects.[41] This can be done only by conferring more resources and opportunities on those who bear the costs of racial injustice.

In Chapter 1, I argued that the pursuit of equal freedom will always involve trade-offs, because people's claims to freedom often conflict. In this case, the *goal* of creating a society in which everyone enjoys equal freedom stands in tension with the *norm* of colorblindness, which forbids that any racial group receive preferential treatment under the law. I argued that such tensions should be resolved in ways that (1) prioritize the freedoms that lie closest to our basic interests and (2) tend to equalize the distribution of freedom in society. Both of these criteria militate against a strict adherence to colorblindness today. I have already shown that the freedoms at stake for Black Americans are absolutely fundamental. Prioritizing these freedoms would also tend to erode deeply entrenched inequalities.

None of this means, of course, that radical liberalism should condone all forms of preferential treatment: remedial policies should impinge as little as possible on other groups' basic interests. For example, the costs of these policies should fall on those who can afford them, not on those who have suffered from economic exploitation and are struggling to stay afloat.

Colorblind liberalism has often drawn support, implicitly or explicitly, from the tendency to imagine that racism itself is reducible to racial animus. If we convince ourselves that racial animus is the main problem, then promoting colorblind attitudes can seem like the ultimate goal. Scholars have shown that this perspective, which some have called "racial liberalism," has dominated the reform agenda in the United States since the mid-twentieth century: white elites in particular have pushed an agenda that emphasizes anti-discrimination, desegregation, and racially inclusive educational curricula at the expense of more ambitious efforts to redress material and political inequalities. "Racial liberalism," writes legal scholar Lani Guinier, "positioned the peculiarly American race 'problem' as a psychological and interpersonal challenge rather than a structural problem rooted in our economic and political system."[42] In our own time, powerful conservative jurists have used this perspective to insist that, absent evidence of intentional discrimination, the courts cannot intervene to redress even glaring patterns of racial inequality (for instance, in the criminal legal system).[43]

Is this position somehow integral to liberalism? Clearly not. Above all, it reflects a willfully simplistic misdiagnosis of the sources of racial hierarchy. Even after racial animus has significantly receded, racial hierarchies are often held in place by the self-interest of dominant groups unwilling to relinquish their advantages. In our society, these advantages run the gamut from privileged access to public goods (such as good public schools) and affluent suburbs, to low tax burdens, to the psychological benefits of belonging to a high-status identity group. Even white voters who pointedly reject racist attitudes have often shown themselves unwilling to relinquish these benefits.[44] In this context, focusing strictly on racial animus tends to reinforce racial hierarchy: it allows white people to reassure themselves that because they do not hold bluntly racist attitudes, they should feel no guilt or obligation to redress racial injustice.[45] None of this is endemic to liberalism—certainly not to radical liberalism. On the contrary, any serious effort to achieve equal freedom must contend with the deep structural sources of racial injustice.

But maybe this more nuanced portrayal is still too simplistic. Maybe liberal ideas encourage us in subtler ways to ignore the reality of structural injustice. Some have argued, for example, that valuing individual freedom as a moral and political goal makes us more likely to believe that social realities are caused by individual choices. One plausible elaboration of this argument goes like this: a culture that values freedom and celebrates individual agency gives rise to a particular kind of esteem. In such a culture, we feel proud of ourselves and win recognition from others when we achieve success through our own efforts. This form of esteem stands in tension, however, with the belief that luck and inherited privilege play significant roles in allocating wealth and status. And this tension in turn leads us to misperceive social reality: to protect our own sense of self-worth, we exaggerate how much control individuals wield over their social and economic fates.[46]

In fact, there is compelling evidence of this cognitive effect in the United States and good reason to believe that it has a significant racial aspect: because white self-esteem is intimately tied to meritocratic ideals, white Americans tend to ignore or downplay the cumulative effects of racial injustice, whether consciously or unconsciously. Sociologist Thomas Shapiro, for example, has found that Americans consistently underemphasize the transformative effects of inherited wealth (and financial assistance from family) in their lives, as well as the disadvantages suffered by those who lack these unearned resources. They do so, he argues, to preserve the powerful meritocratic narrative that sustains their self-respect: we *deserve our position in society because we earned it through tireless effort.*[47] Shapiro shows how this cognitive distortion helps conceal the cumulative effects of racial injustice.

While it seems likely that such distortions will always find fertile soil in our meritocratic culture, it is also important not to overstate the support they draw from liberal ideals. There can be no doubt that freedom connotes responsibility: when I assert that I am a free person, part of what I mean is that I am responsible for my actions. It follows that respecting others as free persons means treating them as responsible agents and not, for example, merely as passive victims of circumstance. (Imagine how it would feel to be treated as though you were not responsible for any of your behavior.) This everyday practice of holding one another responsible is central to relations among free people and therefore to liberalism itself. But we can embrace this practice while also recognizing that our lives are shaped by forces beyond our control. When I praise you for your accomplishments, I am supposing that you have *some* control over the shape of your life. I am not tacitly denying the causal significance of luck or social structure. As a psychological matter, it is possible both to feel pride in our accomplishments *and* to be aware of our own privilege or good fortune—indeed, this is a combination we commonly encourage in our children.

In this time of staggering inequality, more and more Americans are seeing through our meritocratic myths: there is now widespread recognition that wealth derives heavily from "advantages in life" rather than hard work or talent alone.[48] Radical liberalism encourages this recognition. The pursuit of equal freedom demands that we shine a spotlight on the barriers that are holding people down; in this sense, it helps us counteract the cognitive distortions associated with meritocratic esteem. Indeed, there is no credible way to seek equal freedom in the United States without acknowledging—officially and unequivocally—the racial hierarchies that still shape our society and economy, as well as the countless public interventions, from the Homestead Act to the GI Bill, that boosted the fortunes of white Americans. This acknowledgment can help lay the foundation for a reparative politics that is genuinely committed to realizing freedom for all.

The critique of liberal individualism takes other forms, too. Some critics have taken aim at the habit of abstraction that has led so many liberal thinkers to imagine society as a collection of free individuals associating with one another voluntarily. This tendency is evident, for example, in the social contract tradition, which imagines human societies as artifacts of consent among free and equal persons. It is also reflected in the abstract idea of "rational choosers" posited by economists and social choice theorists. Imagining society in these stylized terms leads us to emphasize certain political challenges and ignore others. It suggests that the main work of liberal politics is to devise a set of principles and institutions that can structure the interactions between free individuals. But historically speaking, the individuals who were privileged to interact on these terms—who forged liberal constitutions and bargained as equals in the marketplace— were white men. By imagining whole societies peopled by these abstract individuals, liberal theorists have too often ignored the experiences of enslaved people, women, racial and ethnic minorities, and the propertyless poor. The complex patterns of power and privilege that produce status hierarchies in all existing societies have thus faded from view.[49]

Nowhere are the perils of abstraction clearer than in the market fundamentalism that has done so much to worsen American inequality and stifle the pursuit of racial justice. Begin by imagining society as a group of rational, self-interested individuals. Then construct an idealized model of the free market, which maximizes economic efficiency by rewarding these individuals' effort and ingenuity. Introduce welfare entitlements and social insurance programs into this model, and postulate that they tend to decrease efficiency by weakening incentives to work and reducing the cost (to individuals) of irresponsible behavior. Infer that such programs are therefore counterproductive, not just in your model but also in the real world. Call for them to be weakened or repealed in the name of efficiency and "personal responsibility." And presto! You will have created a picture of social reality so distorted that it is worse than useless. What's missing is *power:* the power that is exercised in both formal and informal ways over vulnerable groups. In Chapter 3, I explored the key role of bargaining power in market economies (and how market fundamentalism conceals it). In this chapter, I described many of the manifestations of racial power. These forms of power pose a direct threat to equal freedom and cry out for ambitious countermeasures.

This final critique of liberal individualism is best understood, then, as an admonition and corrective. It reminds us of the perils of abstraction and the salience of power. Domination and oppression are extraordinarily mutable and resilient, and they continually crop up in new forms. We can understand them only by paying close attention to the lived experience of those who are not free. Many radical critics writing within the liberal tradition have understood as much. In his 1845 *Narrative of the Life of Frederick Douglass: An American Slave,* which remains one of the truly great works of American liberalism, Douglass begins not just with his birth into slavery but also with the fact that he grew up not knowing his own age or birthday and was forbidden even to inquire about them—that is, he begins by exploring the effects of racial power on the mind and character of the enslaved. Mary Wollstonecraft's *A Vindication of the Rights of Woman* (1792)—like Margaret Fuller's *Woman in the Nineteenth Century* (1845)— begins with the several forms of patriarchal power that shaped women's consciousness and habituated them to subordination. None of these writers began by positing a society of abstractly free individuals.

Liberal Exclusions

If excessive individualism has sometimes distorted the liberal perspective, the most profound failures center on exclusion. Any defensible version of liberalism rests on a commitment to the moral equality of persons. In liberal philosophy, this commitment is expressed in the simple yet radical conviction that all people—regardless of race, gender, ethnicity, religion, or any other identity marker—have an equal claim to live freely and therefore an equal claim to fundamental rights, resources, and protections. Internationally, this moral perspective is embodied in the idea of human rights; domestically, it is expressed in the aspiration to extend equal freedom to everyone living within the national territory.[50]

Liberals have too often betrayed this ideal. They have instead extended liberal rights, resources, and protections only to the members of some dominant group or caste: to white people, to Europeans, to men, to Christians or Protestants, to heterosexuals. They have reserved liberal freedoms for some while consigning others to subordination and oppression, and then deployed liberal concepts to justify these exclusions. In the United States, for example, white men have continually mobilized the discourse of individual rights and limited government to protect their power to dominate and oppress women and people of color. At various times, they have deployed it to defend slavery, to reject a radical reconstruction of the South after the Civil War, to resist the desegregation of public schools, and to buttress husbands' control over their wives. In effect, white men have long claimed the *right* to dispose of others at their pleasure.[51]

Some of liberalism's defenders insist that these exclusions were illiberal because they violated some people's rights. I disagree. The history of liberalism can be told as a sustained argument between those pushing for greater inclusion and those trying to hold the line against it, with each side staking out recognizably liberal positions. Advocates on both sides wanted societies marked by expansive personal freedom, buttressed by institutions such as the rule of law, democratic accountability, free media, and an independent judiciary. But they disagreed about who was entitled to this freedom in the first place. To recover a usable liberal past, we must look to the inclusive end of the spectrum: to those deploying liberal ideas to condemn slavery and racial hierarchy, fight patriarchal domination, promote robust anti-poverty programs and reduce economic inequality, assert the rights of LGBTQ people, and more. These liberals genuinely believed in moral equality as a universal value; their victories have brought significant expansions of human freedom.[52]

But the struggle continues. In our time, the impulse toward racial exclusion is manifest, above all, in what Eddie Glaude Jr. has called the "value gap": too many Americans are apathetic or willfully blind when it comes to the persistence of racial hierarchy in their midst.[53] As I argued earlier, extending equal freedom to all citizens means a great deal more than just unwinding overt discrimination in the law. It means building institutions and cultures that extend opportunities equally, that shield people from domination, and that offer recognition to all—and it means pointedly rejecting institutions and cultures that fail to meet these standards. Allowing racial hierarchy to fester, generation after generation, without taking the steps necessary to disrupt it, reflects a fundamental failure to value the lives and freedom of Black Americans on equal terms. It betrays the principle of moral equality that animates the best versions of liberalism.

This betrayal sheds light on an aspect of liberal politics that is not always appreciated: at its best, it is morally and psychologically demanding. To value all citizens' lives equally in a diverse society, we have to empathize with others across group divides. We also have to take responsibility for creating the conditions under which everyone can live freely. Cultivating these virtues, and resisting the pull of self-ishness and tribalism, is difficult work, and it must be undertaken deliberately and collectively. John Stuart Mill, who had no illusions about this, called for a "religion of humanity" that would help us broaden the circle of our sympathies and to care for human beings simply because they are human.[54] A century later, James Baldwin appealed to the transformative power of love in the face of racial injustice—by which he meant not intimate love but a genuine urge to see and care about the suffering of strangers, to see ourselves through their eyes, and to take responsibility for their well-being. Nourishing such love—which is evident, for example, among climate activists today—is an integral yet underappreciated part of the liberal project: we need it to help motivate our collective struggle for equal freedom.[55]

Finally, it is important to see that exclusion is not a uniquely liberal failing. It is, tragically, a *human* failing. Status hierarchies are as old as humankind. Racial and ethnic hierarchies exist and thrive in a great many societies across the world today, including deeply illiberal ones such as China, Russia, and Myanmar, where they tend to be harsher and more brutal. Socialist societies have hardly been immune to them.[56] In the United States today, meanwhile, the loudest voices promoting white supremacy are manifestly anti-liberal: they form part of an upsurge of right-wing, populist authoritarianism that is deeply uninterested in constitutional limits, the rule of law, or the moral dignity of the individual. I say all of this not to excuse liberals for their failures, but to situate them in a broader context. Racial hierarchy draws on deep and complex motives, including our desire for status, profit, and power. It is further amplified by our propensity to form tribal attachments.[57] Anyone who expects to overcome it simply by rooting out liberal ideas has profoundly misdiagnosed the problem.

Liberal Experiments

Racial hierarchy is complex and intractable, and it is held in place by deeply entrenched structural forces. Any plausible effort to dismantle it must target these forces deliberately. As I have done at the end of Chapters 2 and 3, I want to sketch a few of the many possible solutions that are compatible with radical liberalism. This is not a comprehensive or definitive roadmap.

One fundamental driver of racial inequality in the United States has been discriminatory disinvestment: we have failed to invest in the schools, neighborhoods, and public services necessary to create thriving communities and equal opportunities for Black people. Time and again, public money has been denied to Black communities or deliberately redirected. At the broadest level, then, one of the most important remedies is large-scale, sustained investment. In his 1964 book *Why We Can't Wait,* Martin Luther King Jr. called for a "massive program" of "special, compensatory measures" modeled on the Marshall Plan: investments in schools, social workers, jobs programs, homeownership assistance, and other steps designed to counteract the cumulative effects of discrimination and neglect.[58] More recently, philosopher Tommie Shelby has argued that "black metropolitan neighborhoods with high levels of concentrated disadvantage should, on grounds of justice, be abolished."[59] Let us briefly consider what some of the key elements of such an intervention might look like.

Public schools are the place to start. Studies have consistently shown disparities that disadvantage both poor students and students of color: their schools receive less funding, their teachers are less qualified, their facilities are in worse shape. The vast majority of school funding in the United States comes from local property taxes, which means that schools in affluent neighborhoods, where property values are high, tend to receive a great deal more local funding than schools in poor neighborhoods. All states make some effort to close this gap by allocating more state funding to high-poverty schools. But in many states, this redistribution is not enough to achieve parity. In Nevada, Illinois, and North Dakota, where the funding inequalities are greatest, high-poverty school districts are allocated less than three-fourths of the per-student allocation that affluent school districts receive—and this leaves out private fundraising, which serves as another key revenue stream for schools in wealthier neighborhoods.[60] Many states do achieve parity, or close to it, in allocating public funds—but parity itself is the wrong goal. High-poverty schools require a great deal more per student to achieve comparable educational outcomes. According to one rigorous model, it costs around two-and-a-half times *more* to educate students living in poverty to the same standard as their more affluent peers.[61] Dilapidated facilities that have suffered decades of neglect also call for large capital investments. Redressing these disparities would require a massive reallocation of state funds, combined with ambitious federal investment in states without the necessary fiscal capacity.

Public investment is crucial because it *works*. The most rigorous research available shows that schools that spend more per student tend to produce better academic outcomes. Additional funding dedicated to reducing class sizes, raising teacher pay, adding specialist teaching assistants, expanding access to pre-K, and lengthening the school day (and school year) produces sharply positive outcomes. States that spend more per student—such as Massachusetts, New Jersey, and Connecticut—have better-performing educational systems, including in high-poverty neighborhoods with many students of color.[62] Massachusetts offers a model to learn from: between 1995 and 2015, the state ramped up its funding to high-poverty schools and achieved impressive results.[63] We need to go considerably further: schools in high-poverty districts should be the best-provisioned schools in the country, with the highest teacher salaries, the lowest student-to-teacher ratios, and the most comprehensive counseling and after-school programs. Beyond the educational effects of such investments, they would have great symbolic importance.

Schools should be just the beginning. Any serious attempt to revitalize communities blighted by racial injustice would require a wide range of public investments—in community centers, childcare providers, public transit hubs, safe and appealing public housing, parks, libraries, and more. It would require determined efforts to increase Black homeownership and prevent the displacement that occurs when neighborhoods gentrify. As we have seen, housing has been an area of acute racial injustice and a leading driver of the racial wealth gap. Offering rental assistance, down-payment assistance, subsidized mortgages to "legacy" residents, and interest-free loans for home improvements can all form part of the solution. The Roosevelt Institute, for example, has called for a 21st Century Homestead Act that would buy up vacant housing in urban areas and grant it, along with substantial home improvement funding, to people living in historically redlined communities.[64] Nonprofit groups have already begun this work on a small scale. In West Baltimore, a group called Parity buys up and renovates dilapidated homes and, working closely with community partners, helps longtime Black residents purchase them. The Detroit Justice Center sets up locally managed community land trusts to create affordable housing, including democratically governed housing co-ops, in neighborhoods that have suffered long-term disinvestment. Meanwhile, community development finance institutions are finding innovative ways of providing capital and financial services to communities that have been underserved by traditional banks. Such initiatives should be expanded, replicated, and publicly funded.

Policing reform is also an urgent moral priority. While much emphasis has lately been placed on accountability and oversight, these are just one piece of the puzzle. The goals, methods, and training programs that define policing in the United States need to be over-hauled. In too many of our towns and cities, police departments are under pressure to make arrests, and officers are given incentives to make "Terry stops" (named after the 1968 Supreme Court case *Terry v. Ohio*, which established that people can be stopped and detained temporarily when there is reasonable suspicion of a crime). To meet their targets, police train their attention predictably on the populations with the least power to give them political trouble. Officers are also instructed (and outfitted) to be violent enforcers, and they receive too little training in de-escalation techniques or in guarding against implicit racial bias. For many Black Americans, police have become the standing armies that our founders were so anxious to avoid, pa-trolling their neighborhoods like an occupying force. Police are also asked to intervene in a range of situations, including mental health crises and drug addiction, that they are poorly equipped to handle. The main tools at their disposal—arresting or citing people—are not adequate to the task, and police interventions often cause dangerous and unnecessary escalations.

Fortunately, there are alternative models to learn from. In 2002, as part of the settlement of a lawsuit centered on the police depart-ment's long history of racial discrimination, the city of Cincinnati enacted a sweeping set of reforms. It established a citizen complaint authority with broad investigative powers, revised its use-of-force guide-lines, and established a mental-health response team. More funda-mentally, it rethought the purpose of policing: police were tasked not just with arresting criminals, but also with identifying and address-ing the problems that drove criminal behavior in the first place. Po-lice officers were reimagined as community problem-solvers and asked to work closely with community leaders, local business owners, and other local groups to tackle problems at their source. They were asked to cultivate relationships of mutual trust and collaboration with the communities they policed. For years, police resented and resisted these reforms, which succeeded only after determined implementation by committed city leaders. The results have been striking: between 2002 and 2015, use-of-force incidents plummeted, citizen complaints decreased sharply, and both violent crime and misdemeanor arrests fell significantly. Cincinnati's police department is by no means perfect, but the proactive policing methods it has adopted have found broad support among leading criminologists.[65]

Policing reform should be paired with a broader slate of criminal justice reforms aimed at reducing our prison populations and rehabilitating offenders. It is well known that the United States incarcerates more people, per capita, than any other country in the world, even those ruled by repressive dictatorships. When people are convicted of crimes, we sentence them to extraordinarily long prison terms; our prisons are notoriously brutal and degrading, which exacerbates violent behavior; and those released from prison are often saddled with penalties and restrictions that make it difficult for them to get a job, find stable housing, vote, and otherwise reintegrate into society. Meanwhile, our cash bail system imposes harsh burdens on low-income people who cannot afford to pay. On any given day, almost half a million citizens sit in jail—many of them at risk of losing jobs or housing—before they have even been tried.[66] And as we have seen, people of color—Black people in particular—suffer disproportionately from these policies.[67]

The tragedy of mass incarceration is underscored by the fact that we have alternative models at hand that are supported by rigorous research and evidence. All across the country, cities and community groups have pioneered restorative justice models that seek to rehabilitate offenders while also making amends to victims and communities, often with better results for everyone. These groups include Common Justice in New York City, Community Works in Oakland, the Community Justice for Youth Institute in Chicago, and many more.[68] We also need to curb the extraordinary discretion wielded by prosecutors, who compete to position themselves as "tough on crime" by using ever more aggressive tactics to lock people up; and we need to expand funding significantly for public defenders, who in many states are so overworked and underpaid that it makes a mockery of the Constitutional right to a fair trial.[69] None of this will happen, however, unless affluent liberals have the moral discipline to reject politicians who respond to social problems by stoking fear and calling for harsher enforcement.

Our pursuit of equal recognition must also involve explicit acknowledgment of historical injustices. This needs to happen not just nationally but locally too: for cities and police departments to begin rebuilding trust, they must own up to their racist pasts. Many towns and cities have only begun to uncover and recognize the horrific racial abuses—such as the Tulsa Race Massacre of 1921 and the Race Riot of 1898 in Wilmington, North Carolina—that mar their histories.[70] As political theorist Andrew Valls has argued, we can draw ample evidence from the truth commissions that have been used in many countries around the world, most famously in South Africa. These commissions shed light on historical abuses, challenge distorted and mythologized historical narratives, and make it more difficult for these distortions to be taught in schools and affirmed by public officials. Perhaps most importantly, acknowledging wrongdoing and apologizing for it are ways of affirming that everyone's life and freedom matters equally.[71]

Some scholars and activists have called for reparations as a way of making amends for racial injustice. Some have called for the kinds of investments—in neighborhoods and schools, for example—that

I have just laid out; others have advocated for more targeted benefits for individuals whose ancestors were enslaved or who suffered discrimination under Jim Crow. These proposals raise many contentious questions, which I cannot address adequately here. But clearly the principles animating the call for reparations are compatible with radical liberalism. The racial injustices I have described were perpetrated, at nearly every step, with the help of American governments—local, state, and federal. There is no way our governments can extend equal recognition to those who bear the lingering burdens of historical injustice without taking substantial and deliberate steps—not just symbolic gestures—to make amends.[72]

None of the initiatives I have just outlined should be considered in isolation. When Tommie Shelby calls for the abolition of the ghetto, he argues that comprehensive investment in Black neighborhoods and communities must be paired with fundamental changes to the "basic structure of U.S. society."[73] Martin Luther King Jr., Bayard Rustin, and other leading civil rights activists made similar arguments. They are right: without revitalized and racially inclusive unions, without livable wages and affordable housing and healthcare, and without a host of other measures designed to improve workers' bargaining leverage, the initiatives considered in this chapter would be insufficient. By the same token, any serious effort to redress racial hierarchy must also contend with the escalating ecological harms that fall disproportionately on communities of color.

I should reiterate that this chapter offers only a partial glimpse of racial hierarchy in the United States. It focuses on the experience of Black Americans and their relationship to the white majority, and leaves out not only the experiences of other racial groups, but also the complex, intra-racial dynamics that help maintain status hierarchies. A growing body of scholarly literature, for example, documents the socioeconomic effects of "colorism," which refers to stratification according to skin tone, within racial groups.[74] A more complete treatment of our subject would also explore the interactions between race and gender, which expose women of color, for example, to two separate streams of hierarchical power.

Interlude: Gender Hierarchy and Reproductive Rights

Racial hierarchy is just one manifestation of status hierarchy. Among the many others that divide American society, gender hierarchy stands out as especially significant. The ongoing fight to secure equal freedom for women has been one of the defining struggles in the history of American liberalism, from the Seneca Falls Convention of 1848 through the achievement of voting rights in the early twentieth century, the Second Wave feminism of the 1960s, and beyond. More recently, the fight to secure equal rights for transgender and nonbinary people has emerged as a new frontier in this egalitarian project.

As with racial hierarchy, this is an area of tremendous nuance—far too much to fully address here. Instead, I will focus on reproductive rights, which have emerged as a flashpoint in the ongoing struggle to deconstruct gender hierarchy. With the *Dobbs* decision in 2022, the Supreme Court reversed decades of precedent and denied that women have a constitutionally protected right to seek an abortion. Since then, many American states have enacted strict abortion bans, some with virtually no exceptions, even in cases of rape or incest, or to protect the pregnant woman's health.[75]

It should go without saying that these laws have very serious implications for women's freedom. In Chapter 1, where I described the basic human interests that delineate the highest liberal priorities, bodily integrity was the first item on the list. If our bodies are subject to control by others without our consent, then we stand in their power to a frightening extent. This is precisely what happens when government intervenes to force a woman to endure an unwanted pregnancy: it asserts control over the most intimate functions of her body against her will. Pregnancy involves profound physical changes that, beyond the most obvious ones, alter the hormones and brain, the respiratory system, the gastrointestinal system, and more. Some of these effects are permanent. These bodily transformations are compounded by other, deeper changes, which philosopher Margaret Little describes in these terms: "the enterprise of motherhood restructures the self, changing the shape of one's heart, the primary commitments by which one lives one's life, the terms by which one judges one's life a success or failure."[76] This is true, she continues, even for some women who give up their child for adoption. Many women welcome and cherish these changes, but for those who do not, reproductive rights protect their power to make choices about truly fundamental interests.

When women lack this power, they are vulnerable to domination. In fact, the assertion of male control over women's sexuality and fertility is one of the lynchpins of gender hierarchy. Across time, culture, and geography, men have continually asserted ownership over women's bodies and reproductive organs, and in doing so consigned them to subordinate status. The United States is no exception: since the 1960s, the conservative movement has derived significant energy from its dream of reasserting patriarchal control over the family (under the guise of "conservative family values"). Its activists today are fighting not only to extend abortion bans, but also to roll back women's access to contraception and repeal no-fault divorce.[77] The spectacle of predominately male state legislatures enacting draconian abortion laws throws this issue into sharp relief. In Indiana, for example, which enacted an unyielding abortion ban in 2023, just 35 of 150 lawmakers were women. In South Carolina, it was 29 out of 124.[78] There is good reason to see these conservative state legislatures as vectors of patriarchal power.

Pro-life advocates are quick to deflect these accusations by asserting that the fetus's right to life is more fundamental than the mother's interests. In doing so, they sometimes deploy recognizably liberal arguments, centered on the need to protect the fetus's basic interests and its ability (eventually) to live a free life of its own. These arguments raise difficult questions. At what point in its development, and in virtue of what characteristics or capacities, does a fetus acquire interests that a government must protect? Philosophers, scientists, and theologians have long disagreed about this. Nonetheless, the idea that the early stage embryo—without a functioning brain or nervous system—should be regarded as the mother's moral equal, possessed of rights under the law, conflicts deeply with most people's moral intuitions. It is incompatible, for example, with the well-established practice of freezing and storing embryos for in vitro fertilization (IVF), and discarding unneeded embryos afterward.

But there is another, more fundamental point to be made here, which pro-life advocates typically neglect: merely establishing the fetus's right to life is not sufficient to justify banning abortion. The right to life does not grant any of us the right to commandeer another person's body—even if we need it to survive.[79] Yet this is precisely what the pro-life position affirms: that the fetus has not only a general right to live, but also a specific, additional right to grow inside a particular woman's body, to have its blood oxygenated by her lungs, to have its own hormonal development affect her brain and metabolism, and more.[80] In a free society, the idea that pregnant women should have no say in deciding whether to accept this extremely intimate entanglement with another being is truly extraordinary.

As Little points out, this idea is subtly reinforced by popular representations of fetal development. Gestation is often depicted as a biological process in which the fetus grows and matures of its own accord, like a germinating plant, as long as it is not interfered with. From this perspective, abortion looks like a violent intervention into nature's benign trajectory. This picture is fundamentally incomplete: what is missing is the woman's life-sustaining gestational labor. "If, though, gestation belongs to the *woman*," writes Little, "if its essential resources are hers—her blood, her hormones, her energy," then the issue appears in a different light.[81] The key question is whether she should be forced to give this life-preserving labor against her will.

In the twenty-first century, the ideal of equal freedom demands that we protect women's reproductive rights. These rights are fundamental tokens of society's commitment to treat women as equals, with an equal claim to freedom. We can affirm this commitment, moreover, without asserting that women's freedom is the only relevant value, or that the fetus should have no rights in the later stages of pregnancy. We can affirm it without imagining that the decision to have an abortion, at any stage of fetal development, is morally insignificant. There are difficult and complicated moral questions to confront here, which pro-choice advocates too often neglect.[82] But in a society devoted to equal freedom, they must be resolved in a way that does not strip away women's power to govern their own bodies—and shape their own lives.

5

Ecological Degradation

The greatest threat to human freedom in our time lies in the ecological destruction caused by our industrial economies. Our natural environment is inseparable from our freedom. Without clean air to breathe and clean water to drink, without a climate conducive to agriculture and livable temperatures, without stable ecosystems and soils fertile enough to grow abundant food, the range of desirable options available to us contracts sharply. The harsh effects of climate change and toxic pollution are already felt by billions of people around the globe, and on our current trajectory, these effects will worsen dramatically in the coming decades. Like the other dangers we have explored, these harms have fallen disproportionately on poor and vulnerable populations. Mitigating them is essential to any serious effort to promote equal freedom.

The catastrophic degradation of our natural environment offers overwhelming support for one of this book's central theses: in important ways, our current version of capitalism is incompatible with liberal ideals. If anything, our economy today embodies a dangerous mutation of liberalism. The pursuit of economic innovation and efficiency is one of many strategies that liberals have embraced to advance human freedom, but in our present economy, we have supercharged this strategy at the expense of many others. We have facilitated the growth of private economic Leviathans that churn out cheap products and services and contribute billions to our GDP, but also exploit

and impoverish their workers, short-circuit democratic accountability, and exhaust or contaminate the natural resources that people need
to live tolerably free lives. The result has been a wide-ranging assault
on human freedom and a widening gulf between the few who enjoy
an unprecedented range of options and everyone else.

We have no need to invoke exotic theories to recognize the moral
perversity of our degradation of the natural environment. The liberal
ideal of equal freedom is amply sufficient. We do, however, need to
embrace a range of new strategies to pursue this ideal in a world of
growing environmental damage and risk. Radical liberalism demands
that we move aggressively—and quickly—to protect natural resources
from destruction and build ecologically sustainable economies and
societies. We know that liberal societies are capable of significant
change: over the past two centuries they have adapted many times in
response to new dangers and opportunities, and we are in the midst
of another adaptation today. But we are not evolving fast enough,
and with a vocal climate denialist in the White House, we now face
fierce headwinds.

Climate Change and Human Freedom

Ecological degradation takes many forms. Hardly a day goes by
without new evidence of carcinogenic chemicals—including "forever
chemicals"—leaching into our air and water from under-regulated
industrial processes. Toxic algae blooms in our lakes and waterways
and widening dead zones in our oceans speak to the systemic over-
use of chemical fertilizers and pesticides. The billions of tons of plastics that humans have produced are breaking down into microscopic
particles that now saturate the oceans and, increasingly, the human
body itself, with unknown effects. Meanwhile, the aquifers that supply
fresh water to so many American communities—aquifers that formed

slowly underground over thousands of years—are being recklessly depleted by industrial farms, bottled-water producers, and water-guzzling fracking operations as they chase short-term profits.[1] Among these many patterns of destruction, however, the most urgent and most threatening to human freedom is climate change.

In its broad outlines, climate change is now inescapably familiar. As industrial economies continue to pump greenhouse gases like carbon dioxide and methane into the atmosphere, more of the heat rising from the earth's surface is trapped instead of radiating out into space. As a result, the earth's atmosphere has been steadily warming. Over the past sixty years, the concentration of carbon dioxide in the atmosphere has risen from 310–320 parts per million to almost 420. As a direct consequence, average temperatures around the world have increased by around 2 degrees Fahrenheit. Scientists now project that global temperatures will rise between 3.6 and 5.4 degrees before leveling off sometime later this century.[2] These numbers may sound modest, but we now know that the cumulative effects of such warming would be catastrophic.

It turns out that even relatively small changes in the average atmospheric temperature alter the planet's hydrology significantly. Water evaporates from the earth's surface, condenses into clouds, and then falls in the form of rain and snow. This cycle produces most of the fresh water without which human settlements quickly wither and die. Hotter temperatures intensify this cycle: water evaporates faster, and warmer air carries more moisture. The effects of this shift are complex and variable, but on average, storms get more intense, and wet regions of the globe become wetter, while dry regions become more arid. A comprehensive report from the Intergovernmental Panel on Climate Change (IPCC), published in March 2023, focuses considerable attention on these dangers.[3] As rising temperatures dry out entire regions of the earth's surface—including the American Southwest—

they become less hospitable to human life. Wells dry up and rivers run dry, causing property values to fall and livelihoods to disappear. Drier land also tends to burn, as demonstrated by the unprecedented wildfires that have lately ravaged the American West and Canada (among many other places).[4]

Meanwhile, stronger storms are already wreaking havoc. Rising temperatures have brought more intense rainfall, higher storm surges, and more destructive river flooding across many regions of the world, with escalating damage to human settlements and livelihoods.[5] Floods are vectors for serious illness: floodwaters often carry sewage and toxic chemical runoff, and they leave mold and bacteria in their wake. (A 2018 study by the *New York Times* revealed that 2,500 of the country's toxic chemical sites lie in low-lying areas prone to flooding.[6]) In developing countries, floods heighten the risk of cholera and malaria. We are also discovering that most human infrastructure, even in affluent countries, is simply not built to withstand the quantity of water unleashed by the stronger hurricanes and "atmospheric rivers" that climate change is making more common. The cost of remediation and repair is massive: in 2022 alone, the United States suffered eighteen climate disasters that each exceeded $1 billion in costs, for a total of $165 billion—and the annual average is rising fast.[7]

Hotter temperatures also threaten human lives more directly because there is only so much heat a human body can take. In the summer of 2023, many parts of the globe experienced record heat waves. In Phoenix, Arizona, temperatures exceeded 110 degrees for thirty-one days in a row, leading one resident to describe the city as "hell on earth."[8] (In 2024, Phoenix hit 100 degrees for *one hundred* straight days.) The most dangerous heat, however, has been occurring in places like the Persian Gulf, Pakistan, and China, where "wet bulb" temperatures are reaching deadly levels. The wet-bulb index measures heat stress to the human body in direct sunlight and factors in temperature, humidity, and wind. When the wet-bulb index exceeds 95 degrees, it is impossible for the human body to cool down: prolonged exposure leads to heat stroke and death, even in young, healthy people. Even wet-bulb temperatures in the high eighties are very dangerous, especially for people exerting themselves in any way. As global temperatures warm, the number of days that reach these dangerous thresholds is rising quickly, as are heat-related miscarriages, hospitalizations, and deaths.[9] The countries most intensely affected tend to be in poorer equatorial regions where much of the labor force works outside and many people lack access to air conditioning.[10]

Even as the warming atmosphere unleashes more intense climate conditions on land, it is also fundamentally changing the oceans. In the summer of 2023, ocean temperatures off the coast of Florida, which have been rising steadily since the 1970s, reached an astonishing 101 degrees.[11] Warmer temperatures suffocate marine life and destroy marine ecosystems, with stark implications for those who depend on the ocean for food.[12]

Warmer ocean temperatures (along with warmer air) also accelerate the melting of polar ice, causing sea levels to rise. This presents existential dangers to coastal communities everywhere. We do not yet know how much sea levels will rise—a lot depends on our emissions trajectory—but we know that sea levels were *much* higher during earlier periods of the earth's history when temperatures were only slightly warmer than today.[13] A 2022 study by the National Ocean Service, which does not embrace the more extreme projections, estimates that by 2050, "moderate" flooding (which causes damage to coastal communities in the United States) "is expected to occur, on average, more than 10 times as often as it does today."[14]

These far-reaching environmental changes present extraordinary dangers to human freedom. When people's lives are upended by powerful storms and floods, when their land and their wells dry up and become unusable, when their houses or communities burn, when their livelihoods are destroyed or their food prices spike—or when they are stretched to pay for costly mitigation strategies—their range of options contracts, often dramatically. All around the world, extended droughts, floods, and excessive heat are stressing and killing food crops; large swaths of farmland are also being lost to encroaching desert.[15] The IPCC reports that rising temperatures have already exposed "millions of people to acute food insecurity" and warns of escalating risks to the integrity of global food systems.[16] At the same time, desertification, intolerable heat, rising sea levels and soil salinity, and flood risk are rendering whole regions of the earth's surface less habitable and forcing millions of people to leave their homes and communities. An average of twenty million people each year have been displaced by climate conditions since 2008, and that number is projected to rise sharply by 2050.[17] For the poorest climate refugees, this displacement is often catastrophic: they have nowhere to go. Meanwhile, the surge of climate migrants tends to intensify conflict in many parts of the world as competition grows for scarce resources and rising anti-immigrant sentiments fuel authoritarian responses.[18]

Climate change is driven mainly by the burning of fossil fuels, which have otherwise been an extraordinary boon to human civilization. These energy-rich deposits powered the rise of modern societies and fueled tremendous gains in human wealth, health, lifespan, and education. They offered us an invaluable bridge to a clean energy future, but they also became deeply entrenched in our economies and political systems. We rely on oil, gas, and coal to power our energy grids, heat our homes and buildings, and fuel our freight and transportation systems. We use them intensively to produce the commodities most essential to modern society: not just food but also cement, steel, plastics, and much more. Extracting and selling fossil fuels is so profitable that leading companies are still investing heavily in new oil and gas projects even as scientists warn that these projects must stop.[19] These companies are also pumping huge sums into the American political system to protect their profits. Their political clout can be seen in the tens of billions of dollars in annual subsidies that the oil and gas industry still receives from the US government, while their economic clout is reflected in the $4.6 trillion that the world's largest banks poured into fossil fuels between 2016 and 2021, despite a rising chorus of criticism.[20]

Even as our addiction to fossil fuels changes the chemical composition of the atmosphere, we are compounding the problem by destroying the forests, peatlands, and wetlands that pull carbon out of the air and sequester it. The main culprit is industrial agriculture, which by itself accounts for somewhere between a quarter and a third of all greenhouse gas emissions. Meat production is especially damaging: as a rising global middle class demands more meat, industrial producers are scaling up production worldwide. Grazing animals need land to roam; more importantly, feeding them requires huge expanses of cropland. A 2021 study estimated that of all the land currently under cultivation across the world, most is now used to feed livestock.[21] This hunger for land drives deforestation, displaces small farmers, and disrupts local ecosystems, especially in areas that relatively weak states struggle to police. Livestock also emit a great deal of methane, one of the worst greenhouse gases; and the cycle of industrial meat production and processing, with all of its machinery and chemical fertilizers, is highly energy-intensive. It should come as no surprise that meat producers have consistently opposed environmental regulation and innovation. They see climate politics as a threat to their business model, and they wield their substantial lobbying clout to resist new rules and to command a disproportionate share of agricultural subsidies.[22]

Sustainable Liberalism

The ecological damage caused by our capitalist economies imperils equal freedom in obvious ways. In the twentieth century, discussions of the harms of climate change often focused on the interests of "future generations." Today, we need not look so far into the future. Unless we change our emissions trajectory dramatically, hundreds of millions of children alive now will suffer serious harm during their lives. Any political theory that takes their basic interests seriously has strong reason to demand fundamental changes to the status quo.

Some critics have argued that no politics grounded in personal freedom can meet our ecological crisis simply because *freedom* is so often invoked to resist environmental limits.[23] Agribusiness wants to be free from burdensome regulation; developers want to be free to build wherever it is profitable; consumers want to be free to drive gas-guzzling SUVs and use as much energy as they want. If we define freedom narrowly as immunity against government interference, then this criticism makes sense. But principled liberals of every stripe—not just radical liberals—have strong reason to reject this definition. One of the axioms of liberal thought, from its earliest beginnings, is that no one is entitled to do whatever they want heedless of the consequences, especially when these consequences damage other people's freedom or the resources on which it depends. Even John Locke, who is often considered the progenitor of liberal individualism, famously argued that individuals have a right to appropriate natural resources only if they leave "enough and as good" for others. They are not entitled to use up or lay waste to the common store of resources that others need to live freely. If we want to live in a society in which everyone is equally entitled to freedom, we each have to accept limits on the scope of our own liberties. In an age of escalating ecological destruction, liberals have more reason than ever to protect our shared natural environment.

The radical liberalism defended in this book clearly supports such protection. In Chapter 1, I argued that liberals must prioritize the freedoms that are central to human well-being, and I offered a list of basic human interests whose protection should be non-negotiable in any liberal society. These included a fundamental interest in bodily integrity, which includes a claim to be (reasonably) free from invasive toxins and to enjoy access to the resources that healthy bodies need. In fact, virtually all the other basic interests listed there presuppose such access. Our interest in expressing ourselves and affiliating with others, in finding meaningful work, and in enjoying leisure time all depend on our access to life-sustaining natural resources. As our access to these resources is compromised, and as obtaining them grows more costly and difficult, our other basic interests are affected. As the land dries up and burns, for example, livelihoods are endangered, human health suffers, communities begin to disintegrate, and property loses its value.

I also argued that a free person is someone whose options are relatively secure—that is, a person who can reasonably expect that her options will persist over time. Climate change and other forms of ecological degradation undermine this expectation. Many young people today are growing up with a sense of helplessness and dread as they anticipate a future with diminishing options. Consider, to take just one example, the profoundly significant choice of whether to have children (and how many to have). Almost four in ten young people surveyed by a team of researchers in 2021, across many countries, reported that climate change and climate uncertainty make them hesitant to have kids.[24] (I have heard my students express this reluctance as well.) People who feel they cannot in good conscience bring children into this world have suffered an incalculable loss of freedom. More generally, the feeling that we are hurtling toward a scarred and diminished existence gives rise to fatalism and despair and erodes our sense of agency.[25] It is precisely our interest in protecting human freedom that should drive us to take urgent steps to address climate change.

As we have already seen, critics of liberalism often score points by blurring its definition, so that it becomes synonymous with corporate capitalism, unrestrained materialism, or limitless self-gratification. This tendency shows up time and again in academic debates over ecological degradation. In a book-length reflection on liberalism's contribution to our climate crisis, for example, the Marxist scholar Christopher Shaw offers this definition: "the liberalism we are discussing is . . . synonymous with modernity and capitalism. This is a world where belief in God has been replaced with a belief in competitive private enterprise, technology, science and reason."[26] Having given us this overbroad and incoherent definition, he then proceeds to impute to liberals the dogmatic conviction that individuals should be free "from the constraints of obligations to wider society" and therefore free to emit as much carbon into the atmosphere as they like.[27] Little wonder that he finds liberalism incapable of meeting the challenge of a warming planet. Such polemics add nothing to our understanding.

The more cogent ecological critiques of liberalism focus less on the ideal of freedom itself than on the strategies by which liberals have advanced it. Some critics argue that the short election cycles that prevail in liberal democracies give politicians scant incentive to attend to longer time horizons. Others point out that because liberalism developed in tandem with the modern nation-state, it has tended to look to national (and subnational) governments as the bearers of political sovereignty and responsibility. This tendency makes it difficult for liberal institutions to handle ecological challenges that spill across national boundaries. Most importantly, critics rightly argue that some of the core economic strategies adopted in liberal societies—including loosely regulated markets and expansive property rights paired with an expectation of limitless growth—were formulated at a time when humanity was not pressing so hard against the earth's ecological limits. These are powerful criticisms, and they have already compelled left-liberal thinkers and politicians to change course.

The most important idea guiding this change is the principle of sustainability. Broadly speaking, a society is sustainable if the benefits it offers to its members persist over time, and if it does not simultaneously degrade the comparable benefits available in other societies.[28] In liberal theory, this principle's most important implication is to extend the temporal dimension of equal freedom. A sustainable liberalism protects equal freedom not just now, but also into the future. It preserves a world in which our children and grandchildren may live freely too. Understood in this way, the ideal of sustainability can be firmly grounded in liberal ideals: when our grandchildren look us in the eye and demand to know why we chose to exhaust and pollute the common resources they need to live well, they will be pressing their equal claim to freedom and demanding to know why we failed to respect it.[29]

The idea of sustainability is hardly new to liberalism. Many liberal reformers and activists have acknowledged their obligation to future generations. The American founders, for example, were acutely conscious of a duty to lay a foundation on which a free society could stand for generations. A half-century later, the abolitionist activists who popularized the idea of human rights believed they were fighting not just to emancipate enslaved people in their own time, but also to ensure that future generations were not born into bondage. Writing in 1837 in a Philadelphia monthly called *Facts for the People*, one abolitionist put it this way: "*It is for the rights of MAN* that we are contending—the rights of ALL men—our own rights, the rights of our neighbor—the liberties of our country—of our posterity—of our fellow man—of all nations, and of all future generations."[30] The notion that liberal principles stand in tension with our duties to future generations would have astounded him.

While the ideal of sustainability itself is not new, its implications are. As we have seen, our current patterns of ecological degradation are eroding human freedom on a massive scale. In our time, therefore, the ideal of sustainability demands a comprehensive rethinking of liberal strategies: It calls for new political institutions designed to protect those suffering from environmental harms, both today and in the future. It also calls for economies to be rebuilt around an acknowledgment of ecological limits. Because these dangers are relatively recent, and because our understanding of them is evolving so quickly, this rethinking remains a matter of broad disagreement, even among those who acknowledge the need for a major course correction. Although there is broad consensus that liberal societies need to move much faster to solve environmental problems, reformers disagree about how radically we need to reshape our institutional and economic structures, and in what way.

One possible pathway is *ecological modernization.* This involves trying to maintain current levels of economic growth and consumption while shifting aggressively toward renewable energy sources, more efficient energy use (through efficient mass transit, for example, smart grids, and stringently "green" building codes), afforestation, and sustainable agricultural practices. Defenders of this approach point to the substantial progress that countries like Germany, Finland, Switzerland, and the Netherlands have made toward greening their economies. Any defensible version of ecological modernization would also involve a large-scale transfer of green technology and expertise from affluent to developing counties, to help them accelerate their transition away from dirty energy.[31] Put together, these measures require a substantial reimagining of our capitalist economies.

Many environmentalists argue, however, that even the more ambitious visions of ecological modernization do not go far enough. They insist that climate change can be addressed only through more dramatic transformations that would shrink our economies and consumption levels while promoting local and regional self-sufficiency. Let us call this alternative *degrowth,* to use a term that has been adopted by some green critics.[32] The idea of degrowth comes in many different forms, some of them manifestly illiberal. Some activists have pined openly for authoritarian political institutions, for example, that could decisively impose environmental limits on consumers. Some, claiming that sustainability requires a wholesale rejection of capitalist economies, embrace socialism as the only way forward.[33] But many others imagine more modest, local, sustainable societies in distinctly liberal terms—that is, as places with democratic governments subject to constitutional limits, independent judiciaries and free media, market economies restrained by robust ecological limits, and an open civil society.[34] Property rights and other economic rights would be subject to sharper environmental constraints, but citizens would also gain stronger rights to clean air and water, to food uncontaminated by chemicals, and to an unpolluted natural environment.

Both paths seem uncertain at best. On the one hand, ecological modernization is not moving fast enough, even in the countries where it has been embraced wholeheartedly. On the other hand, degrowth seems to face even more daunting challenges, notably the challenge of persuading voters in liberal democracies to accept the privation that would come with economic contraction. As the pain and dislocation of economic downsizing becomes widely felt, it is easy to imagine even enlightened voters embracing opposition parties that promise a return to growth and prosperity. In fact, it is difficult to imagine a majority in any modern electorate accepting such dramatic changes unless they were confronted with something like an existential crisis. Some environmentalists have pointed to emergency economic strategies adopted during World War II to imagine how liberal democracies might eventually respond to the worsening effects of climate change.[35] By then, however, a lot more damage will have been done.

The harsh truth is that if ecological modernization is not sufficient, liberal democracies are unlikely to avert serious climate catastrophe. But before we treat this as a decisive objection to liberalism, we should remind ourselves that other regimes will face comparable if not greater obstacles. The massive challenge of sustaining popular support through long-term economic contraction would confront any government, including a socialist one, that draws its legitimacy from popular consent.[36] Moreover, the deep ideological shifts necessary to lay the groundwork for an eco-socialist society (for example) would take a long time to achieve—more time than we have—and their prospects for success are highly uncertain. Meanwhile, the few defenders of eco-authoritarianism have yet to offer compelling answers to the most basic political questions. How would they ensure that their authoritarian leaders will promote sustainability instead of enriching themselves and retreating to lavish refuges as the world burns? Without the accountability of a liberal democracy, what would prevent these governments from trampling their subjects' rights? Once we bring these obstacles into view, and once we remind ourselves that the European societies on the cutting edge of environmental reform are all liberal societies, the ecological case against liberalism looks a lot weaker.

I have been arguing, so far, that liberal principles can be reimagined in light of our pressing need for ecological sustainability. One area of tension between liberalism and some strains of environmental thought centers on anthropocentrism. Liberalism, as I have defended it here, treats human freedom as the highest political value. This idea of freedom rests on conceptions of agency and dignity that are not easily extended to other species, even less to inanimate nature. From the liberal point of view, we should protect the natural world because its resources and ecosystems are necessary for human freedom and well-being. The fact that so many people value nature gives liberals extra reason to protect it: for many of us, enjoying a broad range of desirable options requires access to unpolluted natural spaces with resilient ecosystems. The destruction of these spaces forecloses desirable options, now and in the future. These arguments will never fully satisfy environmentalists who believe that political systems should recognize the intrinsic value of nature, apart from any value or benefit it brings to humans. But it is worth remembering that liberalism does not offer a comprehensive ethical theory; it is a *political* theory, focused on the challenge of governing the human community. It is possible to hold liberal political convictions while also believing that we have an ethical obligation to respect the natural world as a good in itself.

Liberalism does, however, rest on an acknowledgment of the moral salience of suffering.[37] I argued earlier that freedom is valuable because it shields us from certain predictable forms of suffering—notably those brought by oppression, domination, and deprivation. Suffering, of course, is hardly confined to the human species—and this simple fact gives liberals reason to extend certain protections to other sentient beings. It gives us reason, for example, to abhor the cruelty inflicted on livestock by our industrial animal farms in the name of economic efficiency.

Liberal Experiments

One of the fundamental mistakes we can make, as we try to assess liberalism's viability in the twenty-first century, is to imagine that liberal ideas and institutions are static. In fact, liberal societies have thrived for over two centuries because they have adapted to new challenges. In the early twentieth century, as liberal societies confronted the daunting new problems caused by the rise of industrial capitalism, they developed a host of countermeasures designed to protect people from exploitation and impoverishment, from unsafe factory conditions, from infectious disease, and other hazards. They did this without abandoning their fundamental commitment to protect and expand personal liberty. A similar evolution is under way now, as liberal societies struggle to meet the growing dangers of ecological degradation.

These periods of evolutionary change are typically rife with conflict. Powerful interests that benefit from the status quo move to block meaningful reform, and in liberal societies they tend to invoke older liberal strategies—along with anemic versions of liberal freedom— to defend their interests. We see these tendencies today as business interests mobilize the languages of market freedom, property rights, states' rights, and small government to inhibit reform. But these transitional periods also bring tremendous experimentation and piecemeal reform as diverse constituencies begin to implement new strategies. Today, these experiments are unfolding along many dimensions: technological, economic, and political. Radical liberals should encourage and embrace them.

Freeing ourselves from fossil fuels will involve a comprehensive, multi-faceted effort to embrace clean energy across our economies: to replace dirty power plants with wind and solar installations, create fleets of electric cars and buses, build energy-efficient buildings and source geothermal power to heat them, produce huge quantities of hydrogen fuel to power heavy industry, and more. These efforts are under way all over the world, and the success stories have certain things in common. Most fundamentally, they result from deliberate policy interventions to spur innovation, create and shape markets, and build necessary public infrastructure. New technologies tend to be expensive; they also suffer structural disadvantages when public infrastructure is designed around older energy sources. The costs of new technology fall only after substantial investment has allowed them to scale up and achieve the efficiencies that come with mass production. But the high cost and uncertain future of these fledgling technologies often deter private investors.[38]

Over and over again—from wind turbines and solar panels to electric cars—government intervention has bridged this gap. A combination of subsidies and public investment in research and development, coupled with taxes designed to make older, dirtier technologies more expensive or inconvenient, is crucial. Mandates requiring industries to meet escalating energy efficiency targets, along with robust investments in green infrastructure, have also unlocked private investment and spurred innovation, bringing down costs and accelerating energy transitions. Economist Mariana Mazzucato has argued that the scale of the problem demands a new economic approach: she calls for a "mission-driven" economy in which governments deploy a range of tools—including low-interest loans, grants, innovation prizes, public-private partnerships, and green procurement policies—to direct research and investment toward socially necessary objectives.[39] This approach demands that we streamline and speed up environmental reviews of renewable energy projects so that new construction can happen quickly. We also need to comprehensively reimagine the Farm Bill so that its immense subsidies flow to those farmers who are finding innovative ways to reduce their carbon emissions and chemical pollution and to protect topsoils and ecosystems from degradation.[40] The key, Mazzucato writes, is to reward socially useful innovation "without micromanaging the way in which it is done—so to stimulate as much creativity and innovation [as possible] in multiple actors."[41] Drawing on evidence from the Apollo space program in the 1960s and German *Energiewende* (energy transition) today, she

shows how these strategies can produce decisive results. The Inflation
Reduction Act of 2022, by far the most significant climate bill in US
history, was a significant first step.

Coordinated action is also needed at the state and local levels. A
great deal of the most promising innovation is unfolding in munici-
palities. Cities such as Denver, Columbus, Boston, and Washington,
DC, have created new financing mechanisms, including green banks
and trusts, to help retrofit buildings, modernize electrical grids, re-
train their workforces for green jobs, and invest in green public-transit
projects, including charging infrastructure for electric cars.[42] Meanwhile, by implementing congestion pricing, expanding bike lanes and
(electric) bus lanes, and halting new freeway construction, municipal
governments are beginning to reclaim urban space from cars and shift
commuters toward green transit. There is a great deal to be learned
from European cities, many of which have taken ambitious steps to
move toward carbon neutrality. In Copenhagen, for example, big investments in renewable energy, tree planting and green roofs, a culture of biking and electric-powered public transit, and a system of
advanced sensors that monitor building efficiency have put the city
on track to be carbon neutral within the next decade.[43]

Successful local initiatives typically depend on citizen advocacy
and engagement. In many American cities, grassroots pressure from
organized citizen groups has induced city councilors to take action.[44]
In Oakland, California, for example, a coalition of community-based
groups called the Oakland Climate Action Coalition successfully pres-
sured the city to adopt a more inclusive, bottom-up process for for-
mulating its climate plan. The coalition then drew on the diverse expertise of its member groups to develop a range of ambitious proposals
that combined climate targets with environmental justice goals. The
result was perhaps the most far-reaching set of climate targets in the
country. The coalition also found creative ways of enlisting broader

community engagement and support, from neighborhood workshops and disaster preparedness training (conducted in many languages) to solar-powered concerts designed to enlist young people to join in local climate work. Crucially, the participatory process in Oakland helped community members mobilize their own knowledge and experience, in partnership with scientific and policy experts, to shape local policy so that it reflected the community's needs and priorities.[45]

Local engagement looks different in different constituencies. In Appalachia, local leaders and community groups are focusing on job creation as they work to shift the region's economy from coal to renewables. The Appalachian Climate Technology Coalition (ACT Now), for example—which draws together local universities, nonprofit groups, businesses, and town mayors—is reclaiming abandoned mining lands, cleaning them up, and repurposing them into green energy sites. It is also buying up defunct industrial properties and turning them into training hubs for the solar industry or manufacturing sites for the green economy. The coalition won a $68 million award in 2022 through the Build Back Better Regional Challenge, a federal grant competition launched by the Biden administration to encourage green economic transitions, as well as matching funds from private investors. But the coalition's investments were designed (and will be implemented) by local partners, drawing on their knowledge of local workers and communities. These examples—in Oakland and West Virginia— offer promising alternatives to the top-down, expert-driven models of change that often fail to win local support or to adapt themselves to fit local circumstances.[46]

Yet none of these ideas will go far enough until we figure out how to overcome two other obstacles: the tremendous political power of the fossil fuel industry (and those profiting from it), and the short-term horizons that dominate our political decision-making. The first obstacle brings us back to one of the core themes of Chapters 2 and

3: the overwhelming power of business interests in American politics. The fossil fuel industry wields this power aggressively at all levels of government to block climate policies and preserve its profitability.[47] In Donald Trump, oil and gas companies have a staunch ally who will doggedly advance their agenda even as the world burns. What can we do once saner heads are back in power?

Changing the composition of corporate boards and shifting executives' incentives to encourage them to build long-term value would surely help. But these changes may not be enough. A bolder solution would be to nationalize the largest US fossil fuel companies. Our government could buy up a majority stake in these companies and initiate a phased transition away from fossil fuels, while making provisions for the workers who will lose their jobs. The US government has a long history of nationalizing private businesses temporarily in times of urgent crisis, from World War II to the Great Recession of 2008 (when the automobile industry was bailed out by the Obama administration). The strategy carries considerable risks, but it has a growing number of advocates, and given the scope and severity of the dangers confronting us, it may offer the best path forward.[48] To be clear, the goal would not be to permanently nationalize the energy sector, but to accelerate the transition to a clean energy economy powered by private and community-owned utilities.

Governments must also adopt the longer-term perspective necessary to protect human freedom into the future. They can begin to shift their time frames by empowering new commissioners to protect the interests of future generations. A number of governments— in Sweden, Scotland, and Wales, for example—have already done so. But these experiments are in their infancy. We need to find ways of investing these new voices with real influence without simply creating more veto points that make it harder to pass new laws. Creating new constitutional rights to a stable climate and an unpolluted environment, so that governments can act to fulfill these obligations, is another potential strategy. To date, eleven countries have climate clauses in their constitutions, and in 2023 a group of young plaintiffs in the state of Montana successfully sued the state government for violating their right to a "clean and healthful environment," which is written into the state constitution.[49] Given the difficulty of amending the US federal constitution, state constitutions might be better leverage points for this quintessentially liberal strategy.[50]

Finally, we need to develop a framework of international institutions that can create incentives for green energy transitions and facilitate the transfer of money and technology to developing countries. We need a way of penalizing, through tariffs and other trade barriers, those countries that fail to set ambitious climate targets or that renege on their climate commitments. The European Union recently launched the first phase of its border carbon tariff, for example, which will eventually impose taxes on imported goods produced using dirty energy. We also need a global green bank to finance energy transitions, as well as forest conservation and afforestation, in countries that cannot afford it.[51] And since major climate harms are already being felt, we need compensation schemes for those most affected. The landmark "loss and damage" agreement, ratified by international diplomats in 2022, was a step in the right direction: if successfully implemented, it will require rich countries to compensate their poorer counterparts for the costs of damage wreaked by warmer global temperatures. Once they are fully implemented and funded, these kinds of institutions and policies can help force liberal nation-states (and others) to attend to the global impacts of their economic policies.

One of the problems with global regulatory bodies—and other global institutions and negotiations—is that they suffer from predictable democratic deficits. They operate far from most of their constituents; they often deal with highly technical questions; and their decision-makers are not directly accountable to any particular public. As a result, the voices of affluent power-brokers are consistently over-represented while ordinary people's basic interests are neglected. This has been true, for example, of the many rounds of negotiations over global trade policies, which have been powerfully shaped by big business. But such deficits are not inevitable, and reformers have developed a range of possible solutions. These include strengthening and formalizing the representation of civil society organizations and empowering citizen juries and "mini-publics" to monitor international bodies and judge their policies' fairness. The members of mini-publics are chosen at random from the relevant populations and paid to participate—much like juries in our criminal justice system.[52] These citizen bodies hear from a range of qualified experts and policymakers before making their judgments. Many experiments with citizen juries, assemblies, and mini-publics have already been conducted worldwide, with promising results.[53]

The need for citizen engagement and oversight highlights another important dimension of the fight against climate change: it is an educational project. Too many of our children are raised and educated without any awareness of the land and ecology that sustains them; without spending time on a farm or learning to grow things; without knowing where their water comes from; without cultivating an appreciation for the natural world. They do not learn the value and necessity of stewardship. Citizens raised to think of nature as a storehouse of resources to be extracted and used as efficiently as possible are unlikely to demand that their political leaders adopt longer time horizons or embrace the value of sustainability. Environmental stewardship has never been a strictly partisan value among American voters, and the growing stress on our natural systems will create opportunities to embed it more deeply in our educational curricula.

It is important to acknowledge that many of the measures outlined here will limit people's freedoms. They will, for example, drive up the cost of fossil fuels and of all goods produced with them. They will raise the cost of meat, which will affect many people's diets. They will limit the kinds of homes and buildings that can be built and make it harder and more expensive to drive (and park) cars in urban areas. And much more. The liberal argument for these constraints is that they are necessary to preserve the more fundamental freedoms that will be shattered for billions of people if climate change is not brought under control. Without such constraints, in other words, liberal societies will destroy their own highest moral objective, both at home and abroad. There can be no stronger argument for change. Environmental constraints are necessary, furthermore, to prevent the gross maldistribution of freedom in our world from growing even worse, since the costs of climate change fall most heavily on the poor. To prevent this, we must also ensure that the costs of the energy transition are borne by those who can afford them. This key policy principle, too, is essential to the pursuit of equal freedom.[54]

Containing climate change is so complex and difficult that it often seems impossibly daunting. It could be the greatest challenge humanity has ever faced. As I write this book, it seems unlikely that we will meet this challenge in time to avert catastrophe. But we cannot afford to lapse into despair or resignation. It is well within our power to make the coming crisis less severe. The difference between three degrees Fahrenheit of warming and five is profoundly significant, most of all for the world's poor and vulnerable populations. Every successful climate reform, large or small, will help. I have shown how liberal principles can motivate and guide these reforms, but I want to end on a stronger note. Just as our children—and their children—will need a climate hospitable to human flourishing, they will also need a strong framework of institutions and principles that can protect them from oppression and domination in the increasingly turbulent world they will inherit. To leave them not only a broken natural environment but also a broken, illiberal politics would only compound our moral culpability. We must do everything we can to protect them from this fate.

6

Democracy and Countervailing Power

We are in the midst of several overlapping crises: political, economic, social, and ecological. To address these crises, we need fundamental changes to the basic structure of American society. I have outlined a slate of reforms designed to meet this need, but important questions remain. Can we find the political will to implement these reforms? And if so, can we sustain it long enough to overcome the steep obstacles we now confront? Many critics on both the left and the right have argued that liberal societies—ours in particular—tend to undermine the conditions necessary for ambitious social and political reform. The individualistic tendencies inherent in liberalism, they argue, give rise to a population of politically disengaged citizens who, preoccupied with their own private pursuits, lack the strong social ties or qualities of character necessary to sustain potent political movements.

These criticisms contain elements of truth. By many different measures, our society is fractured and alienated. Our trust in one another is low and declining.[1] Compared to our counterparts fifty years ago, we spend less time involved in civic activities, and most of our engagement with politics is pure spectatorship.[2] Surveys consistently show that we are deeply pessimistic about our political institutions, and this pessimism has bred detachment, anger, and resignation. Moreover, we tend to view citizenship as a status that commands a raft of rights and privileges but imposes few obligations other than (maybe) voting and jury service. Under these circumstances, it makes sense to wonder whether we have the capacity, collectively, to solve the urgent problems that now confront us.

These are questions that liberal thinkers cannot afford to avoid. And yet we do: liberal academics and intellectuals spend a great deal of time thinking about fundamental principles and the policies that might realize them, and far less time thinking about the political power needed to implement and sustain deep change. Refocusing our attention on the question of power helps us see how much the prospect of equal freedom depends on democracy, and especially on the countervailing power exercised by citizens who are engaged, organized, and purposeful.[3] There is no other plausible path forward.

Before exploring this path in more detail, I want to bring the critics' accusations into clearer focus. If they are right—if liberalism saps our political will and leaves us powerless to effect real change— then my whole argument will have been in vain. It is therefore crucial to answer these charges directly. As usual, we have to dig through plenty of exaggeration, willful misrepresentation, and sloppy polemic to locate the kernel of incisive critique that is worth taking seriously.

Liberalism and the Common Good

Some critics have argued that liberal philosophy itself has sapped our capacity to act collectively. The most strident of these critics claim that liberal intellectuals overvalue individual freedom at the expense of all other human goods and therefore offer a deeply impoverished vision of political life. This line of attack is especially popular on the right. In his recent book *Conservatism: A Rediscovery,* for example, Yoram Hazony argues that liberal philosophers see personal freedom as government's "only legitimate purpose" and therefore reject the very idea of a common good. In another widely read attack on liberalism, Patrick Deneen maintains that liberal thinkers are single-mindedly committed to maximizing individual freedom, understood as the gratification of individual appetites and desires.[4] Both writers believe that these ideas, widely diffused in our public culture, have given rise to a population of irresponsibly self-centered individuals who are largely incapable of governing themselves wisely.

These portrayals of liberal philosophy are obviously false and distorted. Countless liberal thinkers have insisted that the pursuit of personal freedom must be balanced by other important public values—including equality and sustainability. Indeed, the ideal of *equal* freedom I have defended here is manifestly incompatible with limitless gratification of individual desire or boundless individual autonomy. Critics like to pretend that the liberal commitment to equality amounts to a minimal constraint on individual freedom—a bare requirement that people not harm one another as they scramble to indulge their desires. But equal freedom requires a great deal more. It requires that people recognize and respect one another despite their differences, and that they not only live peacefully side by side, but also work together on the many joint projects that any flourishing liberal society needs. It requires that they maintain social and economic institutions that meet people's basic needs and guarantee fair opportunity, and that they work together to prevent the concentrations of power that lead to domination. It also requires that they *care* for one another—not just in families but also in schools, neighborhoods, nursing homes, and workplaces—in the ways that make a free and dignified life possible.

This idea of diverse people living together in peace and cooperation, respecting each other as equals, and sharing the fruits of economic prosperity while affording each other room to shape their own lives, amounts to a powerfully appealing idea of the common good. It is what radical liberals mean by *social justice*. This—not limitless choice or boundless self-gratification—is what radical liberalism strives for. Moreover, this vision of the common good demands meaningful constraints on individual freedom. To fund public projects and public goods, to maintain vibrant local institutions, to treat people fairly and correct historical injustices, to achieve ecological sustainability—all of these shared projects require restraint and shared sacrifice. It takes work and joint commitment to maintain the conditions under which equal freedom can flourish.

If radical liberalism contains a distinctive idea of the common good, it also suggests a distinctive ideal of human character. It asks citizens to be tolerant and open-minded. It asks them to cultivate a well-developed sense of fairness and a willingness to take action against unjust structures, policies, and institutions. It asks that citizens develop the self-discipline and personal responsibility required by a free society. Among the privileged, it asks for a humility grounded in the perception that individual success rests, in part, on undeserved advantages. Above all, it asks for empathy, the most important liberal virtue of all. To uphold equal freedom in a diverse society, we must be able to see the world, however imperfectly, through other people's eyes, to empathize with their alienation or deprivation, to feel the urgency of their political grievances—even if, in the end, we do not agree with them. Without empathy, these grievances cannot be fairly evaluated in the first place.[5] James Baldwin argued that the right kind of empathy—which he called love—pushes us to take responsibility for others' well-being and defend them from injustice. None of this is unknown to liberalism's critics: many liberal philosophers have written at length about the qualities of character needed to sustain free and fair societies.[6]

Nor is this interest in moral character confined to academics. Critics of the "woke" left usually fail to appreciate how deeply it is shaped by moral commitment and attention to moral character. Many young people today grew up with a heightened awareness of the moral crises unfolding around them. For some, the graphic footage of police killing unarmed Black men in broad daylight was the key catalyst (others, who had witnessed or experienced police brutality first-hand, had no need of video evidence). The almost daily reports of new climate disasters are another contributor. Young people are trying to figure out how to avoid being complicit in these crises, and they are demanding that their institutions—their schools and universities and local governments—confront this moral challenge too. They are working to cultivate active empathy for those suffering from injustice, and trying to overcome the apathy and willful ignorance they see as widespread among us. Although some expressions of the "woke" impulse have been intolerant and self-righteous, it is at heart an attempt to live morally and create moral communities in an unjust world.[7]

I began this section by defending liberal philosophy against the accusation that it values individual freedom at the expense of all other goods, especially those that encourage social cohesion, community, civic duty, or the common welfare. But many critics of liberalism would respond that the problem lies less with liberal philosophy than with liberal *society*. They would point out that social realities often defy the lofty visions of liberal philosophers. Is it possible, then, that liberal societies *inevitably* weaken human connections and leave people isolated, self-centered, and incapable of governing themselves wisely? If so, there can be little hope of protecting the common good or nurturing the civic virtues I have just described.

When critics shift their attention from liberal philosophy to liberal society, however, they run into analytical problems that tend to vitiate their conclusions. For example: as we take stock of the American status quo, how do we determine which of its problems to attribute to liberalism, and which to other forces (such as capitalism or industrialization)? In fact, many of the tendencies these critics lament—

including the erosion of traditional ways of life, secularization, urbanization and geographic mobility, industrial agriculture and the loss of small family farms, consumerism, ecological degradation, and more—are plainly evident in modern China, a profoundly illiberal society. In their rush to delegitimize liberal politics, these critics tend to attribute any and all pathologies they find in American society to liberalism. In doing so, they stretch its meaning beyond recognition: liberalism simply becomes a catch-all term that encompasses all the evils they see in modern life.[8] This is bad social science.

Another challenge lies in distinguishing among the many strains of liberalism that have shaped American society and culture in different ways. I have argued, for instance, that our current iteration of neoliberal capitalism, which has produced grotesque inequalities, impoverished and exploited working families, and pulled apart so many American communities, stands deeply at odds with the best versions of liberalism. Many liberal thinkers in the first half of the twentieth century would have agreed—and many concur today. American culture also contains resilient strains of antigovernment individualism, embodied for example in our pathological gun culture, our resistance to vaccination, and our zeal to exploit and destroy nature for short-term profit, that a great many liberal thinkers today condemn.[9] These antisocial aspects of American society draw strength from certain elements of the liberal tradition but not others. Radical liberalism lends them little support. To attribute these failures to liberalism in general, then, is to ignore obvious and crucial distinctions.[10]

There is no sense in denying that even radical liberalism would disrupt many forms of human community. Any society premised on equal freedom will tend to dissolve communal arrangements that reflect durable status hierarchies. Any society organized around a dynamic market economy will draw people out of old patterns of interaction and into new ones, for the simple reason that innovation and growth are inherently disruptive. Freedom also engenders cultural, intellectual, and religious diversity, which tends to upend traditional norms and ways of life. In all of these ways, liberalism is a transformative creed whose effects reach far beyond political institutions and into everyday life. Conservatives are right about this. Compared with more static, traditionalist societies, all liberal societies will therefore confront the challenge of creating new forms of community as older ones erode—and some may fail to meet this challenge adequately, especially in times of rapid change. None of this means, however, that liberalism is inimical to human community. Liberal societies have for centuries proved fertile soil for vibrant civil societies containing the widest variety of secular and religious associations. They have a far better track record in this respect than any other type of modern society.

It turns out that when you treat people with respect and protect their rights; create avenues for democratic engagement; invest in neighborhoods and schools; maintain an economy that offers good jobs; and create paths to homeownership, people tend to create their own rich associational life. For all of these reasons, we should resist any attempt to identify liberalism—still less radical liberalism—with the atomistic disintegration of human community.

Elite-Driven Liberalism

There is, however, a narrower criticism of liberalism, embedded in conservative and communitarian broadsides, that is worth taking more seriously. The claim is that liberal intellectuals, because they have placed so much emphasis on improving the quality of our private lives, have too often devalued public virtues and civic commitment. Critics on the left argue that liberal society cannot generate the robust solidarity needed to motivate and sustain movements for social justice. Critics on the right claim that liberalism is incapable of nurturing the civic character required to sustain free societies. They look back with nostalgia at the classical (Greek and Roman) idea of liberty, which was more closely associated with the practice of self-government.

These criticisms have some merit: it is true that liberal intellectuals have often undervalued civic engagement. In our time, this tendency is manifest above all in the elite-driven view of politics embraced by many liberal thinkers. According to this view, constitutions should "lock in" the most important individual rights and freedoms and insulate them from the push and pull of democratic politics. Impartial judiciaries should protect these rights from encroachment, while enlightened regulators and central bankers organize the economy rationally for everyone's benefit. Together, these political elites are supposed to establish the fair and orderly frameworks within which individuals can then go about their lives. With the most important questions taken off the table, politics can then be reimagined as a benign competition among advocacy groups pressing their interests. Political participation thus becomes more a lifestyle choice than an obligation: beyond voting, it is not essential to maintaining a free and fair society. The system largely runs itself, leaving the rest of us free to pursue our private goals.[11]

This elite-driven view comes in many variations. Left-liberals who came of age when Chief Justice Earl Warren presided over an ambitiously progressive Supreme Court came to see the judiciary as the guardian of a just constitutional order against voters still in thrall to racial prejudice. In the 1990s and early 2000s, at the height of neoliberal influence, elites on the right and center-left imagined that the political class, including central bankers and technocrats in the World Bank and World Trade Organization, could calibrate global markets efficiently and protect them from the demands of parochial electorates who stood in the way of progress and economic integration. Today, the rise of right-wing populism has amplified many liberals' yearning for a more civil and reasonable politics overseen by competent elites. Prominent defenders of liberalism have recently described it as an enlightened antidote to churning populist pressures coming from both sides of the political spectrum. From their point of view, liberals are the adults in the room, holding off Trumpist irrationalism on one side and the demands of an illiberal left on the other.[12] Many of these writers appear uneasy about mass political mobilization of any kind.

This uneasiness is as old as liberalism itself. It was felt, for example, by a number of American founders. In the *Federalist Papers*, James Madison explicitly celebrated the Constitution's "TOTAL EXCLUSION OF THE PEOPLE, IN THEIR COLLECTIVE CAPACITY, from any share" in the new government.[13] Like Alexander Hamilton and other influential allies, Madison believed that politics should be conducted by enlightened elites and insulated from popular "passions." In the early nineteenth century, the French thinkers and politicians who first called themselves liberals shared these concerns: they were ambivalent about universal suffrage and worried that the emboldened masses would pursue destructive policies or be seduced by authoritarian demagogues.[14] Liberal freedom would be best preserved, they believed, if important political and economic decisions were shielded from democratic pressures.

There are indeed good reasons to worry about the treatment of minorities by democratic majorities, and liberals rightly emphasize the need for institutional safeguards to protect minority rights. Some of these safeguards inevitably invest unelected elites (such as judges and regulators) with considerable power. But the wholesale embrace of the elite-driven model is a serious mistake. Without the countervailing power of mobilized citizen groups, the rich and well connected invariably bend the constitutional structure to their advantage. They fill the judiciary with their allies, capture or gut regulatory agencies, corrupt public officials, wield the media to their advantage, and close ranks to preserve their privileges.[15] They do this because relentlessly advancing their interests is what they do best. Even the well-intentioned among them have little trouble persuading themselves that their interests ultimately align with the greater good. Fancying themselves visionaries ushering in a more prosperous future over the objections of obtuse politicians, regulators, and workers, they strain self-righteously against political limits.

Meanwhile, politicians who harbor egalitarian ideals lack the political backing they need to hold the line against the relentless pressure (and money) of powerful interest groups and affluent constituents. The resulting politics is fundamentally unbalanced. The rich and powerful get their way, and everyone else suffers the consequences: severe economic inequality and escalating political domination.[16] I already explained how this has happened in the United States over the past forty-five years. Ironically, popular resentment of these tendencies has ignited the very insurgencies the elite-driven model is designed to avoid. As political scientists have begun to recognize, this model tends toward both injustice and self-destruction.[17]

Power-Sharing Liberalism

What does liberalism look like if we dissociate it from the elite-driven model? Part of the answer is, I hope, already outlined in this book. I have emphasized the importance of reinvigorated unions and political parties, worker-owned businesses, community-led climate reforms, and other forms of citizen participation. Once we realize that the elite-driven model ultimately undermines equal freedom, we can see why radical liberalism requires robust citizen engagement and the countervailing power it carries.

In politics, power is the ability to get others to do what you want. It takes many forms. First and most obviously, it is exercised by those who harness the coercive force of government. When a political party, for example, succeeds in passing a new law that cracks down on companies that engage in union-busting, wage theft, and other violations of labor law, it exercises power in this obvious way: if the law is well-designed and enforced, it will force even recalcitrant companies to change their behavior. When a civilian oversight board exercises its subpoena power to investigate police misconduct, it compels the police department to turn over evidence and thus submit to its authority. These fundamental powers—the powers to write the law and enforce it—are rightly seen as critical objectives in any political struggle. They are undeniably crucial to the pursuit of equal freedom.

But these formal exercises of governmental power are just one link in the chain that leads from reformers' aspirations to real political change. Many complementary forms of power are necessary, too. To win control of government in democratic societies, elections must be won. To win elections in the United States, broad coalitions must be built and voters mobilized to support them. And this is hardly the end of it: when both leading parties are deeply beholden to corporate donors, for example, electoral success alone is unlikely to produce legal reforms that shore up organized labor. So political parties must themselves be (re)built around the needs and interests of working people, and grassroots movements must be nurtured that can pull existing parties toward their aims. These parties and movements can, among other things, shift our political discourse. They can draw attention to problems that elites would rather not confront and introduce policy solutions they would rather not discuss—all of which is a necessary prelude to substantial reform. Sociologists and political scientists have long identified agenda control as one of the fundamental dimensions of political power. So long as the agenda is defined by wealthy interests and their proxies, it will typically exclude meaningful economic reform.

Furthermore, to prevent party or movement leadership from being co-opted by the rich and powerful, leaders must be held accountable to rank-and-file members—and this in turn requires a body of citizens who are organized and willing to hold elected officials' feet to the fire when they waver, to attract media attention to their priorities, and to consider becoming leaders themselves. An unorganized, disengaged, uninformed public, vulnerable to mass manipulation and conspiratorial fantasy, has little hope of sustaining such accountability. So we need political parties that rest on a foundation of organized grassroots support, as well as a broader ecosystem of citizen organizations that can recruit and educate members, build their civic capacity, and channel their energies into political action. Together, these ramifying forms of power, exercised by ordinary people through organizations that enable them to act effectively, comprise what I have been calling countervailing power. It offsets the political influence of elites, and its effectiveness is well documented.[18] Without such power, there is little hope of transformative political change.

Countervailing power also operates directly in the economic sphere when workers hold the leverage to exact meaningful concessions from their employers. As I explained in Chapter 3, employees without labor representation typically stand at the mercy of their bosses, especially when they lack highly specialized skills. They can be fired at will, their wages and benefits cut, their hours changed on a whim, their every movement sped up and micromanaged, their access to legal remedies foreclosed. In these contexts, which are pervasive in our economy, individual workers are virtually powerless. By contrast, a unionized workforce that can credibly threaten to strike—with strong legal protections against company retaliation—possesses real power. Because work stoppages inflict significant economic pain on employers, these workers have a real chance to force concessions and improve their wages, their benefits, and their work lives—which is why unions are universally loathed by employers and investors.[19]

One way to tell the story of rising economic inequality and labor exploitation since the late 1970s is to emphasize the steady erosion of countervailing power. We have already seen that labor unions, whose strength and militancy were so important to the New Deal coalition in the 1930s and 1940s, have declined precipitously in the United States, largely because of a sustained assault by the business community and its allies. We have also seen that the Democratic Party, which once plausibly claimed to be the party of working people, came to cater disproportionately to the interests of urban, educated voters and do-nors, while abandoning poor rural constituencies and taking Black and Hispanic voters largely for granted. This shift exacerbated a long-term hollowing out and professionalization of American parties that began in the early twentieth century and accelerated in the 1970s and 1980s. In the nineteenth century, political parties were vibrant mem-bership organizations whose local chapters provided benefits to their members and exercised real power. (For example, they chose delegates for the national convention that would select the party's presidential candidate.) As these benefits and powers were steadily withdrawn—partly out of concerns over corruption and influence-peddling—local party organizations withered. The number of working-class people at-tending Democratic Party conventions and holding important pub-lic offices plummeted.[20]

These changes mirrored a broader shift in American civic culture since the 1960s, which was documented by Theda Skocpol in her 2003 book *Diminished Democracy: From Membership to Management in American Civic Life.* In the mid-twentieth century, Americans still joined large, federated membership organizations by the millions, in-cluding not just unions but also fraternal societies such as the Masons and the Elks, veterans' organizations like the American Legion, and religious associations like the Women's Missionary Union. Although many of these organizations reproduced society's patterns of racial exclusion and gender segregation, they did bring people together across class and partisan divides. Since they were run democratically by their members, they helped train citizens for political leadership. And although most were nonpartisan, they mobilized their members to influence public policy. The American Legion, for example, was instrumental in drafting and winning a GI Bill that was far more generous than the anemic versions then favored by elite opinion.[21] These organizations have declined sharply since the 1960s and have been replaced by nonprofit organizations and advocacy groups run by educated professionals. These newer groups are typically more focused on raising money and influencing elite opinion than on enrolling and mobilizing members. They also tend to focus on issues that are salient to affluent, well-educated donors. Their ascendancy, Skocpol writes, has helped skew national policymaking "toward the values and interests of the privileged."[22]

What we need, then, is a liberal politics that will rebuild, sustain, and institutionalize countervailing power. Following the political theorist Danielle Allen, we might call this "power-sharing liberalism" to distinguish it from elite-driven models.[23] Power-sharing liberalism rests on the belief that equal freedom can be achieved and maintained only when political and economic power is widely shared. If elite-driven liberalism tries to achieve equal freedom by empowering enlightened politicians, judges, and regulators, power-sharing liberalism tries instead to ensure that ordinary people—working-class people in particular—have the ability to impose real costs on political and economic elites, and thus possess the power to change their behavior. With the ability to impose costs comes the possibility of meaningful dialogue, negotiation, and compromise.

Over the past half-century, economic elites have succeeded in insulating themselves almost entirely from these costs. They have stripped unions of power, co-opted and defused the radical grass-roots elements of the civil rights tradition, and secured trade agreements that facilitate the mobility of capital, allowing it to circumvent taxes and regulations. They have removed themselves to affluent suburbs, and their kids to private academies, where they are shielded from the rising social dysfunction unfolding elsewhere—the homelessness, the drug abuse, the failing public schools. They have captured important elements of the Democratic Party (and largely commandeered the Republic Party), gutted local and independent media, and packed the judiciary with judges who share their ideology. The results are unsurprising: leading political scientists have shown that federal lawmakers in recent decades have been wholly unresponsive to the political preferences of constituents on the bottom half of the income spectrum.[24]

Power-sharing liberalism rests on an elementary insight about the effects of concentrated power: people who possess it generally use it to serve their own interests. Writing in defense of democracy in 1861, John Stuart Mill expressed this idea in straightforward terms. He argued that citizens should never expect powerful people (or groups) to serve their interests without being compelled to. "The rights and interest of every or any person," he wrote, "are only secure from being disregarded when the person interested is himself able, and habitually disposed, to stand up for them."[25] The phrase "and habitually disposed" is especially important to my argument here. To protect themselves from domination, citizens need to develop the habit of standing up for their needs, values, and interests. People who have no such habit, and who lack the organization and leadership to act in strategic and disciplined ways in pursuit of their political objectives, pose no credible threat to elite interests. They will never exact significant concessions.

How, then, can countervailing power be built in the United States today? The truth is that there is no easy way. The elite-driven theory is appealing because it offers us a clear path forward: if only we elect (or appoint) the right leaders, they will implement smart policies and change the world. Power-sharing liberalism is more challenging because much of the onus falls on citizens themselves. Organizing large groups of citizens who don't know each other and don't share the same social networks, who are busy and under-resourced, and who are often wary of one another, is difficult. Still, there are steps we can all take. As citizens, we must be willing to join and support organizations whose purpose is to channel popular power, including local party organizations and unions. Helping unionize our workplaces is a vitally important step. The most important challenge lies, however, in helping empower communities that currently lack political leverage, including working-class communities, immigrant communities, and communities of color. All around the country, they are fighting to exercise their political voice in the teeth of voter disenfranchisement and radical gerrymandering, catastrophic disinvestment, workplace and financial exploitation, and a host of other obstacles—and they need allies. College graduates planning their next steps have many different options, including working as organizers, public-interest journalists, movement lawyers, public bankers, or in government itself.[26]

Activists have also begun extending the lessons of union organizing beyond workplaces to build new forms of political solidarity. The Debt Collective, for example, is organizing the huge number of Americans who are in debt so that they can exercise collective power and gain leverage against banks and politicians. It helped organize a "debt strike" among students of the for-profit Corinthian Colleges, for example, to raise awareness of the company's predatory lending practices, and it worked to build support for student loan forgiveness, which was then embraced by the Biden administration and other prominent Democrats. It also tackles medical debt and criminal justice debt.[27] The Los Angeles Tenants Union, the largest of its kind in the country, offers another promising example of countervailing power. It helps tenants fight evictions, resist intimidation and neglect by real estate investors trying to force them out, and build support in city hall for affordable housing measures.[28] Without this kind of organization, renters—like debtors—lack the capacity to act collectively to protect their shared interests. In the longer term, these groups also nourish the character traits that are needed to sustain equal freedom in the face of oligarchic pressures.

Direct action, in the form of peaceful mass protest and civil disobedience, is also a crucial means of catalyzing countervailing power. The dramatic forms of protest and disobedience deployed during the civil rights movement can serve as an important model. More recently, the climate movement has begun to harness this power to tie up and delay fossil fuel infrastructure projects, for example, and make publicity-conscious companies think twice about pursuing them. In a society in which these corporations and their investors exercise hugely disproportionate power, these actions are essential countermeasures. Although the links connecting protest movements to social and political change are complex and variable, scholars have shown that successful social movements carry real power: they can reframe political debates, shift public opinion, give birth to durable new institutions both within and outside government, and win important policy changes.[29] These movements depend on organizations with effective and accountable leaders, who provide the connective tissue between protests and build a coherent movement.

There is also a great deal of policy work to be done. Strengthening labor law to facilitate unionization and labor power is at the very top of the list. So is using tax law and federal procurement policies to encourage worker-owned businesses, farmers' coops, and other organizations that can channel worker power. We also need to establish public banks that can direct a steady flow of capital into these organizations. Public banks are democratically accountable public institutions that would handle deposits for state and municipal governments and use their lending power to serve the needs of local communities. In the United States, the successful Bank of North Dakota is a leading example.[30] Directing public funds through community organizations working in underserved areas is an important strategy that both addresses local problems and empowers citizens. Sara Horowitz, who founded the Freelancers Union and writes eloquently about the power of citizen organizations, points out that they are often starved for funds: private capital tends to flow to organizations that will deliver quick profits, not those designed to provide long-term benefits to communities.[31]

Meanwhile, the Democratic Party could begin rebuilding its support in working-class communities by offering meaningful, direct benefits to constituents. Political scientist Eitan Hersh has suggested, for example, that it spend less money on expensive ads and more money hiring year-round local organizers and cultivating networks of local volunteers who could provide, for example, backup childcare services or run financial literacy clinics. Reimagining party organizations as political communities that engage people in providing for each other and developing their sense of collective efficacy would be a big step in the right direction. Doing so would require that party leaders relinquish top-down control and empower local people rather than simply descending on them during election season with armies of out-of-town volunteers trained to recite campaign scripts. The evidence suggests that these bottom-up strategies would not only build citizens' power and cultivate leaders from different backgrounds, but also bring more voters to the polls.[32]

Creating generous new public benefits can also help generate citizen engagement and power, because people will mobilize to protect valuable entitlements. Social Security is a case in point: since its creation in 1935, citizens have repeatedly beaten back Republican efforts to repeal or privatize it. One important precondition of this kind of mobilization, however, is that the benefits be plainly visible to citizens. American policymakers have often chosen to confer public benefits in ways that are opaque or invisible to most voters: through selective tax benefits such as the home mortgage interest deduction, or by funneling them through private entities like student loan providers Freddie Mac and Sallie Mae. Because these policies are difficult to see and understand, they tend to escape democratic control; as a result, they tend to skew toward wealthy recipients and to enrich special interests. And because even the recipients are not always aware that they are receiving public benefits, they also fail to generate public trust, allegiance, or mobilization.[33] People who benefited from the GI Bill understood that they were receiving government support; they valued it and were drawn into the political process.[34] By contrast, people who benefit today from the massive health insurance subsidies granted to private employers tend to regard their healthcare as "private." Progressive lawmakers should ensure that public benefits are administered directly by public agencies and communicated clearly. This too is a key strategy for generating countervailing power on the left.

All of these expressions of countervailing power depend, fundamentally, on the institutional architecture of democracy itself: on voting rights, free and competitive elections, and majority rule. Elected officials have strong incentives to listen to citizens who are active and organized only when these citizens are voting constituents—or when they have the ear of voting constituents. This incentive is intensified when politicians are engaged in competitive elections in which they stand a chance of losing power. Where politicians have insulated themselves from meaningful challenge—through gerrymandering, voter suppression, or corruption of the electoral process—they can afford to ignore the voices of citizen groups. Likewise, when they can drown out these voices with a flood of money from wealthy donors, the bonds of democratic accountability begin to fray.

There is, of course, a chicken-and-egg problem to confront. After decades of erosion, countervailing power needs to be buttressed and enhanced by policy interventions. But these policy interventions are likely to succeed only if they are backed by countervailing power. There is no general answer to this conundrum other than strategic opportunism. It often takes a political crisis to dislodge existing patterns of thought and power and send people looking for other solutions. When they do, organized citizen groups can help change the conversation, even when they represent a minority of the electorate. When the financial crisis rocked the global economy in 2007–2008, Wall Street's own voices dominated the policy debates in Washington. In the wider media landscape, however, it was the Tea Party that successfully channeled and amplified the voices of a small slice of the electorate. Scholars have shown that the Tea Party derived real power from grassroots organization and mobilization (along with substantial support from conservative elites and media networks).[35]

In the coming years, the Trump administration's cruelty and corruption, along with its powerful authoritarian impulses, will likely precipitate serious chaos and backlash. Meanwhile, the effects of climate change are likely to create another set of crises: ecological, agricultural, economic, and demographic. In the political tumult and uncertainty these crises will bring, we should stay laser-focused on securing the policy shifts that will help build and institutionalize countervailing power: this is the key that can unlock the structural changes we need. Every step of the way, we should expect coordinated opposition from business interests warning of economic apocalypse (as they always do when facing policy interventions that would impose costs on them). In response, we must remind ourselves of the economic and ecological carnage our current version of neoliberal capitalism has already inflicted on many millions of people, and the dystopian future it portends. We must also remember that thriving liberal economies come in many different forms, including Northern European versions that grant significantly more power, and deliver significantly more benefits, to working people.

A Democratic Media

The exercise of countervailing power depends, crucially, on citizens' access to relevant and reliable information. If the public cannot identify pressing threats to equal freedom, it stands little chance of defeating them. In America today, citizens' access to sound information has been compromised by several crises afflicting our news media and the practice of journalism. No theory of power-sharing liberalism would be complete without some attention to the purpose and proper structure of a democratic media.

It is widely understood that the press serves an essential civic function in any well-functioning democratic society. To act effectively in pursuit of their own interests and values, citizens need access to trustworthy information. To establish political goals and priorities, they need to know what is happening in their community and society, and how these events have been shaped by political choices. To hold public officials accountable, they need reliable information about what their local, state, and federal governments are doing, how public officials are being influenced, and how their policies compare to possible alternatives. More broadly, to think critically about their politics, citizens need access to multiple intelligent perspectives "about how things are, how they have been, and even how they might be."[36] We should expect the media to deliver this information, and this range of perspectives, to citizens.

The commercial media in the United States have never served this purpose perfectly. From the hyper-partisan newspapers of the Jacksonian Era to the dominant network newscasts of the mid-twentieth century, American media have always been shaped by commercial pressures, private ownership patterns, partisan forces, and other influences that compromised their objectivity and interfered with their civic mission. Moreover, the concerns of affluent, white communities have always received more attention than those of poor communities and people of color. Yet even when we keep these historical imperfections in mind, it is fair to say that our media's capacity to serve their fundamental democratic purpose faces unprecedented challenges. They have two main sources: the collapse of the business model that sustained newspaper journalism for over a century, and the virulent spread of misinformation in our new media landscape.

Newspapers have been the leading source of news in the United States since its founding. Until recently, they employed far more journalists than other media organizations, and they still produce better, more comprehensive news coverage than any rival.[37] Their reporting reaches readers and subscribers directly, but it also feeds the larger ecosystem of radio, television, and online news. Today newspapers are dying at an unprecedented rate. Between 2005 and 2020, a fourth of the nation's newspapers closed their doors, and many others were gutted by mass layoffs of journalists. In the decade preceding 2020, the number of newspaper journalists in the United States fell by half—from 71,000 to 35,000.[38] For over a century, newspapers stayed afloat by capturing steady revenue streams from both subscribers and local advertisers. The rise of the internet has compromised both: since readers can get news online for free, fewer are paying for newspaper subscriptions. More importantly, advertising revenue has plummeted as advertisers have shifted online. Websites such as Craigslist destroyed the classified ad business, and massive online platforms—mainly Google and Facebook—have used their monopoly power as digital "entry points" to capture the lion's share of online advertising revenue. To make things worse, many struggling newspapers have been bought up by a handful of publicly traded companies and hedge funds that have stripped them down to cut costs. These new mega-owners typically have no connection to the communities their newspapers serve and no commitment to any civic mission—their purpose is only to maximize profits.[39]

The collapse of newspaper journalism has already had serious consequences for American democracy, the most important of which is the atrophy of local and state-level news. Covering state and local news is labor-intensive. Journalists have to be present at city council meetings, PTA meetings, zoning board meetings, court hearings, and other places where important decisions are discussed, made, and communicated. To report accurately about environmental hazards, public health crises, public corruption or influence peddling, union-busting, or anything else that affects local populations, reporters have to collect and sift data, conduct interviews, comb through police reports, and develop deep familiarity with the communities they cover. The precipitous decline of American newspapers has left millions living in "news deserts," where there are not enough journalists to generate these kinds of information.[40] Two-thirds of American counties now have no daily newspaper, while two hundred have no newspaper at all—and the number keeps growing.[41] Unsurprisingly, rural counties and poor communities are most affected. Expanding news deserts thus exacerbate growing inequalities in information access. At a time when niche policy publications are flourishing behind expensive paywalls, catering to affluent clients with specialized policy interests, less affluent voters are losing access to political reporting about issues of vital interest to them.[42]

As readers have moved online, and as viewers have shifted to twenty-four-hour cable news outlets, they have also begun receiving news from sources that, from a democratic point of view, are far inferior to most local newspapers. A great deal has now been written about the circulation of viral misinformation and conspiracy theories through social media platforms, whose algorithms are designed to promote sensational and outrage-inducing content. A 2018 study by the journal *Science* found, for example, that across all subject areas, lies outperform truth by a wide margin on Twitter (X): they circulate "farther, faster, deeper, and more broadly" than accurate information, and the disparity is especially pronounced for political news.[43] Online platforms and cable news also tend to funnel readers—especially right-leaning readers—into partisan echo chambers that confirm and then radicalize their preexisting viewpoints.[44] These platforms have also compromised free expression in other ways: speakers who express the wrong opinions are frequently drowned out by a cacophony of threats, lies, defamation campaigns, lurid conspiracy theories, and other aggressive techniques that flourish under cover of online anonymity.[45] None of these threats are new—misinformation, partisan bias, and intimidation have existed for a very long time—but good research suggests that our new media environment has exacerbated all of them. The situation has been worsened immeasurably by the radicalization of the Republican Party, which has become a vehicle for mass deception comparable to authoritarian parties in Hungary, Turkey, and other failing democracies.[46]

This is not the place for a detailed examination of these trends. My point is that healthy, diverse, and responsible news media are indispensable to the ideal of power-sharing liberalism and to the broader project of realizing equal freedom. In this area, as in so many others, a complacent faith in the market has proven very costly. Since the 1980s, throughout the period of neoliberal ascendancy, regulators have tended to assume that market competition and business innovation were the keys to helping commercial media deliver the information that citizens need, and that government should therefore refrain from interfering. The broader American discourse about media and journalism is also shot through with market fundamentalist assumptions, which suggest that news, like other media outputs, is a commodity to be bought and sold. It follows that if customers are not willing to pay enough to sustain it, we should simply reconcile ourselves to journalism's decline, much as we accept the decline of door-to-door milk delivery or the full-service gas station.[47]

These assumptions are false and pernicious. It now looks, in hindsight, like the market's capacity to sustain diverse, high-quality journalism—especially at the state and local levels—was a historical accident. So long as newspapers were the dominant means of reaching local populations, advertisers had little choice but to place their ads there. The quasi-monopoly power exercised by newspapers allowed them to command prices high enough to subsidize their civic mission. Seen in economic terms, writes media scholar Victor Pickard, high-quality news was a precarious "by-product . . . [of] the primary exchange between media owners and advertisers."[48] Once technologies shifted and advertisers found more efficient ways of reaching people, newspaper revenues collapsed. Advertisers were never committed to subsidizing responsible news.

In fact, there is good reason to view our current journalistic crisis as a classic case of market failure. High-quality journalism is a public good: virtually everyone benefits from its production and dissemination, but many people will receive these benefits without paying. When reporters at the *Buffalo Evening News* broke a story, after months of investigative work, about how pilot fatigue and deficient training helped cause the crash of a commercial airliner in 2009, their findings featured prominently in the sweeping reforms enacted by Congress.[49] The story was picked up by many other media outlets, so that many people accessed it for free. Millions of passengers then benefited from the Congressional reforms, but very few of them paid anything to support journalists at the *Evening News*. More generally, we all benefit (for free) when our fellow citizens are better informed and therefore less likely to vote for irrational policies or unqualified candidates. It is well understood that markets tend to underprovide public goods: because so many of the benefits produced by good journalism are uncompensated, those who produce it have trouble receiving a fair return on their investment, and too little money flows into news production. In our current technological environment, where people expect to get news for free on social media platforms, and where these platforms capture most of the available advertising revenue, this shortfall has grown more severe.[50]

Free-market thinking has also corrupted our view of the media's democratic function. The "marketplace of ideas" has played a prominent role in American discourse about political speech ever since Supreme Court Justice Oliver Wendell Holmes introduced it in a First Amendment case in 1919.[51] The phrase has been used repeatedly to suggest that truth will triumph over falsehood in open competition, and that democracy is therefore best served by allowing market forces to determine the flow of information. In its infamous *Citizens United* ruling in 2010, the Court used this rationale to strike down longstanding limits on political spending and allow corporations and other groups to spend as much as they want to influence American elections. Today, most can do so without even disclosing their identities to viewers. As countless critics have pointed out, the Court's reasoning vastly underestimates the threats to democratic deliberation that are *produced* by the marketplace.[52] Market forces are gutting local newspapers and funneling untold millions of dollars of dark money—in the form of advertisements paid for by political action committees—into our election cycles, and if we have learned anything from the spread of viral misinformation online, it is that truth does not necessarily triumph in a market saturated with algorithmically enhanced lies. More fundamentally, the metaphor of the marketplace invites a deeply impoverished view of democratic debate in which citizens "shop" for the information and viewpoints that best serve their interests. From this perspective, what could be wrong with micro-targeted political disinformation that reliably gives consumers the emotional rush and sense of tribal belonging they crave?

Scholars and reformers have many ideas about how to revitalize American news media. It helps to recognize that when compared to other liberal democracies, our media environment is an outlier. It is dominated by a handful of massive corporations; it is only lightly regulated by public interest provisions; and it is relatively starved of public funding.[53] Many European countries offer generous public subsidies or tax credits to newspapers, for example, while also maintaining firewalls that preserve media independence from political control. To further reinforce media independence, some advocates have proposed publicly funded news vouchers (worth, say, fifty dollars a year) for every adult citizen, which they would allocate to local news organizations of their choice, provided these met certain basic eligibility requirements. The vouchers could be paid for by taxes on the social media giants that have done so much to undermine responsible journalism.[54] Reformers have also proposed strong antitrust measures to limit consolidated media ownership, along with tax incentives to help shift local news organizations from for-profit to nonprofit models and encourage local ownership.[55]

Media scholars have also offered a raft of proposals aimed at reducing the spread of misinformation online, including robust transparency requirements that would make companies disclose how they are manipulating users' newsfeeds, who is paying for online ads, and which audio and video files have been digitally altered. Others have proposed regulations requiring these platforms to privilege credible information and diverse perspectives, or laws that claw back some of the legal immunity that social media platforms enjoy for harmful and defamatory content, especially when this content is enhanced by company algorithms.[56] It seems clear, in any case, that social media giants need far stronger incentives to protect the public interest. Meta's craven decision to discontinue independent fact-checking on Facebook and Instagram just days before Trump took office illustrates this point: here is an immensely powerful profit-making engine that thinks nothing of destabilizing our democracy to protect its bottom line.

Finally, journalists, anchors, and media producers must embrace their role as partisans for democracy. Perhaps the most fundamental mission, for any democratic media, is to report on threats to democracy itself. In the words of award-winning journalist, editor, and media critic Margaret Sullivan, "journalism, practiced in a democratic crisis, *is* a form of activism."[57] Although some journalists have internalized this mission, many more have not: as I was writing this book, too many journalists were still covering the 2024 election cycle as though it was business as usual and devoting most of their attention to the horse race. Too many were also accusing both sides of the same sins (such as "polarization" and "tribalism"). Determined to avoid the appearance of bias, they found themselves unable to speak plainly about the threat that a second Trump presidency would pose to democracy in the United States, or about the increasingly fascist tenor of his campaign.[58] Too often, they resorted to "sanewashing": by translating Trump's barely-coherent ramblings into standard journalistic copy, they made him seem far more rational than he is.

Media reform can help reinvigorate our democracy, but it cannot *create* an informed and responsible public. If citizens are unable or unwilling to distinguish fact from fiction or lack the attention span to digest in-depth reporting, then such reform will ultimately prove fruitless. In this sense, a democratic media depends on educational institutions that prepare citizens to participate responsibly in public life. This is not the place to develop a theory of liberal education, but it is worth outlining a few of its fundamental requirements. First, if countervailing power is necessary to prevent liberal societies from slouching toward oligarchy, then civic education is vitally important. A public educational system that does not prepare its students to exercise power—and do so responsibly—fails to lay the necessary groundwork for the perpetuation of liberal values and institutions. Second, while civic education in liberal democracy must be framed in a way that respects diverse values, identities, and ways of life, it must insist on certain fundamentals. Students must learn to respect others as free and equal persons, and this means developing the character traits— most importantly, a capacity for empathy, a sense of fairness, and an aversion to cruelty—that undergird this respect. They must learn how power works in a liberal democracy, and how citizens harness this power to bring change. Crucially, they must also learn, as a matter of personal integrity, to form their public judgments on the basis of fact and evidence, and to navigate the onslaught of misinformation and AI-generated "hallucinations" with savvy and skepticism.[59]

There is no sense in pretending that countervailing power always serves progressive purposes. In the United States, organized citizen groups include anti-vax and anti-trans groups, "parents' rights" organizations trying to ban books from school libraries and propagate whitewashed visions of American history, and others whose efforts only exacerbate the crises we face. Grassroots mobilization on the right has produced remarkable successes of late, especially in the gun rights and anti-abortion movements, both of which developed through local, chapter-based organizations that enlisted scores of volunteers to work incrementally at the local and state levels. To infer from such examples, however, that public policy is better left to experts or elites, and that we should strive to insulate government from popular passions or pressures, is to draw exactly the wrong lesson. This defensive posture might be appropriate if we were trying to protect a (mostly) just status quo from corruption. But we are not. We stand in need of fundamental change, and I have yet to read any persuasive account of how such change might happen without significant democratic pressure.

Power-sharing liberalism aims to rechannel the popular anger that is currently roiling our politics and focus it on shared economic and ecological objectives. When people organize themselves as employees, co-owners, renters, farmers, or just as people sharing the burdens of environmental pollution and degradation, they can build alliances across cultural and demographic divides and begin wresting control of public policy from economic elites. This is one of the hopeful lessons of the Progressive Era and the New Deal, which were times of substantial citizen mobilization and worker activism. The flip side of this hope is the fear that if these popular resentments are not redirected, they will continue to be harnessed and weaponized by an increasingly authoritarian political right.

Crucially, power-sharing liberalism need not depend on utopian assumptions about how mobilized citizens are likely to behave. It does not suppose that they will always be enlightened, rational, or progressive. It does, however, suppose that citizens organized around shared economic or ecological interests will be more knowledgeable and strategic, and less prone to manipulation and deception, than unorganized masses. The history of organized labor offers ample support for this supposition. Power-sharing liberalism is about giving citizens and workers a seat at the table and trusting that they will be able to defend their interests. It is about offsetting the power that wealthy elites inevitably exercise in modern societies, and forcing them to negotiate with the people affected by their decisions. In this sense, it has a greater claim to realism than the elite-driven model, which ultimately rests on the naive hope that powerful people will choose, even without robust accountability to the rest of us, to serve the public interest, keep watch over each other, and resist collusion and corruption.[60]

Finally, power-sharing liberalism does not assume that the liberal left's priorities always fit neatly together. Conflicts will inevitably arise between different mobilized constituencies. The aims of organized labor, for example, will not always coincide with the goals of environmental activists. Such tensions are unavoidable because peoples' basic interests are not always aligned. Even those committed to equal freedom will often disagree about which freedoms (and whose interests) to prioritize. Limited public resources—and the public's limited appetite for higher taxes—will also force us to make difficult choices. The only way forward is through negotiation and compromise. Building countervailing power will not, by itself, produce consensus. But in giving more groups a seat at the table, it will ensure that their interests are not entirely neglected. Power-sharing liberalism is no sure bet—there is no such thing in politics—but it represents our best hope of achieving the deep policy shifts that are needed to realize equal freedom in our time.

CONCLUSION
What Should We Do?

To save liberal democracy in the United States, we need to make deep changes to the status quo. We have to attack the massive inequalities in power, wealth, and status that are pulling our country apart and lay new foundations for a more egalitarian and sustainable future. Over the past six chapters, I have outlined a set of ideals and strategies that can guide us in this effort. Radical liberalism shows us what a truly free society could look like. It promises people the power to make choices and to shape their lives in ways that matter, and it extends this promise to everyone on equal terms. It aims, especially, to expand freedom for those who have the least of it. To accomplish these goals, it seeks to build countervailing power and to cultivate citizens who can exercise it responsibly.

What can we do—each of us—to play our part in this struggle? And what *should* we do? I pose these questions with some trepidation, because people in our society are so differently situated. In our economy, many of us cannot afford to spend time or resources on politics. Many also go through stages of life—raising young children, for example, or caring for ailing parents—in which private duties crowd out many public obligations. One way to acknowledge these realities is to treat the obligations discussed in this chapter as *defeasible,* meaning they can be overridden by extenuating circumstances. Happily, a great deal can be accomplished if, at any point in time, a determined minority of like-minded people throw their energies into the fight.

Engaged Citizenship

In this dark time, our first obligations are defensive. Thwarting the Trump administration's worst impulses will require strategic acts of resistance, which will depend on our willingness to stay engaged. In our federal system, state and municipal officials—including governors, attorneys general, and mayors—have considerable power to push back. They can refuse to allow local law enforcement officers, for example, to carry out Trump's vindictive agenda; they can also challenge the administration in court. Members of Congress also have substantial leverage. Even though they are in the minority, Democrats could hold informal hearings across the country to expose Trump's abuses and throw sand in his administration's gears at every opportunity. Because the GOP's majorities in Congress are slim, moderate Republicans hold even greater power. Most of these officials will take action only if they believe that their own political survival depends on it. We have to let them know what we expect of them—by inundating them with phone calls, writing personalized emails, and attending town hall meetings. Similar pressure can be applied to the leaders of prominent civil society organizations, from universities to the AARP.

There is a flood of litigation under way to defend our rights, our Constitution, and our democracy from this administration's brazen attacks. But given Trump's willingness to defy judges and flout the law, litigation alone may not be enough. Citizens can join the fight by taking to the streets. Scholars who study authoritarian takeovers have shown that popular mobilization matters: mass protest deflates the regime's confidence, punctures the illusion that it speaks for "the people," and gives others the courage and permission to speak out. It is a way of recruiting and building power in the face of tyranny.[1]

All of this depends on our refusal to normalize Trump's behavior. Trump and his enablers are borrowing openly from the authoritarian playbook that has already undermined liberal democracy in many other countries, from Hungary to India to Venezuela. His apologists are continually trying to convince us that this is just business as usual. We cannot allow ourselves to be deceived. In the twenty-first century, liberal democracy tends to die gradually, by a thousand small cuts, inflicted by elected officials who claim to be doing the people's work.[2]

To help build countervailing power, we also have to join organizations and movements that are focused on winning political power and using it for good. These operate at many levels, from local to global. They include, for example, citizens organizing to pressure city councilors to adopt green building codes, scrutinize their policing policies, or revise zoning rules to expand affordable housing and allow greater building density. They include climate organizations such as 350.org and the Sunrise Movement, which organize actions and protests nationally and globally, and labor coalitions mobilizing workers. They include Indivisible and other activist coalitions mobilizing resistance to Trump's abuses of power. They also include the Democratic Party, which needs to be wrested back from wealthy donors and overpaid consultants and steered—firmly and constantly—toward the goal of equal freedom. Crucially, citizen engagement means more than just cutting a check or signing an online petition. Countervailing power dissipates unless citizens are willing to attend meetings, participate in strategy discussions, help recruit other members, and meet with legislators.

If we are serious about achieving equal freedom, we must also adopt sound political strategies. Political scientists have often described politics as a competition for power in which rival groups adopt different strategies, with varying degrees of success. In this sense, it can be understood as a complex game—albeit with very high stakes—that can be played well or poorly. Too many of us on the left have been making clumsy or counterproductive moves. We should learn from successful activists—and the scholars who study them—and become savvier and more deliberate about the choices we make.

One key insight is that winning power in any liberal democracy means assembling a broad political coalition. This is especially true for the left in the United States, where the Senate and the Electoral College overrepresent rural, conservative populations. To win power at the federal level, the left must hold together a coalition of voters who comprise several percentage points more than half the population. And this means, in the near term at least, that any winning coalition will include people who hold moderate or even conservative views on many issues. Scholars who study effective grassroots movements emphasize the importance of "bridging" ties that link people across social and ideological divides.[3] So we should ask ourselves: are we doing anything to help forge such ties?

A related insight is that the pursuit of equal freedom must unfold across two different time frames—the long term and the short term—which call for different strategies. In the long term, American public opinion has to be shifted substantially to the left. The ultimate goal is to unify a winning coalition around a comprehensive program of egalitarian reforms. But opinions do not change overnight. The profound shifts we have seen around LGBTQ rights, for example, or climate change, reflect decades of activism and outreach. Right-wing activists too have long seen the need for a coherent, long-term strategy designed to shift the political consensus in their direction. They call it "metapolitics," and they understand that it requires strategic outreach to voters who are not presently in their political camp, with the aim of eventually moving them to the right. In recent years, they have found success among blue-collar white voters who were once drawn to the left by their pro-union sympathies. The left has to play this long game too—and play it better.

In the short term, however, elections have to be won. Every year, elections are held that determine the balance of power in our local, state, or federal governments. A great deal hangs in the balance in these elections: housing and zoning policy, the regulation of hazardous pollution, the accessibility of healthcare, the attitude and approach of district attorneys, the prospects for meaningful climate action, the integrity of our democratic institutions. Those who have the most to lose (or gain) are often the most vulnerable among us. Before the 2024 election, some of my students had convinced themselves that elections make little difference because both parties are in thrall to wealthy donors and corporate interests. This attitude was irresponsible even then. Today, it is unconscionable: we cannot hope to curb Trump's abuses of power or rebuild our democracy until we break his hold on Congress and elect people who will stand up to him. This will mean defeating MAGA candidates in red states and swing districts in 2026 and 2028. Elections matter.

These two different time frames sometimes generate conflicting strategies. To achieve long-term shifts in public opinion, for example, we need public figures to stake out positions that fall considerably left of the mainstream, to broaden the spectrum of acceptable views and shift our national debate over time—much like Bernie Sanders did in 2016. To win in the short term and avoid alienating moderate partners, however, politicians may need to distance themselves from some of these ambitious positions and compromise on important political priorities. They may also have to remain deliberately vague on certain subjects to avoid taking sides between fractious coalition partners.

Politics is, of course, a team game, and it calls for substantial role differentiation.[4] Good players recognize this fact and do their best to excel in their own role while also staying out of their teammates' way. Insisting on ideological purity or homogeneity, for example, is not just antithetical to liberal ideals; it's also bad strategy. So is vilifying those who forge difficult compromises or build bridges with more moderate constituencies. This is a point emphasized by many seasoned progressive activists: an ideologically pure progressive party may carry the day in Berkeley or Ann Arbor, but it will lose statewide and lose badly at the federal level.[5] A 2021 study by the Pew Foundation suggests that fewer than a fifth of American voters hold uniformly progressive views. A far larger number hold progressive opinions on *some* issues and moderate views on others.[6] In our current political climate, alienating these voters will only gift power to right-wing candidates whose policy agenda is morally catastrophic.

Savvy players will also strive to manage disagreements in a way that leaves the door open for future cooperation. Catholic Latino voters, for example, are important coalition partners for the left because many hold fairly progressive views on economic justice. But they also tend to hold conservative views on abortion. The point here is not that progressives should stay silent about what they believe or stop pushing for deep change. The issue is how disagreement should be expressed. The long-term goal is to welcome more people into the coalition and persuade them to embrace more progressive positions. Vilifying others as sexist or bigoted—or as "deplorables," in Hillary Clinton's unfortunate phrasing—is likely to drive them away. Successful organizers understand this: Ernesto Cortés Jr. and the highly effective Industrial Areas Foundation, for example, have adopted the mantra that there are "no permanent enemies." What this means, in practice, is that they work hard to "depolarize" after political fights by initiating dialogue with persuadable opponents.[7] This can be difficult and infuriating work, and it calls for patience and self-restraint. But successful organizers understand that their opponents in one fight may be partners in the next one.

In the past decade or so, scholars and activists have learned a great deal about how people change their minds on political questions.

A crucial first step is establishing personal trust and rapport. Without it, any possibility of persuasion evaporates, no matter how conclusive one's evidence or arguments. Progressive activists working to shift opinion on gay marriage and transgender rights, for example, have deployed a door-to-door method called "deep canvassing," which centers on nonjudgmental listening and personal story-sharing, with the goal of building trust and empathy and inviting people to reflect on the sources of their political convictions. For trans activist Vivian Topping, it comes down to what she calls "giving grace," which means "being able to hear someone say something that can be hurtful, and trying to think about how to have a real conversation and connect with them."[8] Such grace is not always the appropriate response to political conflict—and sometimes it is too much to ask. But the scholars who have studied deep canvassing report that it has achieved successes far beyond any other known method of political persuasion.[9]

Good strategists also seek to ground their political arguments in widely shared interests or experiences that can unify diverse coalition partners. Economic interests are absolutely essential for this purpose. The experience of economic insecurity is widely shared in America today, as is the experience of low-wage work and the perception that rich people have rigged the economy in their favor. These are critical sources of solidarity for any coalition of the left, and they can unify people around a range of ambitious liberal objectives. As we have seen, economic exploitation and impoverishment lie at the heart of many forms of status hierarchy, including racial hierarchy.[10] As Touré Reed has argued in his book *Toward Freedom,* a politics that focuses on mobilizing particular identity groups without also anchoring itself in an analysis of class is unlikely to build enough cross-group solidarity to knit together a diverse coalition; it is also unlikely to formulate solutions that address the sources of our current crises—including racial injustice.

Emphasizing economic inequality and insecurity does not, however, mean staying silent about race or status hierarchy. The scholar and activist Ian Haney López has shown that a broad slice of the American electorate is responsive to a "race-class" narrative that weaves the two together. This narrative begins by highlighting the ways in which wealthy elites and their lobbyists have bent the rules in their favor even as they push to gut the services that working people depend on, such as public schools, Social Security, and Medicare. It then pivots and shows how these elites, working through their proxies in the Republican Party, have tried to blame recent immigrants and people of color for the country's problems, with the aim of stoking antagonisms among working people and preventing them from unifying around shared objectives. From this race-class perspective, healing racial injustice forms part of a wider effort to lift up working people of all backgrounds.[11] López's focus-group research shows that this narrative is more effective in reaching "persuadable" voters than stories that focus on class or race alone. It is also historically accurate: economic elites in America have often moved to defuse economically egalitarian movements by stoking racial division.[12]

To broaden its reach in this precarious moment, the American left must also overcome its discomfort with the language and symbols of American patriotism. Love of country is a powerful political motive, and it can be used for both just and unjust purposes. We cannot afford to let the MAGA movement own it. Successful organizers throughout American history—from the Knights of Labor to the civil rights movement—have understood the need to articulate an alternative vision of American nationality, which celebrates equality, diversity, and freedom for all. Embracing this alternative does not mean accepting whitewashed or uncritical views of the American nation or its history. Instead, it means identifying ourselves—vocally and publicly—with what's best in our national inheritance and fighting to expand and improve it.

A number of political scientists have lately emphasized the key role of informal norms in maintaining healthy liberal democracies and preventing democratic decline. They praise parties and politicians who respect these norms—including civility and bipartisan cooperation—and resist the temptation to play "constitutional hardball" by doing everything they legally can to defeat and frustrate their opponents.[13] They rightly warn that widespread contempt for democratic norms weakens and hamstrings democratic institutions and facilitates the emergence of authoritarian power. There is no question that the MAGA movement's contempt for the most fundamental democratic norm of all, the peaceful transfer of power through elections, has brought our society to a dangerous political precipice.

What these scholars too often fail to emphasize, however, is that these same norms tend to frustrate change across virtually all policy areas, including those that lock in minority rule and elite domination. The Republican Party's current authoritarian tilt, along with its open pandering to billionaire donors and fossil fuel executives, all but guarantees that it will continue to attack democracy, entrench exploitation and inequality, and accelerate climate catastrophe. Meanwhile, gerrymandered districts and overrepresented rural voters make it very difficult for Democrats to win commanding majorities in Congress and statehouses, even when the GOP is unpopular. So long as Democrats are committed to exercising restraint when they are in power, they will likely find their agenda blocked. I would therefore argue for an important exception: when they have the opportunity to enact reforms that would substantially enhance democracy itself, Democrats should set aside their procedural scruples. They should also use even narrow Congressional majorities to strengthen voting rights, expand the composition of the Senate by granting statehood to Puerto Rico and the District of Columbia, enhance unions and democratize corporate power, and weaken the influence of money in politics. The long-term health and even survival of liberal democracy in America may depend on it.[14]

Deepening democracy in these ways may also unlock other legislative priorities. Throughout this book, I have advocated a long list of systemic reforms, many of which will be expensive and require substantial shifts in public opinion. We cannot pursue all of them at once, nor hope to achieve them all in the short term. As we choose which ones to prioritize, we will have to make difficult compromises—or risk getting nothing at all. Choosing those reforms that broaden the electorate and build countervailing power is a good place to start. These are the changes that can lay the political groundwork for a deeper realignment.

There are plenty of reasonable debates to be had, of course, about political strategy and messaging. I am neither a political strategist nor a public opinion expert, and I cannot resolve those disagreements here. It seems clear, however, that many of us on the left have developed the habit of speaking and acting—both online and in person—with no discernible strategy at all: instead, we use our political platforms to vent our emotions, burnish our political bona fides with like-minded peers, or make ourselves feel pleasantly righteous.[15] Or we embrace strategies that are manifestly incompatible with the goal of assembling a broad coalition of people with different backgrounds and perspectives. College progressives, for example, are often led astray by political instincts honed within highly homogeneous peer groups. Many of them have become intolerant of disagreement on too many issues and have embraced unnecessarily strident political languages. Or they have adopted insular jargon, devised by humanities professors at elite universities, that potential allies find alienating.[16] In our time of crisis, with so much hanging in the balance, we cannot afford these missteps.

I began this discussion of political strategy by describing politics as a complex, high-stakes game. But of course it is other things, too. Liberal thinkers have long insisted that politics should embody, as much as possible, relationships of mutual respect among free and equal persons. This moral commitment limits the range of strategies that radical liberals can or should employ. First, it demands that we ground our public arguments in sound reasoning and evidence. We live in an age of rampant misinformation, corrosive conspiracy-mongering, and growing indifference to truth. This problem is exacerbated by social media algorithms pushing inflammatory content and by the use of generative AI and doctored videos to produce "news" content tailored to our emotional needs. Many of us become accomplices when we retweet, share, or "like" news stories without verifying their accuracy; when we continue to spend valuable time on manipulative, conspiracy-filled platforms like X; or when we allow our judgments to be swayed by flimsy evidence or unchecked confirmation bias.[17] Responsible citizenship rests on an *ethics of belief:* we must strive to get our political information from outlets that employ professional journalists and fact-checkers, or from credentialed researchers. Engaged citizens are, in effect, trying to exercise power over others. To do so based on flimsy assertions or obviously defective evidence is to do wrong, because power unconstrained by fact and evidence is arbitrary and illegitimate.

Second, any plausible ethics of belief also demands that we embrace our differences. We must be willing to engage with a broad range of perspectives, including perspectives at odds with our own. This means not just tolerating but actively eliciting diverse points of view, without which we are condemned to see the world through a narrow lens. As we have seen, there are limits to the liberal embrace of diversity: liberals should not welcome—or tolerate—hate speech, harassment, or threats of violence. We should not accept those who refuse to treat other speakers and listeners as equals. But we must also take care to define these exceptions narrowly so that they do not become means of silencing or intimidating those who do not conform to our orthodoxies. When we move to shut down wide-ranging debates over, for example, abortion rights or the politics of Israel and Palestine, or when we make devoutly religious people feel unwelcome, we not only damage our own capacity to understand the world and act effectively in it; we also fail to respect our peers' fundamental expressive freedoms.

It should go without saying, however, that for people who have suffered oppression and marginalization, politics can be a place to express anger, anguish, and indignation. Asking that these sentiments always be carefully calibrated to meet strategic objectives—or even to adhere to norms of civility—can be not just tone-deaf but wrong: it can exacerbate failures of recognition.

Liberalism or Socialism?

I want to end this book where it began, by returning briefly to the meaning of liberalism. Many of the policy positions I have defended fall far left of the American political mainstream and considerably left of the Democratic Party establishment. Some of them have been embraced, at various times, by people who identify as social democrats or even democratic socialists. Readers who tend to identify liberalism with the status quo might wonder whether my proposals should be called *liberal* at all, and whether, in calling them liberal, I am stretching the term beyond recognition. I would respond that liberalism is a broad and diverse tradition. Some versions of it offer no deep criticism of our current iteration of capitalism; some convey reactionary agendas that would deepen the exploitation and inequality that pervade modern life. My goal here was not to reconstruct these versions or to summarize liberalism in its entirety, but to offer an account of *radical* liberalism. This alternative vision of liberalism has a long pedigree, stretching back through the civil rights movement and the New Deal to the Progressive Era and beyond, and it draws support from the writings of many liberal philosophers and political theorists today.[18]

It also helps to remember that all of these terms—not just liberalism but also social democracy and democratic socialism—are broad, contested labels whose meaning varies from one writer and politician to the next. There is simply no way to draw clear boundaries between them. In the Introduction, I argued that most European social democrats are best understood as left-liberals whose economic vision runs close to Franklin Roosevelt's. Meanwhile, many who call themselves democratic socialists in the United States today have retreated significantly from the state socialist program that wreaked so much havoc in the twentieth century. Instead, they call for the kinds of reforms popularized by Bernie Sanders, including revitalized unions, worker representation on corporate boards, universal healthcare, and ambitious criminal justice reform.[19] All of these reforms are compatible with the liberal principles laid out in this book.

This "softening" of socialism is a testament to liberal democracy's success: over time, more and more socialists have foresworn violent revolution and minority rule and committed themselves to reform through democratic means. Many have also embraced liberal institutions: they now acknowledge the need for individual rights, independent judiciaries, checks and balances, economic markets, free media, and open civil societies.[20] Whether these people call themselves socialists, social democrats, radical liberals, or progressives, many have absorbed liberalism's most important principles and commitments.

We should welcome these developments and—no matter what labels we apply to ourselves—join forces to fight for a freer and more egalitarian future.

Yet while these softer forms of socialism overlap with liberalism, other versions still stand opposed to it. Throughout much of the twentieth century, leading socialists called for wholesale nationalization of the economy, which would then be subject to comprehensive planning by public officials. This vision was premised on an extraordinary consolidation of power: government would own all land and natural resources and all productive assets in a given territory; government agencies would determine what goods and services were produced and in what quantities; government would also allocate housing to residents, determine how much workers were paid, and a great deal more. This impulse toward consolidation survives today. In his popular 2019 *Socialist Manifesto,* for example, Bhaskar Sunkara concedes that worker-owned firms should be subject to market competition: they should produce goods and services for sale on the market, so that only efficient and innovative firms survive. But he also argues that these firms would have to rent land, building space, and equipment from government, which would own all these resources. And he insists that capital markets should be fully nationalized: public banks, with elected boards, would decide how to allocate capital flows in their state or region. In other words, anyone who needed a loan to start or expand a business would have to persuade elected officials of the worthiness of their business plan.[21]

Liberals have always rejected this vision of concentrated power, largely because of its potential for tyranny and political domination. A government that commands complete control over everyone's livelihood can too easily pacify and subdue its population. A political party that sweeps into power, winning majorities on legislatures and bank boards alike, could entrench itself permanently, partly by starving its political opponents of economic opportunities. One way to encapsulate this divide is to say that egalitarian liberals and social democrats (and the more moderate socialists who have joined them) are trying to reimagine capitalism, to rewrite its source code in ways that promote equality and sustainability. Hardline socialists, on the other hand, are trying to abolish capitalism altogether and subject economic decision-making to comprehensive political control.

I have argued that radical liberalism must be resolutely evidence-based. This standard has always posed a problem for socialists who call for the wholesale abolition of capitalism. In the history of modern societies, they have only a litany of failures to point to—many of them morally catastrophic. Yet there is plenty of evidence that capitalism can be successfully reimagined. The New Deal was one such reimagining. The so-called "Nordic model" embraced by Scandinavian countries is another. Both achieved significant expansions of human freedom. And while there is much to learn from these examples, our task today is not simply to reproduce them. We must develop new models, inspired by these older ones, that fit the challenges and circumstances of our time.

In this book, I have outlined a strain of liberalism that can offer us hope in today's troubled world. I call it "radical" because it offers an ambitiously egalitarian vision of the future. It demands broad and far-reaching reforms designed to empower people, on equal terms, to live freely. It insists on freedom for all, not just for the few.

This vision is too often lacking in our public discourse. The left is quick to identify inequalities and injustices that it aims to dismantle—from poverty and political oppression to patriarchy and heterosexism—but it is far less adept at articulating what a good or just society might look like. Many on the left have convinced themselves that liberalism offers them no help in imagining a better future, so they have turned to political theories that are utopian, vague and underdeveloped, or otherwise disconnected from reality. Meanwhile, those who have spoken up to defend liberalism in this time of rising authoritarian peril have too often settled into a defensive crouch: they have praised liberalism as a reasonable, time-tested doctrine and a recipe for mutual toleration, sensible compromise, and incremental change.[22] If they offer us a vision of the future, it looks far too much like the present.

I have argued for a more compelling tradition of liberal thought that is not only bold in its purposes but also realistic, innovative, and deeply grounded in values and beliefs that are widely shared in our society. Radical liberalism is realistic in that it recognizes the need for new institutional foundations, backed by sound evidence, that will expand freedom for those who have the least of it. It insists that these institutions include robust precautions against the abuse of power. It also holds that real change will happen only if we correct the power imbalances that now distort our economy and politics, and empower people to solve problems in their own communities and workplaces. Radical liberalism maintains, in other words, that any blueprint for a more just and equal society will remain hopelessly unrealistic unless it is anchored in a sober analysis of institutions and power relations.

Radical liberalism is innovative in that it embraces one of the great strengths of liberal societies: their capacity for change. It looks for solutions in the diverse experiments that are already unfolding, on various scales, in liberal societies today. I have highlighted a number of these experiments in the preceding chapters—and these represent just a small slice of the many new initiatives currently under way. Together, they can not only inspire us to think in new ways about the challenges we face, but also offer us hope in a time of rising resignation and despair.

Finally, radical liberalism draws strength from the language of personal freedom that still resonates deeply in American political culture, on the left and right alike. I hope to have shown that this liberal language is pregnant with emancipatory possibility. Interpreted in the right way, it can underwrite transformative change. It can tap the commonsense moral and political intuitions that many Americans hold dear and use them to build an argument for ambitious political, economic, and social reform. There is no better way forward.

Acknowledgments

Many people helped make this book possible. I am grateful to Sarah Wood, who worked as my research assistant in the summer of 2023 and contributed valuable evidence and insights. I am also thankful for the many people who read and commented on parts of the manuscript: Will Barndt, Pablo Bose, Michele Commercio, Larry Croner, Bill Curtis, Leslie Duhaylongsod, Alec Ewald, Michael Frazer, Randall Harp, Lisa Holmes, Minh Ly, Steve Macedo, Leigh Raymond, Ethan Schoolman, Benna Trachtenberg, and my brother, Michael. I benefited immensely from their suggestions. I am especially indebted to those few people who took the time to read the entire draft and share their thoughts: Patrick Neal, Bob Taylor, Andrew Valls, my wife, Tess, and my mother, Laura. I am also grateful for the Yale political theory workshop and all of its participants, who hosted me graciously in the fall of 2023 and gave me a lot to think about.

The ideas in this book were shaped by countless conversations, over many years, about the meaning and value of liberal politics. I am indebted to the many teachers and friends who contributed to these conversations, including Eric Beerbohm, Denise Dutton, David Erdos, Joel Greifinger, John Holzwarth, George Kateb, Steve Macedo, Susan McWilliams, Pratap Mehta, Shmulik Nili, Philip Pettit, Jennifer Pitts, Jedediah Purdy, Tamsin Shaw, Jeff Stout, Micah Watson, Keith Whittington, Mariah Zeisberg, and many others.

I want to thank my editor at Yale University Press, Bill Frucht, for his careful edits and suggestions (and for our lengthy back-and-forth about the title). It was a pleasure to work with him throughout the process of seeing this book into print.

Finally, I would like to thank my colleagues in the University of Vermont's Department of Political Science and College of Arts and Sciences for their support and encouragement. Over the years it took to write this book, UVM has been a wonderful place to think and work.

Notes

Introduction

1. Pew Research Center, *1999 Millennium Survey;* Chambers, "Americans Are Overwhelmingly Happy."

2. Borelli, *Americans Are Split;* Daniller, *Americans Take a Dim View.*

3. Nussbaum, *Sex and Social Justice,* 57.

4. See, for instance, Gopnik, *Thousand Small Sanities;* Fukayama, *Liberalism and Its Discontents;* Craiutu, *Why Not Moderation?;* Mounk, *People vs. Democracy.* One notable exception is Daniel Chandler's excellent 2023 book, *Free and Equal.*

5. I draw this term from New Left activist and intellectual Arnold Kaufman. See Kaufman, *Radical Liberal.*

6. For a succinct overview of recent research in this area, see Hacker et al., "American Political Economy."

7. This book reflects the influence of many contemporary liberal theorists, including Elizabeth Anderson, Danielle Allen, Michael Walzer, Martha Nussbaum, Amartya Sen, Philippe Van Parijs, Paul Starr, and many others. Many of the endnotes throughout this book reveal my intellectual debts to a wider range of liberal thinkers and reformers as well.

8. This point is confirmed by scholars who study successful social movements; see, for instance Woodly, *Politics of Common Sense.*

9. For further discussion, see Zakaras, *Roots of American Individualism.*

10. The use of the term "classical liberal" to describe nineteenth-century free-market enthusiasts is an invention of the libertarian right. Libertarians have used it to try to claim that the original or essential form of liberalism was centered on free markets. In fact, many nineteenth-century liberals—from the early French liberals to the American Whigs to John Stuart Mill himself—were not free-market doctrinaires.

Chapter 1. Equal Freedom

1. The term "elites" appears fairly often in this book. I typically use it to describe two groups of people: *economic elites*, that is, wealthy business owners, investors, or corporate managers who command significant decision-making power in our economy and who tend to be well-connected to the political class; and *political elites*, that is, political power-brokers, be they elected officials, cabinet appointees, or powerful regulators and judges, whose voices carry significant political weight.

2. Pettit, *Just Freedom*, 34–35.

3. A paradigmatic expression of this view can be found in Berlin, "Two Concepts of Liberty." Some have gone so far as to argue that freedom simply means "the absence of a particular obstacle—*coercion* by other men" (Hayek, *The Constitution of Liberty*, 19, emphasis mine). Proponents of this negative definition, including libertarians and other Cold War liberals, worried that a more expansive idea of freedom would license broad political interventions in the economy and society. It might require, for example, that government provide free healthcare to protect us from illness, or provide generous welfare benefits to protect us from deprivation.

4. Pettit, *Just Freedom*, 36–37.

5. Pettit, *Just Freedom*, 36.

6. Some might try to rescue negative freedom by arguing that it was intended strictly as a *political* standard. That is, they might accept my broader definition of freedom but insist that it has no place in politics. In politics, they might argue, we should confine it to a narrower goal: protecting people from unwanted interference by others. There are strong reasons to reject this view, which I explore in this chapter and again in Chapter 4. Mainly, it would consign huge numbers of people to needless deprivation, exploitation, and diminished opportunity.

7. The availability of a range of options also addresses a problem posed by what philosophers call "adaptive preferences." We tend to reject the view that people can render themselves free by shifting their preferences to match whatever options are available to them, however meager those options are. If this were true, a man serving a life sentence could become free simply be ceasing to desire anything not available to him in his cell.

8. By "reasonable" here I mean that the expectation is well-grounded in reality; it is not delusional.

9. One of the seminal statements of this early liberal impulse can be found in John Locke's *A Letter Concerning Toleration* (1689).

10. To describe power as *arbitrary* is to say that it is completely untethered from the interests of those it affects; it need not give them any moral "weight" whatsoever.

11. Shklar, "Liberalism of Fear," 27.

12. Roosevelt, "Topeka, KS—Campaign Speech. September 14, 1932."

13. Agency should not be confused with the more ambitious ideal of personal autonomy. An autonomous person is a person who has, as much as possible, *chosen* her own identity and values instead of passively inheriting them from her culture, peers, or family. Agency, by contrast, describes a more modest threshold. A person who is conscious of making choices in keeping with her own values, for example, is an agent—even if these values were largely inherited from others. Indeed, most of us make reflective choices without submitting our entire value system to sustained philosophical scrutiny or experimental reconstruction.

14. For one compelling elaboration of the meaning and significance of human dignity from a liberal perspective, see Kateb, *Human Dignity.*

15. Some such idea of basic interests has been embraced by a range of different liberal thinkers, including John Rawls, Joseph Raz, David Johnston, Martha Nussbaum, and William Galston.

16. This view of rights has been ably advanced, for example, by philosopher Martha Nussbaum; see Nussbaum, "Capabilities and Human Rights."

17. This point is forcefully developed in Waldron, "Homelessness and the Issue of Freedom."

18. Pettit, *Just Freedom,* 81.

19. Fraser, "Social Justice," 28–29.

20. Elassar, "US Muslims Reflect"; Bayoumi, "Dangerous Outsiders and Exceptional Citizens"; Desmond-Harris, "9 Devastating, Revealing Stories."

21. Of course, opportunities can never be literally equal simply because people are different: their abilities and experiences vary widely, and these differences invariably produce inequalities in the opportunities available to them. In this context, the term "equal" is best understood to mean "fair and substantial." This is what most of us mean when we talk about equal opportunity.

22. This evidence is laid out in Chapter 4.

23. I use the term *compete* very broadly. It does not just describe competition for jobs at leading firms, for example. In fact, many of our life choices include some competitive element: there are always others who would want to live in the same places, to carve out similar economic niches, etc. Opening a small brewery or bakery

in Vermont, for example, is a highly competitive proposition. Equal opportunity means having a fair chance at carving out the life you want for yourself.

24. See Van Parijs and Vanderborght, *Basic Income,* 103–109.

25. Even if it was carried out in a decentralized way—in small, anarcho-communist collectives, for example—it would empower local communities to exercise tremendous power over their members.

26. Mishel and Wolfe, *CEO Compensation;* Kiatpongsan and Norton, "How Much (More) Should CEOs Make?," 587.

27. I borrow this basic idea—that society is a system of cooperation, and that we must structure it fairly—from philosopher John Rawls, one of the leading liberal thinkers of the twentieth century.

28. This point is ably developed in Lefebvre, *Liberalism as a Way of Life.*

Chapter 2. Tyranny

1. Associated Press, "Kremlin Crackdown."

2. Balevic, "Moscow Police."

3. Freedom House, *Freedom in the World, 2022: Russia.*

4. Freedom House, *Freedom in the World, 2022: Russia.*

5. Using this definition, not all authoritarian regimes are tyrannical. An absolute ruler who used his power to protect his subjects' basic interests would not count as a tyrant.

6. Through intimidation, imprisonment, ballot stuffing, and the arbitrary disqualification of opposition candidates, Putin's allies ensure that they never lose. Freedom House, *Freedom in the World, 2021: Russia.*

7. These states were, of course, nowhere close to fully democratic: their systematic denial of political rights (including speech and associational rights) to African Americans vitiates their claim to democratic legitimacy.

8. Freedom House, *Freedom in the World, 2022: Russia.*

9. Ginsburg and Huq, *How to Save a Constitutional Democracy,* 95–101; Naím, *Revenge of Power,* 3–105; Diamond, *Ill Winds,* 59–80.

10. For a seminal discussion of the norms implicit in the ideal of the rule of law, see Fuller, *Morality of Law.*

11. Ginsburg and Huq, *How to Save a Constitutional Democracy,* 108–109.

12. Diamond, *Ill Winds,* 62–66; Ginsburg and Huq, *How to Save a Constitutional Democracy,* 78–82. For a more detailed discussion, see Müller, *What Is Populism?*

13. Žižek, *First as Tragedy,* 90, 99–101, 102, 121. Like many Marxists, Žižek com-

bines incisive criticisms of modern capitalism with fantastic, ill-defined visions of communist politics and society.

14. For further discussion, see Hirschmann, *Subject of Liberty*, 103–137.

15. See book 8 of Plato's *Republic*.

16. Emerson, "Address on the Anniversary," 17.

17. Mill, *On Liberty*, 2.

18. See, for instance, Norris and Inglehart, *Cultural Backlash*; Mounk, *People vs. Democracy*; Levitsky and Ziblatt, *Tyranny of the Minority*; Galston, *Anti-Pluralism*; Frum, *Trumpocracy*.

19. Gold, "After Calling Foes 'Vermin'"; Stone, "Openly Authoritarian Campaign."

20. Liptak, "Defiance and Threats"; Reporters Without Borders, "One Month of Trump."

21. Bumiller, "People Are Going Silent."

22. Seven Republicans voted to adopt the second article of impeachment, pertaining to the abuse of presidential power.

23. Skelley, "How the Republican Push." Although their effects have so far turned out to be weaker than expected, scholars have shown repeatedly that these restrictions disproportionately affect voters of color, further weakening the voting power of groups who have already suffered a litany of abuses and exclusions. See Brennan Center for Justice, *Fact Sheet*.

24. Brennan Center for Justice, *Voting Laws Roundup*. See also the 2023 report, "Replacing the Refs," produced by the election integrity center, States United Action.

25. For an assessment of civil and political freedom in Hungary see Freedom House, *Freedom in the World, 2024: Hungary*.

26. Grumbach, "Laboratories of Democratic Backsliding."; Drutman, Diamond, and Goldman, *Follow the Leader*.

27. Ginsburg and Huq, *How to Save a Constitutional Democracy*, 68–119.

28. Daniel, "Rogue Bureaucracy." This episode was also featured in Rachel Carson's seminal 1962 book *Silent Spring*.

29. Shaw and Younes, *Most Detailed Map*.

30. Song and Younes, *Air Monitors Alone*.

31. Steinzor, *Why Not Jail?*, 22–27.

32. See Garrett, *Too Big to Jail*; Coffee, *Corporate Crime and Punishment*.

33. Quoted in Garrett, *Too Big to Jail*, 290–291.

34. Garrett, *Too Big to Jail*, 291–295. For a broader discussion of this dynamic in capitalist democracies, see Lindblom, "Market as Prison."

35. Saitone, Schaefer, and Scheitrum, "COVID-19 Morbidity."

36. Select Subcommittee on the Coronavirus Crisis, *Now to Get Rid of Those Pesky Health Departments.*

37. Drutman, *Business of America Is Lobbying,* 13. Of the top one hundred lobbying organizations in Washington in any given year, at least ninety are business organizations.

38. See for instance Drutman, *Business of America Is Lobbying;* Nownes, *Total Lobbying;* Kaiser, *So Damn Much Money.*

39. The role of Super PACs is ably summarized in an amicus brief to the US Supreme Court, written in 2020 by a team of political scientists: see Baker et al., "Brief of Amici Curiae Political Scientists."

40. Drutman, *Business of America Is Lobbying,* 236. See also Grim and Siddiqui, "Call Time for Congress."

41. For insight into these coordinated activities, see for instance Mayer, *Dark Money.*

42. See Michaels, *Triumph of Doubt.*

43. See, for instance, Woods, "An Environmental Race to the Bottom?"; Konisky, "Regulator Attitudes."

44. See, for example, Stokes, *Short Circuiting Policy.* Like tobacco companies, the fossil fuel industry has been deliberately misleading the public. Since the late 1970s, for example, Exxon executives have known—because their own scientists were telling them—about the dangers of climate change. Banerjee, Song, and Hasemeyer, "Exxon's Own Research."

45. See, for instance, Intergovernmental Panel on Climate Change, *Climate Change 2022.*

46. Stiglitz et al., *Rewriting the Rules,* 50.

47. This shift in corporate strategy is traceable to the so-called "shareholder revolution" of the 1980s, which turned corporate managers away from other, longer-term stakeholders. For further analysis, see Stiglitz et al., *Rewriting the Rules,* 49–57. It has its roots, before that, in shifting management practices (and the consultants who tirelessly promoted them) in the 1970s; see Hyman, *Temp.*

48. See, for instance, Zuboff, *Age of Surveillance Capitalism;* Bilott, *Exposure;* Lewis, *Big Short;* Keefe, *Empire of Pain;* Elmore, *Seed Money;* Leonard, *Meat Racket;* Bogdanich and Forsythe, *When McKinsey Comes to Town;* Gillam, *Whitewash;* Goswami and Woods, *Waste Deep;* Davies et al., "Uber Files"; Morgenson and Rosner, *These Are the Plunderers;* Robison, *Flying Blind;* Coll, *Private Empire;* Steinzor, *Why*

Not Jail?, 67–75; Hopkins, *Disastrous Decisions;* Mayer, *Dark Money,* 146–171; Bakan, *The Corporation;* Punch, "Suite Violence"; Girion, *Johnson & Johnson Knew;* Buell, *Capital Offenses.*

49. Henderson, *Reimagining Capitalism,* 7–29; Bakan, *Corporation,* 28–59.

50. See, for instance, Lears, *Rebirth of a Nation.*

51. The Clinton administration, which aggressively courted the business community, was in fact one of the most successful promoters of deregulation; the ideological fruit of the Reagan years finally ripened in the 1990s.

52. For an authoritative study of the rise of deregulatory ideology in the United States, see Gerstle, *Rise and Fall of the Neoliberal Order.*

53. For a seminal contribution to this debate, see Carpenter and Moss, *Preventing Regulatory Capture.*

54. For an overview, see Ginsburg and Huq, *How to Save a Constitutional Democracy,* 164–204.

55. On the threat of executive aggrandizement, see Riedl et al., "Pathways of Democratic Backsliding." On emergency powers, see Goitein, "Alarming Scope," and Brennan Center for Justice, "Executive Power."

56. See Levitsky and Ziblatt, *Tyranny of the Minority,* 198–223.

57. See, for instance, Inglehart and Norris, "Trump"; Berman, "Causes of Populism."

58. Since 2009, Democrats have lost significant support among both white and Hispanic voters who do not have a college degree; see Pew Research Center, *Changing Partisan Coalitions,* 17. These trends were plainly evident in the 2024 election returns. For more insight, see Jennifer Medina, "For Minority Working-Class Voters."

59. See, for instance, Hersh, *Politics Is for Power,* 160–181.

60. See Tomasky, "Why Does No One Understand." For a more detailed look at the effects of disinformation and propaganda in our politics, see McQuade, *Attack from Within.*

61. For a cogent articulation of these privileges and their benefits, see Ciepley, "Beyond Public and Private."

62. Ciepley, "Beyond Public and Private."

63. British Academy, *Principles for Purposeful Business.*

64. Warren, "Companies Shouldn't Be Accountable Only to Shareholders." Warren's proposal applied only to corporations with over $1 billion in gross receipts— so only very large corporations.

65. See for instance Greenfield, *Failure of Corporate Law,* 125–152.

66. For a more detailed discussion, see Chandler, *Free and Equal,* 250–257.

67. The "Responsible Corporate Officer Doctrine," which allows corporate officers to be prosecuted for certain kinds of egregious misconduct on their watch even if they had no knowledge of it, offers one interesting precedent. Another possibility is reinvigorating the legal doctrine of *ultra vires,* which was used historically to prevent corporations from betraying the public purposes for which they were chartered. See, for instance, Greenfield, *Failure of Corporate Law,* 73–105.

68. See, for instance, Bruner, "Corporate Governance Reform," 1266–1275; Strine, *Toward Fair and Sustainable Capitalism.*

69. Such an agenda has been laid out, for example, in Wu, *Curse of Bigness.*

70. This argument has been persuasively developed by Elizabeth Anderson; see Anderson, *Private Government.*

71. For an overview, see, for instance, Norris and Abel van Es, *Checkbook Elections?*

72. Norris and Abel van Es, *Checkbook Elections?,* 263.

73. For a detailed discussion, see Teachout, *Corruption in America.*

74. See Carpenter and Moss, *Preventing Regulatory Capture,* 451–465.

Chapter 3. Exploitation

1. Saez and Zucman, "Wealth Inequality."

2. Kent and Ricketts, *U.S. Wealth Inequality.*

3. Autor, Mindell, and Reynolds, *Work of the Future,* 19. It remains too early to tell whether this recent wage growth is a temporary effect of the post-pandemic economy. It has not, in any case, put much of a dent in the broader trends discussed in this chapter.

4. For an overview of these economic changes, see Howe, *What Hath God Wrought,* 525–569.

5. For a classic discussion, see, Appleby, "Commercial Farming.'"

6. Lincoln, "Address," 479.

7. Colton, *Junius Tracts,* vol. 7: *Labor and Capital,* 9. Emphasis in the original.

8. Economic historians tend to agree that this was a time of abundant opportunity and mobility for white workers; see, for instance, Pope, "Inequality"; Appleby, *Inheriting the Revolution.*

9. For further discussion, see Zakaras, *Roots of American Individualism;* Anderson, "When the Market Was 'Left.'"

10. For further discussion, see Foner, *Reconstruction,* 102–110, 128–142. For more

details about women's rights advocates and Native American advocates appealing to the ideal of independence, see Zakaras, *Roots of American Individualism,* 68–80.

11. For an excellent discussion, see Gourevitch, *From Slavery to the Cooperative Commonwealth.*

12. Although he reaches different political conclusions, Alan Wertheimer offers a useful, philosophically rigorous exploration of the idea of exploitation; see Wertheimer, *Exploitation.*

13. A fully articulated theory of exploitation would need to define each of these conditions much more precisely. "Reasonable" options would have to be defined in relative terms—relative, that is, to the standard of living that prevails in the society in question. Otherwise, virtually all paid work in poor societies would qualify as exploitative.

14. In one respect, however, it still falls short of the small farmer's. In theory at least, the small farmer did not have to engage in market transactions for his economic livelihood, because he could live off his farm. The Vermont contractor has no such independent source of sustenance.

15. Autor, Mindell, and Reynolds, "Work of the Future," 19.

16. For analysis of declining economic mobility in the United States, see Corak, "Income Inequality"; Bratberg et al., "Comparison of Intergenerational Mobility"; Mitnik and Grusky, *Economic Mobility;* Chetty et al., "Fading American Dream"; Ferrie, "History Lessons." Further evidence about the economic struggles and insecurity of low-wage workers will be laid out in detail later in this chapter.

17. For further reading, see Guendelsberger, *On the Clock;* Tirado, *Hand to Mouth;* Genoways, *The Chain;* Wood, *Despotism on Demand;* Head, *New Ruthless Economy;* Shipler, *Working Poor;* Greenhouse, *Big Squeeze;* McClelland, "I Was a Warehouse Wage Slave."

18. Douglas and Leonard, "Is the US Chicken Industry Cheating Its Farmers?"

19. Leonard, *Meat Racket,* 24. Leonard's book offers a devastating study of Tyson and American meat production more generally.

20. See also Lakhani, "'They Rake in Profits.'"

21. Stone and Colvin, *Arbitration Epidemic,* 21–23.

22. Hamaji, Deutsch, and Nicolas, *Unchecked Corporate Power.*

23. Desmond, *Poverty, by America,* 63–70.

24. See Kasakove, "Investors Are Buying Mobile Home Parks"; Kolhatkar, "What Happens."

25. Adding up overdraft fees and interest on payday loans, Desmond estimates

that $61 million is being extracted *each day*, mainly from low-income Americans. Desmond, *Poverty, by America*, 71, 77. For more detail, see Baradaran, *How the Other Half Banks*, 102–161; Pascale, *Living on the Edge*, 54–75.

26. Tirado, *Hand to Mouth*, 23.

27. For a classic articulation of this view, see Friedman, *Capitalism and Freedom*, 14–15. For a more recent iteration, see McCloskey, *Why Liberalism Works*.

28. For more detail, see Zakaras, *Roots of American Individualism*, 132–159.

29. For a succinct overview of these and other policy strategies that have depressed wages in the United States, see Mishel and Bivens, *Identifying the Policy Levers*.

30. Williamson, "Radical Taxation."

31. For a seminal discussion of these falsehoods, see Polanyi, *Great Transformation*. For an updated version, see Anderson, *Hijacked*, ix–xviii, 254–283.

32. For one recent discussion of how American pharmaceutical companies manipulate patents and secure windfall profits at the expense of patients' interests, see Robbins, "How a Drug Company Made $114 Billion."

33. Reich, *Saving Capitalism*, 16–28.

34. This point is developed at length in Reich, *The System*.

35. Anyone who doubts that there are fundamental similarities between our economy and the economy of the first Gilded Age should pick up Walter Weyl's incisive 1912 book *The New Democracy*.

36. For further discussion and evidence, see Piketty, *Brief History*.

37. Hyman, *Temp*, 41.

38. Bureau of Labor Statistics, *News Release*.

39. Stiglitz et al., *Rewriting the Rules*, 71–74; Greenhouse, "'Old-School Union Busting.'"

40. One 2020 study found that the average out-of-pocket costs associated with pregnancy and childbirth exceed $4,500 for women *with* employer-subsidized health plans. See Moniz et al., "Out-of-Pocket Spending."

41. Hacker, *Great Risk Shift*, 77.

42. See Hertel-Fernandez, "Dismantling Policy."

43. Stiglitz et al., *Rewriting the Rules*, 78–79.

44. For in-depth studies of this economic transformation, see Weil, *Fissured Workplace*; Hyman, *Temp*.

45. See for instance Ravenelle, *Hustle and Gig*; Rosenblat, *Uberland*. People using these platforms selectively to supplement other, regular income also enjoy greater autonomy and satisfaction than those who depend on them entirely. See, for

instance, Schor et al., "Dependence and Precarity." That so many workers feel the need to supplement their regular incomes speaks to the unfairness of the economy as a whole.

46. Kerwin et al., *U.S. Foreign-Born Essential Workers,* 2. See also Svajlenka, *Protecting Undocumented Workers.*

47. Ferriss and Yerardi, *Wage Theft Hits Immigrants—Hard.*

48. Villavicencio, *Undocumented Americans,* 10–11.

49. For one fairly sophisticated version of this argument, see McCloskey, *Why Liberalism Works.*

50. OECD, *OECD Employment Outlook, 2022,* 345. See also Ross and Bateman, *Meet the Low-Wage Workforce.*

51. Karpman, Zuckerman, and Gonzalez, *Material Hardship,* 2. For more detail about working poverty in America, see, for instance, Greenhouse, *Big Squeeze;* Shulman, *Betrayal of Work.*

52. Cardoso and Wichman, "Water Affordability."

53. Lakhani, Singh, and Kamal, "Almost Half a Million U.S. Households."

54. Coleman-Jensen et al., *Household Food Security,* 7.

55. For a grim overview, see, for instance, Goldblum and Shaddox, *Broke in America.*

56. Dobkin, "US Homelessness Surged."

57. For more detail, see, for instance, Desmond, *Evicted;* Kozol, *Rachel and Her Children.* In California, which is the epicenter of the crisis of American homelessness, the growing mismatch between wages and housing costs is a leading cause; see Levin, "'We Have Failed.'"

58. Hacker, *Great Risk Shift,* 86.

59. In addition to Jacob Hacker's book, this insecurity is ably documented in Gosselin, *High Wire.*

60. "Being poor," write Sendhil Mullainathan and Eldar Shafir in their landmark study, "reduces a person's cognitive capacity more than going one full night without sleep." Mullainathan and Shafir, *Scarcity,* 13. See also Geronimus, *Weathering.*

61. Schneider and Harknett, "Consequence of Routine."

62. See, for instance, Woo and Postolache, "Impact of Work Environment"; Goh, Pfeffer, and Zenios, "Relationship between Workplace Stressors."

63. Schor, "(Even More) Overworked American," 6–11.

64. For more background, see Hunnicutt, *Free Time.*

65. These findings can be explored through the work of Opportunity Insights,

a nonprofit that studies economic opportunity and its distribution in the United States: https://opportunityinsights.org. See also Autor, Mindell, and Reynolds, "Work of the Future," 24–25. The erosion of stability and opportunity for middle-class families is also explored in detail in Hacker, *Great Risk Shift*.

66. See for instance Walker, *Shame of Poverty*; Marmot, *Status Syndrome*. For reflections on poverty and shame in the United States, see Tirado, *Hand to Mouth*; Pascale, *Living on the Edge*, 119–139.

67. This point is ably developed in Starr, *Freedom's Power*.

68. See Williamson, *Read My Lips*.

69. The billionaire investor Warren Buffett made a similar point while speaking to a group of students at the University of North Carolina in 1996: "If you stick me down in the middle of Bangladesh or Peru or someplace," he said, "you'll find out how much this talent is going to produce in the wrong kind of soil. I will be struggling thirty years later." https://www.youtube.com/watch?v=xFpEGLyymxw.

70. See for instance Moller, *Governing Least*, 70–73.

71. This view is ably developed in Murphy and Nagel, *Myth of Ownership*. See especially pp. 31–37.

72. Piketty, *Brief History*, 131. For useful discussions of this data, see Piketty, *Brief History*, 121–149; Saez and Zucman, *Triumph of Injustice*, 32–44.

73. States such as California and Massachusetts have developed enforcement strategies that enlist the help of in-state labor organizations in identifying corporate offenders, which is a step in the right direction. Block and Sachs, *Clean Slate for Worker Power*, 88–91.

74. See also Kirsch, *Future of Work in America*; Stiglitz et al., *Rewriting the Rules*, 70–79, 139–143; Block and Sachs, "Clean Slate for Worker Power."

75. Blasi, Freeman, and Kruse, *Citizen's Share*, 181–182, 263–264; Blasi and Kruse, *Employee Ownership and ESOPs*.

76. For an excellent discussion of this history and these experiments and policy ideas, see Blasi, Freeman, and Kruse, *Citizen's Share*.

77. Whittaker, "Idea That Raising Wages."

78. For a gut-wrenching account of these practices, which have become commonplace in the industry, see Ballou, *Plunder*.

79. Frank, "Wealthiest 10%."

80. See, for instance, Goshen and Levit, "Agents of Inequality," 57–69; Foroohar, *Makers and Takers*, 148–151, 315–326; Ballou, *Plunder*, 215–246.

81. For one detailed set of proposals, see Frison and Jacobs, *From Uniformity to Diversity*. See also Holt-Giménez, *Can We Feed the World without Destroying It?*

82. For one insightful discussion, see Schuetz, *Fixer-Upper*.

83. For more on postal banking, see Baradaran, *How the Other Half Banks*, 183–209.

84. Sawhill, *Forgotten Americans*, 112–113.

85. Autor, Mindell, and Reynolds, "Work of the Future," 53–69.

86. See, for instance, Sadowski, "Why Silicon Valley Is Embracing Universal Basic Income."

87. For more details, see Van Parijs and Vanderborght, *Basic Income;* Hasdell, *What We Know about Universal Basic Income;* West et al., *Preliminary Analysis*.

88. See, for instance, Tanden, Martin, and Jarsulic, *Toward a Marshall Plan*.

89. For one comprehensive proposal (offered by two highly respected economists), see Saez and Zucman, *Triumph of Injustice*.

90. See, for instance, Saez and Zucman, *Triumph of Injustice;* Piketty, *Brief History;* Banerjee and Duflo, *Good Economics for Hard Times*, 236–262.

91. Pew Research Center, *Biden, Trump Supporters;* Gilberstadt, *More Americans Oppose*.

Chapter 4. Racial Hierarchy

1. Kochhar and Moslimani, *Wealth Surged,* 14, 13; Perry, Stephens, and Donoghoe, *Black Wealth*.

2. Moore, *State Unemployment by Race*.

3. See, for instance, Mahajan et al., "Trends in Differences in Health Status."

4. Human Rights Watch/ACLU, *Racial Discrimination,* 63–69; García, *Schools Are Still Segregated;* Frankenberg et al., *Harming Our Common Future*.

5. Sharkey, *Stuck in Place,* 27–28; Zhong and Popovich, "How Air Pollution across America Reflects Racist Policy."

6. Sharkey, *Stuck in Place,* 33–46. See also Massey and Denton, *American Apartheid*.

7. Nellis, *Color of Justice;* Western and Simes, "Criminal Justice"; Hinton, Henderson, and Reed, *Unjust Burden;* Goff et al., *Science of Justice;* Ciccolini and Sawyer, *'Kettling' Protesters in the Bronx*.

8. Craigie, Grawert, and Kimble, *Conviction, Imprisonment, and Lost Earnings*.

9. Zhou, "How Trump's DOJ."

10. See, for instance, Baptist, *Half Has Never Been Told;* Beckert and Rockman, *Slavery's Capitalism.*

11. For a detailed discussion of race and racism in the politics of the New Deal, see Katznelson, *Fear Itself;* Katznelson, *When Affirmative Action Was White.*

12. Rothstein, *Color of Law,* 70–73.

13. This sordid story is told in detail by Richard Rothstein in his book *Color of Law.* See also Coates, "Case for Reparations." Restrictive covenants were struck down by the Supreme Court in 1948, but many white communities simply found other ways to enforce racial exclusion.

14. Sharkey, *Stuck in Place,* 47–90; Massey and Denton, *American Apartheid.* For a brilliant reflection on the many overlapping forms of injustice that gave rise to concentrated urban poverty, and on the moral principles that ought to inform our response, see Shelby, *Dark Ghettos.*

15. Historically Black Colleges and Universities.

16. Brown, *Whiteness of Wealth,* 80–81.

17. See for instance Chetty et al., "Race and Economic Opportunity," 714; Sharkey, *Stuck in Place,* 114–116.

18. For a thorough discussion, see Eberhardt, *Biased.*

19. See for instance Beck and Blumstein, "Racial Disproportionality"; Rehavi and Starr, "Racial Disparity"; Hinton, Henderson, and Reed, "Unjust Burden." See also Alexander, *New Jim Crow,* 97–139.

20. Brown, *Whiteness of Wealth,* 80–87; Rothstein, *Color of Law,* 110–112.

21. Bertrand and Mullainathan, "Are Emily and Greg More Employable Than Lakisha and Jamal?"; Quillian et al., "Meta-Analysis of Field Experiments."

22. Sullivan et al., *Not Only Equal Paychecks;* Brown, *Whiteness of Wealth,* 132–165.

23. Data from the 2020 census reveals that around 13 percent of the 9.7 million Americans who identify as American Indian and Alaskan Native lived on reservations or other trust lands.

24. Pettit et al., *Continuity and Change;* Clarren, "How America Is Failing."

25. Chetty et al., "Race and Economic Opportunity"; Sharkey, *Stuck in Place,* 91–116.

26. Chetty et al., "Race and Economic Opportunity," 758–760.

27. Sullivan et al., *Not Only Equal Paychecks.*

28. For a powerful exploration of the "afterlife" of incarceration and its devastating effects on Black communities, see Miller, *Halfway Home.*

29. Alexander, *New Jim Crow,* 97–139.

30. Wolfe, "'A Profound Betrayal of Trust'"; Goldberg, "Funds to Aid Jackson's Water System"; Demashkieh et al., *Flint Water Crisis;* Beaumont, "Flint Residents Grapple."

31. Fraser, "Social Justice," 28–29.

32. Fraser, "Social Justice," 18–20. See also Canaday, *Straight State.*

33. Coates, *Between the World and Me,* 20–21, 103, 71.

34. For another powerful discussion of this fundamental "value gap," see Glaude Jr., *Democracy in Black,* 29–50.

35. For an insightful exploration of this tendency, see Brown, *In the Ruins.*

36. If this "best version" were a radical outlier, embraced by virtually no one, then it might be fair to treat it as irrelevant here. But this is clearly not the case when it comes to liberalism today: *many* of the intellectuals who have recently defended liberalism in the context of racial injustice—including Danielle Allen, Andrew Valls, Charles Mills, Tommie Shelby, and others—have shown that it can support strongly egalitarian conclusions.

37. Bonilla-Silva, *Racism without Racists,* 79–103.

38. *Parents Involved v. Seattle School District No. 1,* 551 US 701 (2007). https://www.loc.gov/item/usrep551701/.

39. Oxner, "Texas Agriculture Commissioner." Whether or not affirmative action or loan forgiveness to farmers are the best ways to seek racial justice is, of course, a matter of legitimate debate. My quarrel here is with the effort to invalidate *all* public programs that selectively target African Americans on the grounds that they are discriminatory.

40. This point is forcefully developed in Loury, *Anatomy of Racial Inequality,* 109–154.

41. This argument is developed from a liberal point of view, for example, in Valls, *Rethinking Racial Justice.*

42. Guinier, "From Racial Liberalism to Racial Literacy," 100. See also Darda, *Strange Career of Racial Liberalism.*

43. See Alexander, *New Jim Crow,* 109–139.

44. See, for instance, Marble and Nall, "Where Self-Interest Trumps Ideology."

45. See Bright, "White Psychodrama"; Guinier, "From Racial Liberalism to Racial Literacy." Scholars have also suggested that the pressure to achieve quantifiable rigor in social scientific analysis drove mid-century social scientists to focus on mea-

surable attitudes instead of messier and more complex social structures. See Gordon, *From Power to Prejudice.*

46. These tendencies are discussed, for example, in Sandel, *Tyranny of Merit,* 59–80, 124–125.

47. Shapiro, *Hidden Cost,* 60–84. Similar insights can be gleaned from Arlie Hochschild's work; see Hochschild, *Strangers in Their Own Land,* 135–203.

48. Pew Research Center, *Most Americans.* See also Piston, *Class Attitudes.*

49. Mills, "Racial Liberalism"; Mills, "'Ideal Theory' as Ideology." See also Loury, *Anatomy of Racial Inequality,* 110–154.

50. By "living" I mean to describe long-term residents of the territory. We saw in Chapter 2 that equal freedom requires that we avoid creating second-class citizens. To consign immigrants who live and work in the national territory long-term to second-class citizenship is to violate this moral requirement.

51. See, for instance, Stovall, *White Freedom.*

52. Almost all of these liberals, even those on the exclusive end of the spectrum, tended to use universalistic language to express their moral and political principles. But they didn't really mean it: their soaring, universalistic proclamations masked deeply hierarchical views about who deserved full moral and political consideration.

53. Glaude, *Democracy in Black,* 29–50.

54. See Mill, "Utility of Religion."

55. See for instance Baldwin, *Fire Next Time,* 8, 95, 104; Rogers, *Darkened Light of Faith,* 279–285. Mill and Baldwin are hardly alone among liberal thinkers in arguing that liberalism is morally demanding, and more specifically that it depends on the cultivation of empathy and a willingness to protect others from injustice. More recent examples include Isaiah Berlin, Michael Ignatieff, Judith Shklar, Richard Rorty, Martha Nussbaum, Sharon Krause, Michael Frazer, and others.

56. See Law, *Red Racisms.*

57. For a searching analysis of these complex roots, see Wilkerson, *Caste.*

58. King Jr., *Why We Can't Wait,* 124–131.

59. Shelby, *Idea of Prison Abolition,* ix. This idea is laid out more comprehensively in Shelby, *Dark Ghettos.*

60. Baker, Sciarra, and Farrie, *Is School Funding Fair?,* 11, 14–18. See also Weathers and Sosina, "Separate Remains Unequal"; Baker and Corcoran, *Stealth Inequities;* Roza et al., "How within-District Spending"; EdBuild, *Nonwhite School Districts.*

61. Duncombe and Yinger, "How Much More," 522, 525.

62. For a comprehensive summary of this research, see Baker, *Educational In-*

equality, 81–101, 210–211; Jackson, "Does School Spending Matter?" The Department of Defense has also achieved exceptional results in the roughly fifty schools it runs on military bases, which are highly integrated racially and socioeconomically. Its strategies for success are unsurprising: good salaries for teachers, relatively high per-student spending, and support for the families (a salary, affordable housing, and access to healthcare). See Mervosh, "Who Runs the Best U.S. Schools?"

63. Baker, *Educational Inequality,* 87–88.

64. Baradaran, *Homestead Act.*

65. See, for instance, Weisburd and Majmundar, *Proactive Policing;* Lum, "Perspectives on Policing"; Engel, Isaza, and McManus, "Owning Police Reform." For further discussion of Cincinnati's police reforms, see Semuels, "How to Fix"; Worden and McLean, *Mirage of Police Reform,* 189–196.

66. Wykstra, "Bail Reform."

67. For a powerful overview, see Howard, *Unusually Cruel.*

68. See Sered, *Until We Reckon.* For thoughtful reflections on what works and what doesn't, see also Strang and Sherman, "Morality of Evidence"; Baliga, Henry, and Valentine, *Restorative Community Conferencing.*

69. These are among the recommendations offered by leading criminologist John Pfaff; see Pfaff, *Locked In,* 203–232.

70. This occurred in Wilmington, North Carolina.

71. For further discussion, see Valls, *Rethinking Racial Justice,* 44–75.

72. For sophisticated recent treatment of the issue, see Valls, *Rethinking Racial Justice,* 16–43; Darity Jr. and Mullen, *From Here to Equality.*

73. Shelby, *Dark Ghettos,* 275–284.

74. See Monk Jr., "Unceasing Significance of Colorism"; Reece, "Future of American Blackness."

75. For updated state-by-state information, see Kaiser Family Foundation, "Policy Tracker."

76. Little, "Moral Permissibility of Abortion," 155.

77. North, "Christian Right Is Coming." No-fault divorce allows people to end their marriages without having to prove, in a court of law, that they have been mistreated. The advent of no-fault divorce in the 1970s, which allowed women to escape abusive husbands without costly court proceedings, coincided with reductions in domestic violence and spousal murder. See Stevenson and Wolfers, "Bargaining in the Shadow."

78. Willingham, "Gender Divide Prominent." In both states, women legislators

voted differently than men; in South Carolina, male legislators had to overcome a filibuster staged by the five women senators (three of them Republicans).

79. This point is often associated with Judith Jarvis Thomson; see Thomson, "In Defense of Abortion." In my view, a more persuasive articulation can be found in Little, "Abortion, Intimacy."

80. Little, "Abortion, Intimacy," 299.

81. Little, "Moral Permissibility of Abortion," 152–153.

82. For a sophisticated, in-depth treatment, see Greasley, *Arguments about Abortion.*

Chapter 5. Ecological Degradation

1. On groundwater depletion, see Rojanasakul et al., "America Is Using," 10–33, 52–72; Philpott, *Perilous Bounty.* On microplastics, see Pinto-Rodrigues, "Microplastics Are in Our Bodies"; Sharma et al., "Understanding Microplastic Pollution." On dead zones, see Kirchman, *Dead Zones.* On carcinogens, see Casey, "EPA Proposes Banning"; Tingley, "Forever Chemicals."

2. Wallace-Wells, "Beyond Catastrophe."

3. For an overview, see Intergovernmental Panel on Climate Change, *Climate Change 2022,* 44–68.

4. See for instance Barbero et al., "Climate Change Presents." Already, major home insurance companies have begun pulling out of California and other western states because of the high risk of wildfires.

5. Intergovernmental Panel on Climate Change, *Climate Change 2022,* 605–608.

6. Tabuchi et al., "Floods Are Getting Worse."

7. National Oceanic and Atmospheric Administration, *Billion-Dollar Weather and Climate Disasters.*

8. Canon, "Hell on Earth."

9. See, for instance, Powis et al., "Observational and Model Evidence."

10. Raymond, Matthews, and Horton, "Emergence of Heat and Humidity"; Kommenda et al., "Where Dangerous Heat Is Surging." See also Romanello et al., "2022 Report," 1624–1625.

11. NASA, "Ocean Warming."

12. Cornwall, "Breathless Oceans."

13. During the Last Interglacial period, which ended some 115,000 years ago, sea levels were 20–30 feet higher than they are today, although it was only very slightly warmer. Intergovernmental Panel on Climate Change, *Ocean and Cryosphere,* 55.

14. National Oceanic and Atmospheric Administration, *Technical Report Overview*. For the full report, see Sweet et al., *Global and Regional Sea Level Rise Scenarios*.

15. Lesk, Rowhani, and Ramankutty, "Influence of Extreme Weather"; Nicas, "Slow-Motion Climate Disaster."

16. McKibben, *Falter*, 36–39; Intergovernmental Panel on Climate Change, *Climate Change 2022*, 9, 60, 713–906.

17. Intergovernmental Panel on Climate Change, *Climate Change 2022*, 52. See also Lustgarten, "Great Climate Migration."

18. See, for instance, Koubi, "Climate Change and Conflict."

19. See, for instance, Gelles, "Fossil Fuels."

20. Rothfeder and Maag, "How Wall Street's Fossil-Fuel Money."

21. Xu et al., "Global Greenhouse Gas Emissions." For a broader discussion, see Weis, *Ecological Hoofprint*.

22. See, for instance, Carrington, "'Gigantic' Power of Meat Industry."

23. See, for instance, Dobson, *Green Political Thought*, 149–158.

24. See Hickman et al., "Climate Anxiety in Children."

25. See Holland, "Environment as Meta-Capability."

26. Shaw, *Liberalism and the Challenge of Climate Change*, 4.

27. Shaw, *Liberalism and the Challenge of Climate Change*, 4, 26.

28. This definition draws from the seminal 1987 report of the United Nations Brundtland Commission, which defined sustainable development as "development that meets the needs of the present without compromising the ability of future generations to meet their own needs." United Nations, *Our Common Future*.

29. For further reflection on liberalism and sustainability, see Barry and Wissenburg, *Sustaining Liberal Democracy*, especially the chapters written by Barry and Wissenburg themselves.

30. Anon., "Our Objects," 4. Emphasis in the original.

31. For further discussion of ecological modernization as a political paradigm, see Dryzek, *Politics of the Earth*, 165–183.

32. For a seminal discussion of these more radical political programs, see Dobson, *Green Political Thought*. The dichotomy between ecological modernization and degrowth is obviously very broad and rough; in fact, there exists a broad spectrum of views on this question.

33. For authoritarian strains, see Shearman and Wayne-Smith, *Climate Change Challenge*; Hickman, "James Lovelock.'" For socialist degrowth, see, for instance, Saitō, *Slow Down*.

34. Bill McKibben's writing offers one prominent example of this view; see, for instance, McKibben, *Deep Economy.*

35. See, for instance, Brinn, "Path Down to Green Liberalism"; Cox, *Any Way You Slice It.*

36. Even the Chinese government, which is highly authoritarian, believes that its legitimacy depends on its ability to maintain robust rates of economic growth.

37. This acknowledgment has a long history in liberal ideas, dating back to liberal utilitarians such as Jeremy Bentham and John Stuart Mill.

38. See Harvey and Gillis, *Big Fix,* 9–35; Victor, Geels, and Sharpe, *Accelerating the Low Carbon Transition.*

39. Procurement refers to the purchase of goods and services by government agencies. The Buy Clean California Act, for example, requires that low-emissions materials be used for construction projects funded by the state government.

40. Leaving aside SNAP benefits (food stamps), the current Farm Bill is among the most morally inexcusable major items in the US budget, and it receives far too little attention from those interested in social and environmental justice. For one comprehensive reform proposal, see the National Sustainable Agriculture Coalition's "2023 Farm Bill Platform."

41. Mazzucato, *Mission Economy,* 127. See also Harvey and Gillis, *Big Fix,* 165–238.

42. George, Kane, and Tomer, *How US Cities Are Finding Creative Ways.*

43. See for instance Stratton, "Carbon-Free Copenhagen." The city had hoped to reach full carbon neutrality by 2025 but has since extended its deadline.

44. Harvey and Gillis, *Big Fix,* 117–139; Tura and Ojanen, "Sustainability-Oriented Innovations."

45. See Mendez, *Climate Change from the Streets,* 91–114.

46. See Pace, "New Coalition"; Frischen and Zakaras, *America's Path Forward,* 99–110.

47. For one telling example of this immensely destructive power at the local level, see Leber, "Attack on American Cities." For an index of its global power, we need only consider that more fossil fuel lobbyists were granted access to the crucial climate negotiations at COP 28 in Dubai than representatives from the ten most climate-vulnerable countries *combined.* Lakhani, "Record Number of Fossil Fuel Lobbyists."

48. See, for instance, Pollin, "Nationalize the U.S. Fossil Fuel Industry"; Becker, "Why We Must Nationalize Big Oil"; Paul, Skandier, and Renzy, *Out of Time;* Alperovitz, Guinan, and Hanna, "Policy Weapon."

49. See Toral et al., "11 Nations."

50. For further reflections on these various strategies, see Smith, *Can Democracy Safeguard the Future?*

51. William Ruto, the president of Kenya, has lately emerged as a leading advocate for a strong global green bank. See Carr, "Kenya's Proposal for a Green Bank."

52. More precisely, the mini-publics are chosen using a "stratified random sampling" technique that ensures that they will reflect the key social and demographic characteristics of the population at large.

53. The seminal work in this area is James Fishkin's; see Fishkin, *Democracy When People Are Thinking.* For a broader discussion of the democratization of global governance, see Dryzek et al., *Deliberative Global Governance;* Baber and Bartlett, *Consensus and Global Environmental Governance.*

54. The idea of a "just" energy transition has received considerable attention from scholars and policy analysts. For a brief introduction, see, for instance, Carley and Konisky, "Justice and Equity Implications."

Chapter 6. Democracy and Countervailing Power

1. Rainie, Keeter, and Perrin, *Trust and Distrust in America*, 35.

2. See Hersh, *Politics Is for Power*, 3.

3. I draw the term "countervailing power" from economist John Kenneth Galbraith, who used it in his 1952 book *American Capitalism: The Concept of Countervailing Power.* See also Reich, *The System*, 54–69.

4. Hazony, *Conservatism*, 223; Deneen, *Why Liberalism Failed*, 48, 21–42.

5. Empathy can, of course, distort moral judgment if it is selectively applied. If we empathize mainly with members of our own social group or class, we will remain morally blinkered.

6. These include such canonical thinkers as Adam Smith and John Stuart Mill, as well as a host of more recent liberal thinkers, including Stephen Macedo, Martha Nussbaum, Stephen Holmes, Nancy Rosenblum, Amy Gutmann, Alexandre Lefebvre, and many others.

7. Conservative critics thus find themselves in the peculiar position of arguing that liberalism is a nihilistic free-for-all on the one hand, and that it gives rise to excessive moralism and intolerance on the other.

8. Deneen's work exemplifies this sloppiness on the right; see Deneen, *Why Liberalism Failed.*

9. For more detail, see Zakaras, *Roots of American Individualism.*

10. Some critics insist that that these competing strains of liberalism are ultimately reducible to the same thing: a celebration of limitless individual autonomy. See, for instance, Deneen, *Why Liberalism Failed*, 43–63. For reasons explored throughout this book, this argument strains credulity.

11. Jedediah Purdy has rightly criticized this view as a kind of anti-political fantasy; see Purdy, *Two Cheers for Politics*, 13–25.

12. Purdy, *Two Cheers for Politics*. In *Liberalism and Its Discontents*, for example, Francis Fukuyama takes aim at "the right-wing populist and left-wing progressive movements that threaten liberalism today." Fukayama, *Liberalism and Its Discontents*, 17. See also Mounk, *People vs. Democracy*.

13. This line appears in *Federalist Papers*, no. 63, emphasis in the original. Available online at https://avalon.law.yale.edu/18th_century/fed63.asp.

14. See, for instance, Rosenblatt, *Lost History of Liberalism*, 88–128, 156–193.

15. The highly successful activities of the Federalist Society are a case in point: over time, through the concerted and lavishly funded activism of economic elites, it has changed the composition of the American judiciary, filling it with judges who are hand-picked for their fealty to business interests.

16. See for instance Bartels, *Unequal Democracy;* Gilens and Page, "Testing Theories."

17. Political scientist Sheri Berman, for example, emphasizes both rising economic inequality and the declining responsiveness of political institutions (due to elite capture) as key drivers of populist sympathies. See Berman, "Causes of Populism."

18. There are many scholarly studies of what I am calling countervailing power, which document its effectiveness in local, state, and national politics. See, for instance, Han, McKenna, and Oyakawa, *Prisms of the People;* Stout, *Blessed Are the Organized;* McAlevey, *No Shortcuts;* Woodly, *Reckoning;* Payne, *I've Got the Light of Freedom.*

19. For insightful analysis, see McAlevey, *No Shortcuts.*

20. Hersh, *Politics Is for Power,* 147–196; Polsby, *Consequences of Party Reform.*

21. Skocpol, *Diminished Democracy,* 242–243.

22. Skocpol, *Diminished Democracy,* 236.

23. Allen, *Justice by Means of Democracy,* 57–60.

24. Bartels, *Unequal Democracy;* Gilens and Page, "Testing Theories."

25. Mill, "Considerations," 224.

26. For more on movement lawyering, see the Movement Law Lab (https://movementlawlab.org). For more on public banking, see, for instance, Public Bank L.A. (https://publicbankla.com), and Dēmos, *Banking for the Public Good.*

27. See Coleman, "How a Group of Student Debtors."

28. See Ross, "In Los Angeles."

29. For a cogent overview, see, for instance, Meyer, *Politics of Protest,* 227–250, 145–171.

30. See, for instance, Dēmos, *Banking for the Public Good.*

31. Horowitz, *Mutualism.*

32. Hersh, *Politics Is for Power,* 210–215.

33. See Mettler, *Submerged State.*

34. Mettler, *Submerged State, 27.*

35. See Skocpol and Williamson, *Tea Party.*

36. Rosenfeld, *Democracy and Truth,* 30.

37. See Napoli and Mahone, *Local Newspapers Are Suffering;* Mahone et al., *Who's Producing Local Journalism.*

38. These losses were not offset by the modest hiring increases at digital sites and TV news stations. Overall, 24,000 journalism jobs disappeared. Abernathy, *News Deserts and Ghost Newspapers,* 8, 25.

39. Abernathy, *News Deserts and Ghost Newspapers,* 7–35; Pickard, *Democracy without Journalism?,* 43–45, 70–89; Coppins, "Secretive Hedge Fund." The top three owners now control almost a thousand newspapers between them. Abernathy, *News Deserts and Ghost Newspapers,* 31–35.

40. Penelope Muse Abernathy defines a "news desert" as "a community, either rural or urban, where residents have very limited access to the sort of credible and comprehensive news and information that feed democracy at the grassroots level." Abernathy, *News Deserts and Ghost Newspapers,* 18.

41. Abernathy, *News Deserts and Ghost Newspapers,* 19.

42. Pickard, *Democracy without Journalism?,* 87–88.

43. Vosoughi, Roy, and Aral, "Spread of True and False News," 1146. For an in-depth study of Facebook's role in the spread of misinformation, see Vaidhyanathan, *Anti-Social Media.*

44. For an extended discussion, see Benkler, Faris, and Roberts, *Network Propaganda.*

45. For further discussion of these speech-suppressing strategies and their implications for political expression, see, for instance, Wu, "Is the First Amendment Obsolete?"

46. For an insightful discussion of right-wing conspiracism and its effects in our time, see Muirhead and Rosenblum, *Lot of People Are Saying.*

47. Pickard, *Democracy without Journalism?*, 47–63; Baker, *Media, Markets, and Democracy,* 3–19.

48. Pickard, *Democracy without Journalism?*, 65.

49. See Sullivan, *Newsroom Confidential,* 38–39.

50. For a seminal analysis, see Baker, *Media, Markets, and Democracy,* 3–95.

51. *Abrams v. United States* (1919). Both the phrase and the idea have been repeatedly—and falsely—traced back to liberal philosopher John Stuart Mill. Not only does Mill never use the metaphor of the market; he also rejects the claim that truth will triumph automatically. "I acknowledge that the tendency of all opinions to become sectarian," writes Mill, "is not cured by the freest discussion, but is often heightened and exacerbated thereby; the truth which ought to have been, but was not, seen, being rejected all the more violently because proclaimed by persons regarded as opponents." Mill, *On Liberty,* 49.

52. See for instance Wu, "Is the First Amendment Obsolete?"; Baker, *Media, Markets, and Democracy.*

53. Pickard, *Democracy without Journalism?*, 136–138.

54. For one version of this proposal, see Rolnik et al., *Protecting Journalism,* 34–43. Similar proposals are advanced in Chandler, *Free and Equal,* 157–162.

55. See, for instance, Rolnik et al., *Protecting Journalism,* 43–49; Cagé, *Saving the Media,* 1–11, 89–137. For an in-depth discussion of emerging models of local ownership, see Kennedy, *Wired City.*

56. See, for instance, Benkler, Faris, and Roberts, *Network Propaganda,* 351–380; Reich, Sahami, and Weinstein, *System Error,* 213–230; Minow, *Saving the News,* 101–144; Couric, Krebs, and Robinson, *Final Report.*

57. Sullivan, *Newsroom Confidential,* 204.

58. See, for instance, Bunch, "Journalism Fails Miserably."

59. For one thoughtful discussion of these questions, see Gutmann, *Democratic Education.*

60. Purdy, *Two Cheers for Politics,* 244.

Conclusion

1. See, for instance, Snyder, *On Tyranny*; Riedl et al., "Pathways of Democratic Backsliding."

2. See Levitsky and Ziblatt, *How Democracies Die.*

3. See, for instance, Han, McKenna, and Oyakawa, *Prisms of the People,* 144–150; Garza, *Purpose of Power,* 136–137; Walzer, *Political Action,* 25–28.

4. This point is thoughtfully developed in Sabl, *Ruling Passions.*

5. See, for instance, Giridharadas, *Persuaders,* 15–81. See also Garza, *Purpose of Power,* 82–83, 136–137, 182.

6. This tally includes voters who fall into two separate categories devised by Pew researchers: the "progressive left" (6 percent) and the "outsider left" (10 percent, comprised of younger, left-leaning voters who express deep alienation from the Democratic Party). Pew Research Center, *Beyond Red vs. Blue,* 75–100. See also Drutman, "Moderate Middle."

7. Stout, *Blessed Are the Organized,* 114–124, 237. This is not the appropriate response with all opponents. Hardened white supremacists are not going to be converted to progressive ideals, and the right response to them is sharp antagonism. Good strategists learn to conduct what activist Loretta Ross calls accurate "threat assessment": to tell the difference between persuadable opponents and political enemies. Giridharadas, *Persuaders,* 53.

8. Quoted in Resnick, "How to Talk Someone out of Bigotry."

9. See McRaney, *How Minds Change,* 14–53, 218–258.

10. See Reed, *Toward Freedom.*

11. This is also the message of Heather McGee's powerful book *The Sum of Us.* See McGhee, *Sum of Us.*

12. López, *Merge Left.* For one excellent study of this pattern in the second half of the nineteenth century, see Richardson, *Death of Reconstruction.*

13. See, for instance, Levitsky and Ziblatt, *How Democracies Die.*

14. For an insightful reflection on the debate over norms, see Purdy, *Two Cheers for Politics,* 93–120.

15. For an incisive discussion of this tendency in our debates over racial justice, see Bright, "White Psychodrama."

16. See Giridharadas, *Persuaders,* 33–34.

17. Confirmation bias is the tendency to accept evidence that supports our pre-existing beliefs while discounting or ignoring evidence that contradicts them.

18. It draws inspiration, for example, from the writings of liberal intellectuals—such as Walter Weyl and Leonard Hobhouse—in the early twentieth century, and from Elizabeth Anderson, Martha Nussbaum, Danielle Allen, Tommie Shelby, and other liberal thinkers today.

19. See, for instance, Aronoff, Dreier, and Kazin, *We Own the Future;* Robertson, "What Would a Socialist America Look Like?"

20. German socialist Eduard Bernstein was an early exemplar of these revi-

sionist trends. His influential treatise, *Evolutionary Socialism,* was published in 1899.

21. Sunkara, *Socialist Manifesto,* 18–26. I too support public banking (as I indicated in Chapter 6). The difference is that I do not call for the wholesale elimination of private banking or investing.

22. See Moyn, *Liberalism against Itself,* 1–11, 169–176.

Bibliography

Abernathy, Penelope Muse. *News Deserts and Ghost Newspapers: Will Local News Survive?* Chapel Hill, NC: Hussman School of Journalism and Media, 2020.

Abrams v. United States, 250 U.S. 616 (1919).

Alexander, Michelle. *The New Jim Crow: Mass Incarceration in the Age of Colorblindness.* New York: New Press, 2012.

Allen, Danielle. *Justice by Means of Democracy.* Chicago: University of Chicago Press, 2023.

Alperovitz, Gar, Joe Guinan, and Thomas S. Hanna. "The Policy Weapon Climate Activists Need." *The Nation,* April 26, 2017.

Anderson, Elizabeth. *Hijacked: How Neoliberalism Turned the Work Ethic against Workers and How Workers Can Take It Back.* Cambridge, UK: Cambridge University Press, 2023.

Anderson, Elizabeth. *Private Government: How Employers Rule Our Lives (and Why We Don't Talk about It).* Princeton, NJ: Princeton University Press, 2017.

Anderson, Elizabeth. "When the Market Was 'Left.'" Pp. 1–36 in Anderson, *Private Government: How Employers Rule Our Lives (and Why We Don't Talk about It).* Princeton, NJ: Princeton University Press, 2017.

Anonymous. "Our Objects." *Colored American,* July 8, 1837, p. 1.

Appleby, Joyce. "Commercial Farming and the 'Agrarian Myth' in the Early Republic." *Journal of American History* 68, no. 4 (Mar. 1982): 833–849.

Appleby, Joyce. *Inheriting the Revolution: The First Generation of Americans.* Cambridge, MA: Harvard University Press, 2000.

Aronoff, Kate, Peter Dreier, and Michael Kazin, eds. *We Own the Future: Democratic Socialism—American Style.* New York: New Press, 2020.

Associated Press. "Kremlin Crackdown Silences War Protests, from Benign to Bold." *AP News,* April 14, 2022. https://apnews.com/article/russia-ukraine-europe-moscow-347cf5d867eb34b1e8469f942685b673.

Autor, David, David Mindell, and Elisabeth Reynolds. 2020. *The Work of the Future: Building Better Jobs in an Age of Intelligent Machines.* Cambridge, MA: MIT Task Force on the Work of the Future, 2020.

Baber, Walter F., and Robert V. Bartlett. *Consensus and Global Environmental Governance: Deliberative Democracy in Nature's Regime.* Cambridge, MA: MIT Press, 2015.

Bakan, Joel. *The Corporation: The Pathological Pursuit of Profit and Power.* New York: Free Press, 2004.

Baker, Anne, et al. "Brief of Amici Curiae Political Scientists" for *Representative Ted Lieu et al. v. FEC,* 2020. https://www.fec.gov/resources/cms-content/documents/lieu_political_scientists_amici_brief.pdf.

Baker, Bruce D. *Educational Inequality and School Finance: Why Money Matters for America's Students.* Cambridge, MA: Harvard University Press, 2018.

Baker, Bruce D., and Sean P. Corcoran. *The Stealth Inequities of School Funding.* Washington, DC: Center for American Progress, 2012.

Baker, Bruce D., David G. Sciarra, and Danielle Farrie. *Is School Funding Fair? A National Report Card.* New Brunswick, NJ: Education Law Center, 2014.

Baker, C. Edwin. *Media, Markets, and Democracy.* Cambridge, UK: Cambridge University Press, 2002.

Baldwin, James. *The Fire Next Time.* New York: Vintage Books, 1993 [1963].

Balevic, Katie. "Moscow Police Are Stopping People and Demanding to Read Their Text Messages, Reporter Says." *Business Insider,* Mar. 6, 2022.

Baliga, Sujatha, Sia Henry, and Georgia Valentine. *Restorative Community Conferencing: A Study of Community Works West's Restorative Justice Youth Diversion Program in Alameda County.* Oakland, CA: Impact Justice, 2017.

Ballou, Brendan. *Plunder: Private Equity's Plan to Pillage America.* New York: PublicAffairs, 2023.

Banerjee, Abhijit V., and Esther Duflo. *Good Economics for Hard Times.* New York: PublicAffairs, 2019.

Banerjee, Neerla, Lisa Song, and David Hasemeyer. "Exxon's Own Research Confirmed Fossil Fuels' Role in Global Warming Decades Ago." *Inside Climate News,* September 16, 2015.

Baptist, Edward E. *The Half Has Never Been Told: Slavery and the Making of American Capitalism.* New York: Basic Books, 2014.

Baradaran, Mehrsa. *A Homestead Act for the 21st Century.* New York: Roosevelt Institute, 2019.

Baradaran, Mehrsa. *How the Other Half Banks: Exclusion, Exploitation, and the Threat to Democracy.* Cambridge, MA: Harvard University Press, 2015.

Barbero, R., J. T. Abatzoglou, N. K. Larkin, C. A. Kolden, and B. Stocks. "Climate Change Presents Increased Potential for Very Large Fires in the Contiguous United States." *International Journal of Wildland Fire* 24 (July 2015): 892–899.

Barry, John, and Marcel Wissenburg, eds. *Sustaining Liberal Democracy: Ecological Challenges and Opportunities.* London: Palgrave, 2001.

Bartels, Larry. *Unequal Democracy: The Political Economy of the New Gilded Age.* 2nd ed. Princeton, NJ: Princeton University Press, 2016 [2008].

Bauer, Bob, Cristina Rodríguez, and Kate Andrias. *Final Report.* Washington, DC: Presidential Commission on the Supreme Court of the United States, 2021.

Bayoumi, Moustafa. "Dangerous Outsiders and Exceptional Citizens: Being Muslim American since 9/11." *The Guardian,* Sept. 10, 2021.

Beaumont, Hilary. "Flint Residents Grapple with the Water Crisis a Decade Later: 'If We Had the Energy Left, We'd Cry.'" *The Guardian,* Apr. 25, 2024.

Beck, Allen J., and Alfred Blumstein. "Racial Disproportionality in U.S. State Prisons: Accounting for the Effects of Racial and Ethnic Differences in Criminal Involvement, Arrests, Sentencing, and Time Served." *Journal of Quantitative Criminology* 34 (2018): 853–883.

Becker, William. "Why We Must Nationalize Big Oil." *The Hill,* June 25, 2022.

Beckert, Sven, and Seth Rockman, eds. *Slavery's Capitalism: A New History of American Economic Development.* Philadelphia: University of Pennsylvania Press, 2016.

Benkler, Yochai, Robert Faris, and Hal Roberts. *Network Propaganda: Manipulation, Disinformation, and Radicalization in American Politics.* New York: Oxford University Press, 2018.

Berlin, Isaiah. "Two Concepts of Liberty." Pp. 166–217 in Henry Hardy, ed., *Liberty.* Oxford, UK: Oxford University Press, 2002 [1958].

Berman, Sheri. "The Causes of Populism in the West." *Annual Review of Political Science* 24 (2021): 71–88.

Bertrand, Marianne, and Sendhil Mullainathan. "Are Emily and Greg More Employable Than Lakisha and Jamal? A Field Experiment on Labor Market Discrimination." *American Economic Review* 94, no. 4 (2004): 991–1013.

Bilott, Robert. *Exposure: Poisoned Water, Corporate Greed, and One Lawyer's Twenty-Year Battle against DuPont.* New York: Atria Books, 2019.

Blasi, Joseph R., Richard B. Freeman, and Douglas L. Kruse. *The Citizen's Share: Putting Ownership Back into Democracy.* New Haven: Yale University Press, 2013.

Blasi, Joseph R., and Douglas L. Kruse. *Employee Ownership and ESOPs: What We Know from Recent Research.* Washington, DC: Aspen Institute, 2024.

Block, Sharon, and Benjamin Sachs. *Clean Slate for Worker Power: Building a Just Economy and Democracy.* Cambridge, MA: Center for Labor and a Just Economy, Harvard Law School, 2020.

Bogdanich, Walt, and Michael Forsythe. *When McKinsey Comes to Town: The Hidden Influence of the World's Most Powerful Consulting Firm.* New York: Doubleday, 2022.

Bonilla-Silva, Eduardo. *Racism without Racists: Color-Blind Racism and the Persistence of Racial Inequality in America.* 6th ed. Lanham, MD: Rowman & Littlefield, 2022.

Borelli, Gabriel. *Americans Are Split over the State of the American Dream.* Washington, DC: Pew Research Center, 2024.

Bratberg, Espen, et al. "A Comparison of Intergenerational Mobility Curves in Germany, Norway, Sweden, and the U.S." *Scandinavian Journal of Economics* 119, no. 1 (2017): 72–101.

Brennan Center for Justice. *Fact Sheet: The Impact of Voter Suppression on Communities of Color.* New York: Brennan Center for Justice, 2022.

Brennan Center for Justice. *Voting Laws Roundup: June 2023.* New York: Brennan Center for Justice, 2023.

Brennan Center for Justice. "Executive Power." Accessed Feb. 2, 2025. https://www.brennancenter.org/issues/bolster-checks-balances/executive-power.

Bright, Liam Kofi. "White Psychodrama." *Journal of Political Philosophy* 31, no. 2 (2023): 198–221.

Brinn, Gearóid. "The Path Down to Green Liberalism." *Environmental Politics* 31, no. 4 (2022): 643–662.

The British Academy. *Principles for Purposeful Business: How to Deliver the Framework for the Future of the Corporation.* London: British Academy, 2019.

Brown, Dorothy. *The Whiteness of Wealth: How the Tax System Impoverishes Black Americans—and How We Can Fix It.* New York: Crown, 2022.

Brown, Wendy. *In The Ruins of Neoliberalism: The Rise of Antidemocratic Politics in the West.* New York: Columbia University Press, 2019.

Bruner, Christopher M. "Corporate Governance Reform and the Sustainability Imperative." *Yale Law Journal* 131, no. 4 (2022): 1217–1277.

Buell, Samuel W. *Capital Offenses: Business Crime and Punishment in America's Corporate Age.* New York: W.W. Norton, 2016.

Bumiller, Elisabeth. "'People Are Going Silent': Fearing Retribution, Trump Critics Muzzle Themselves." *New York Times,* Mar. 6, 2025.

Bunch, Will. "Journalism Fails Miserably at Explaining What Is Really Happening In America." *Philadelphia Inquirer,* Aug. 27, 2023.

Bureau of Labor Statistics. "News Release: Union Members—2023." Washington, DC: Bureau of Labor Statistics, Jan. 23, 2024.

Cagé, Julia. *Saving the Media: Capitalism, Crowdfunding, and Democracy,* trans. Arthur Goldhammer. Cambridge, MA: Harvard University Press, 2016.

Canaday, Margot. *The Straight State: Sexuality and Citizenship in Twentieth-Century America.* Princeton, NJ: Princeton University Press, 2011.

Canon, Gabrielle. "'Hell on Earth': Phoenix's Extreme Heatwave Tests the Limits of Survival." *The Guardian,* July 14, 2023.

Cardoso, Diego S., and Casey J. Wichman. "Water Affordability in the United States." *Water Resources Research* 58, no. 12 (2022): e2022WR032206.

Carley, Sanya, and David M. Konisky. "The Justice and Equity Implications of the Clean Energy Transition." *Nature Energy* 5 (2020): 569–577.

Carpenter, Daniel, and David A. Moss, eds. *Preventing Regulatory Capture: Special Interest Influence and How to Limit It.* New York: Cambridge University Press, 2014.

Carr, Earl. "Kenya's Proposal for a Green Bank: The IMF, World Bank, and China's Role." *Forbes,* Sept. 15, 2023.

Carrington, Damian. "'Gigantic' Power of Meat Industry Blocking Green Alternatives, Study Finds." *The Guardian,* Aug. 18, 2023.

Casey, Michael. "EPA Proposes Banning Cancer-Causing Chemical TCE Used in Automotive Care and Other Products." *Washington Post,* Oct. 23, 2023.

Chambers, Chris. "Americans Are Overwhelmingly Happy and Optimistic about the Future of the United States." *Gallup News Service,* Oct. 13, 2000.

Chandler, Daniel. *Free and Equal: A Manifesto for a Just Society.* New York: Knopf, 2024.

Chetty, Raj, David Grusky, Maximilian Hell, Nathaniel Hendren, Robert Manduca, and Jimmy Narang. "The Fading American Dream: Trends in Absolute Income Mobility since 1940." *Science* 356, no. 6336 (2017): 398–406.

Chetty, Raj, Nathaniel Hendren, Maggie R. Jones, and Sonya R. Porter. "Race and Economic Opportunity in the United States: An Intergenerational Perspective." *Quarterly Journal of Economics* 135, no. 2 (2020): 711–783.

Ciccolini, Julie, and Ida Sawyer. *"Kettling" Protesters in the Bronx: Systemic Police Brutality and Its Costs in the United States.* New York: Human Rights Watch, 2020.

Ciepley, David. "Beyond Public and Private: Toward a Political Theory of the Corporation." *American Political Science Review* 107, no. 1 (2013): 139–158.

Clarren, Rebecca. "How America Is Failing Native American Students." *The Nation,* July 24, 2017.

Coates, Ta-Nehisi. *Between the World and Me.* New York: One World, 2015.

Coates, Ta-Nehisi. "The Case for Reparations." *Atlantic Monthly,* June 15, 2014.

Coffee, John C. *Corporate Crime and Punishment: The Crisis of Underenforcement.* Oakland, CA: Berrett-Koehler, 2020.

Coleman, Aaron Ross. "How a Group of Student Debtors Took on Their Banks—and Won." *GQ,* Oct. 8, 2019.

Coleman-Jensen, A., M. P. Rabbitt, C. Gregory, and A. Singh. *Household Food Security in the United States in 2015.* Washington, DC: US Department of Agriculture, Economic Research Service, 2015.

Coll, Steve. *Private Empire: ExxonMobil and American Power.* New York: Penguin, 2012.

Colton, Calvin. *Junius Tracts,* vol. 7: *Labor and Capital.* New York: Greeley and McElrath, 1844.

Coppins, McKay. "A Secretive Hedge Fund Is Gutting News Rooms." *Atlantic Monthly,* Oct. 14, 2021.

Corak, Miles. "Income Inequality, Equality of Opportunity, and Intergenerational Mobility." *Journal of Economic Perspectives* 27, no. 3 (2013): 79–102.

Corasaniti, Nick, and Reid J. Epstein. "G.O.P. and Allies Draft 'Best Practices' for Restricting Voting." *New York Times,* Mar. 23, 2021.

Cornwall, Warren. "Breathless Oceans." *Science,* Feb. 2, 2023.

Couric, Katie, Chris Krebs, and Rashad Robinson. *Final Report of the Commission on Information Disorder.* Washington, DC: Aspen Institute, 2021.

Cox, Stan. *Any Way You Slice It: The Past, Present, and Future of Rationing.* New York: New Press, 2013.

Craigie, Terry-Ann, Ames Grawert, and Cameron Kimble. *Conviction, Imprisonment, and Lost Earnings: How Involvement with the Criminal Jus-*

tice System Deepens Inequality. New York: Brennan Center for Justice, 2020.

Craiutu, Aurelian. *Why Not Moderation? Letters to Young Radicals.* Cambridge, UK: Cambridge University Press, 2024.

Daniel, Pete. "A Rogue Bureaucracy: The USDA Fire Ant Campaign of the Late 1950s." *Agricultural History* 64, no. 2 (1990): 99–114.

Daniller, Andrew. *Americans Take a Dim View of the Nation's Future, Look More Positively at the Past.* Washington, DC: Pew Research Center, 2023.

Darda, Joseph. *The Strange Career of Racial Liberalism.* Redwood City, CA: Stanford University Press, 2022.

Darity, William A., Jr., and A. Kirsten Mullen. *From Here to Equality: Reparations for Black Americans in the Twenty-First Century.* 2nd ed. Chapel Hill: University of North Carolina Press, 2022.

Davies, Harry, Simon Goodley, Felicity Lawrence, Paul Lewis, and Lisa O'Carroll. "The Uber Files: Uber Broke Laws, Duped Police, and Secretly Lobbied Governments, Leak Reveals." *The Guardian,* July 11, 2022.

Demashkieh, Rasha, Laura Reyes Kopack, Mumtaz Haque, Athur M. Horwitz, Deloris Hunt, Ricardo Resio, Linda Lee Tarver, and Bradley Voss. *The Flint Water Crisis: Systemic Racism through the Lens of Flint.* Detroit: Michigan Civil Rights Commission, 2017.

Dēmos. *Banking for the Public Good: Public Bank NYC.* New York: Dēmos, 2022. https://www.demos.org/sites/default/files/2022-05/Demos_Public Banking_CaseStudy_FA.pdf.

Deneen, Patrick. *Why Liberalism Failed.* New Haven: Yale University Press, 2018.

Desmond, Matthew. *Evicted: Poverty and Profit in the American City.* New York: Crown, 2016.

Desmond, Matthew. *Poverty, by America.* New York: Crown, 2023.

Desmond-Harris, Jenée. "9 Devastating, Revealing Stories of Being Muslim in Post-9/11 America." *Vox,* Sept. 11, 2016.

Diamond, Larry. *Ill Winds: Saving Democracy from Russian Rage, Chinese Ambition, and American Complacency.* New York: Penguin, 2019.

Dobkin, Rachel. "US Homelessness Surged 18% in 2024." *Newsweek,* Dec. 27, 2024.

Dobson, Andrew. *Green Political Thought.* 4th ed. London: Routledge, 2007.

Douglas, Leah, and Christopher Leonard. "Is the US Chicken Industry Cheating Its Farmers?" *The Guardian,* Aug. 2, 2019.

Drutman, Lee. *The Business of America Is Lobbying: How Corporations Became Politicized and Politics Became More Corporate.* Oxford, UK: Oxford University Press, 2015.

Drutman, Lee. "The Moderate Middle Is a Myth." *FiveThirtyEight,* Sept. 24, 2019.

Drutman, Lee, Larry Diamond, and Joe Goldman. *Follow the Leader: Exploring American Support for Democracy and Authoritarianism.* Washington, DC: Democracy Fund Voter Study Group, 2018.

Dryzek, John S. *The Politics of the Earth.* 3rd ed. Oxford, UK: Oxford University Press, 2013.

Dryzek, John S., Quinlan Bowman, Jonathan Kuyper, Jonathan Pickering, Jensen Sass, and Hayley Stevenson. *Deliberative Global Governance.* Cambridge, UK: Cambridge University Press, 2019.

Duncombe, William, and John Yinger. "How Much More Does a Disadvantaged Student Cost?" *Economics of Education Review* 24, no. 5 (2005): 513–532.

Eberhardt, Jennifer. *Biased: Uncovering the Hidden Prejudice That Shapes What We See, Think, and Do.* New York: Penguin, 2019.

EdBuild. *Nonwhite School Districts Get $23 Billion Less Than White Districts Despite Serving the Same Number of Students.* Washington, DC: EdBuild, 2019. https://edbuild.org/content/23-billion.

Elassar, Alaa. "US Muslims Reflect on How 9/11 Changed Their Lives and What the Future Holds for Them." *CNN,* Sept. 7, 2021. https://www.cnn.com/2021/09/07/us/muslims-relationship-with-america-september-11/index.html.

Elmore, Bartow J. *Seed Money: Monsanto's Past and Our Food Future.* New York: W.W. Norton, 2021.

Emerson, Ralph Waldo. "Address on the Anniversary of the Emancipation of the Negroes in the British West Indies." Pp. 7–33 in Len Gougeon and Joel Myerson, eds., *Emerson's Antislavery Writings*. New Haven: Yale University Press, 1995 [1844].

Engel, Robin S., Gabrielle T. Isaza, and Hannah McManus. "Owning Police Reform: The Path Forward for Practicioners and Researchers." *American Journal of Criminal Justice* 47 (2022): 1225–1242.

Ferrie, Joseph. "History Lessons: The End of American Exceptionalism? Mobility in the United States since 1850." *Journal of Economic Perspectives* 19, no. 3 (2005): 199–215.

Ferriss, Susan, and Joe Yerardi. *Wage Theft Hits Immigrants—Hard*. Washington, DC: Center for Public Integrity, 2021.

Fishkin, James S. *Democracy When People Are Thinking: Revitalizing Our Politics Through Public Deliberation*. Oxford, UK: Oxford University Press, 2020.

Foner, Eric. *Reconstruction: America's Unfinished Revolution*. Updated ed. New York: HarperPerennial, 2014 [1988].

Foroohar, Rana. *Makers and Takers: How Wall Street Destroyed Main Street*. New York: Crown Business, 2016.

Frank, Robert. "The Wealthiest 10% of Americans Own a Record 89% of all U.S. Stocks." *CNBC,* Oct. 18, 2021.

Frankenberg, Erica, Jongyeon Ee, Jennifer B. Ayscue, and Gary Orfield. *Harming Our Common Future: America's Segregated Schools 65 Years after Brown*. Los Angeles: Civil Rights Project, UCLA, 2019.

Fraser, Nancy. "Social Justice in the Age of Identity Politics: Redistribution, Recognition, and Participation." Pp. 7–109 in Nancy Fraser and Axel Honneth, *Redistribution or Recognition? A Political-Philosophical Exchange,* trans. Joel Golb, James Ingram, and Christiane Wilke. London: Verso, 2003.

Freedom House. *Freedom in the World, 2021: Russia*. Washington, DC: Freedom House, 2021.

Freedom House. *Freedom in the World, 2022: Russia*. Washington, DC: Freedom House, 2022.

Freedom House. *Freedom in the World, 2024: Hungary.* Washington, DC: Freedom House, 2024.

Friedman, Milton. *Capitalism and Freedom.* Chicago: University of Chicago Press, 2002 [1962].

Frischen, Konstanze, and Michael Zakaras. *America's Path Forward: Conversations with Social Innovators on the Power of Communities Everywhere.* Washington, DC: Georgetown University Press, 2023.

Frison, Emily, and Nick Jacobs. *From Uniformity to Diversity: A Paradigm Shift from Industrial Agriculture to Diversified Agroecological Systems.* Brussels: International Panel of Experts on Sustainable Food Systems, 2016.

Frum, David. *Trumpocracy: The Corruption of the American Republic.* New York: HarperCollins, 2018.

Fukayama, Francis. *Liberalism and Its Discontents.* New York: Farrar, Straus and Giroux, 2022.

Fuller, Lon. *The Morality of Law.* Rev. ed. New Haven: Yale University Press, 1969.

Galbraith, John Kenneth. *American Capitalism: The Concept of Countervailing Power.* New York: Houghton Mifflin, 1952.

Galston, William. *Anti-Pluralism: The Populist Threat to Liberal Democracy.* New Haven: Yale University Press, 2018.

García, Emma. *Schools Are Still Segregated, and Black Children Are Paying a Price.* Washington, DC: Economic Policy Institute, 2020.

Garrett, Brandon L. *Too Big to Jail: How Prosecutors Compromise with Corporations.* Cambridge, MA: Harvard University Press, 2014.

Garza, Alicia. *The Purpose of Power: How We Come Together When We Fall Apart.* New York: One World, 2021.

Gelles, David. "Fossil Fuels Aren't Going Anywhere." *New York Times,* Oct. 12, 2023.

Genoways, Ted. *The Chain: Farm, Factory, and the Fate of Our Food.* New York: HarperCollins, 2014.

George, Caroline, Joseph W. Kane, and Adie Tomer. *How US Cities Are Finding Creative Ways to Fund Climate Progress.* Washington, DC: Brookings Institution, 2023.

Geronimus, Arline T. *Weathering: The Extraordinary Stress of Ordinary Life in an Unjust Society.* New York: Little, Brown Spark, 2023.

Gerstle, Gary. *The Rise and Fall of the Neoliberal Order: America and the World in the Free Market Era.* New York: Oxford University Press, 2022.

Gilberstadt, Hannah. *More Americans Oppose Than Favor the Government Providing a Universal Basic Income for All Adult Citizens.* Washington, DC: Pew Research Center, 2020.

Gilens, Martin, and Benjamin I. Page. "Testing Theories of American Politics: Elites, Interest Groups, and Average Citizens." *Perspectives on Politics* 12, no. 3 (2014): 564–581.

Gillam, Carey. *Whitewash: The Story of a Weed Killer, Cancer, and the Corruption of Science.* Washington, DC: Island Press, 2017.

Ginsburg, Tom, and Aziz Z. Huq. *How to Save a Constitutional Democracy.* Chicago: University of Chicago Press, 2018.

Giridharadas, Anand. *The Persuaders: At the Front Lines of the Fight for Hearts, Minds, and Democracy.* New York: Vintage Books, 2022.

Girion, Lisa. *Johnson & Johnson Knew for Decades that Asbestos Lurked in Its Baby Powder.* Los Angeles: Reuters, 2018.

Glaude, Eddie, Jr. *Democracy in Black: How Race Still Enslaves the American Soul.* New York: Broadway Books, 2016.

Goff, Phillip Atiba, Tracey Lloyd, Amanda Geller, Steven Raphael, and Jack Glaser. *The Science of Justice: Race, Arrests, and Police Use of Force.* Denver: Center for Policing Equity, 2016.

Goh, Joel, Jeffrey Pfeffer, and Stefanos A. Zenios. "The Relationship between Workplace Stressors and Mortality and Health Costs in the United States." *Management Science* 62, no. 2 (2016): 608–628.

Goitein, Elizabeth. "The Alarming Scope of the President's Emergency Powers." *Atlantic Monthly,* Jan./Feb. 2019.

Gold, Michael. "After Calling Foes 'Vermin,' Trump Campaign Warns Its Critics Will Be 'Crushed.'" *New York Times,* Nov. 13, 2023.

Goldberg, Michael. "Funds to Aid Jackson's Water System Held Up as Mississippi Governor Tate Reeves Rose." *Clarion Ledger* (Jackson, MS), Sept. 27, 2022.

Goldblum, Joanne Samuel, and Colleen Shaddox. *Broke in America: Seeing, Understanding, and Ending U.S. Poverty.* Dallas: BenBella Books, 2021.

Gopnik, Adam. *A Thousand Small Sanities: The Moral Adventure of Liberalism.* New York: Basic Books, 2019.

Gordon, Leah N. *From Power to Prejudice: The Rise of Racial Individualism in Midcentury America.* Chicago: University of Chicago Press, 2015.

Goshen, Zohar, and Doron Levit. "Agents of Inequality: Common Ownership and the Decline of the American Worker." *Duke Law Journal* 71, no. 1 (2022): 1–69.

Gosselin, Peter. *High Wire: The Precarious Financial Lives of American Families.* New York: Basic Books, 2008.

Goswami, Omanjana, and Stacy Woods. *Waste Deep: How Tyson Foods Pollutes U.S. Waterways and Which States Bear the Brunt.* Cambridge, MA: Union of Concerned Scientists, 2024.

Gourevitch, Alex. *From Slavery to the Cooperative Commonwealth: Labor and Republican Liberty in the Nineteenth Century.* New York: Cambridge University Press, 2015.

Graham, David A. "The Threat to Democracy Is Still in Congress." *Atlantic Monthly,* Dec. 2022.

Greasley, Kate. *Arguments about Abortion: Personhood, Morality, and Law.* Oxford, UK: Oxford University Press, 2017.

Greenfield, Kent. *The Failure of Corporate Law: Fundamental Flaws and Progressive Possibilities.* Chicago: University of Chicago Press, 2006.

Greenhouse, Steven. *The Big Squeeze: Tough Times for the American Worker.* New York: Alfred A. Knopf, 2008.

Greenhouse, Steven. "'Old-School Union Busting': How US Corporations Are Quashing the New Wave of Organizing." *The Guardian,* Feb. 26, 2023.

Grim, Ryan, and Sabrina Siddiqui. "Call Time for Congress Shows How Fundraising Dominates Bleak Work Life." *Huffington Post,* Jan. 8, 2013.

Grumbach, Jacob. "Laboratories of Democratic Backsliding." *American Political Science Review* 117, no. 3 (2023): 967–984.

Guendelsberger, Emily. *On the Clock: What Low-Wage Work Did to Me and How It Drives Americans Insane.* New York: Back Bay Books, 2019.

Guinier, Lani. "From Racial Liberalism to Racial Literacy: *Brown v. Board of Education* and the Interest-Divergence Dilemma." *Journal of American History* 91, no. 1 (2004): 92–118.

Gutmann, Amy. *Democratic Education.* Princeton, NJ: Princeton University Press, 1999 [1987].

Hacker, Jacob S. *The Great Risk Shift: The New Economic Insecurity and the Decline of the American Dream.* Rev. ed. New York: Oxford University Press, 2019 [2006].

Hacker, Jacob S., Alexander Hertel-Fernandez, Paul Pierson, and Kathleen Thelen. "The American Political Economy: Markets, Power, and the Meta Politics of U.S. Economic Governance." *Annual Review of Political Science* 25 (2022): 197–217.

Hamaji, Kate, Rachel Deutsch, Elizabeth Nicolas, Celine McNicholas, Heidi Shierholz, and Margaret Poydock. *Unchecked Corporate Power: Forced Arbitration, the Enforcement Crisis, and How Workers Are Fighting Back.* Washington, DC: Economic Policy Institute, 2019.

Han, Hahrie, Elizabeth McKenna, and Michelle Oyakawa. *Prisms of the People: Power and Organizing in Twenty-First Century America.* Chicago: University of Chicago Press, 2021.

Haney López, Ian. *Merge Left: Fusing Race and Class, Winning Elections, and Saving America.* New York: New Press, 2019.

Harvey, Hal, and Justin Gillis. *The Big Fix: Seven Practical Steps to Save Our Planet.* New York: Simon & Schuster, 2022.

Hasdell, Rebecca. *What We Know about Universal Basic Income: A Cross-Synthesis of Reviews.* Palo Alto, CA: Stanford Basic Income Lab, 2020.

Hayek, Friedrich. *The Constitution of Liberty.* Chicago: Henry Regnery Co., 1960.

Hazony, Yoram. *Conservatism: A Rediscovery.* Washington, DC: Regnery Gateway, 2022.

Head, Simon. *The New Ruthless Economy: Work and Power in the Digital Age.* Oxford, UK: Oxford University Press, 2003.

Henderson, Rebecca. *Reimagining Capitalism in a World on Fire.* New York: PublicAffairs, 2020.

Hersh, Eitan. *Politics Is for Power: How to Move beyond Political Hobbyism, Take Action, and Make Real Change.* New York: Scribner's, 2020.

Hertel-Fernandez, Alexander. "Dismantling Policy through Fiscal Constriction: Examining the Erosion in State Unemployment Insurance Finances." *Social Service Review* 87, no. 3 (Sept. 2013): 438–476.

Hickman, Caroline, Elizabeth Marks, Panu Pihkala, Susan Clayton, Eric Lewandowski, Elouise E. Mayall, Britt Wray, et al. "Climate Anxiety in Children and Young People and Their Beliefs about Government Responses to Climate Change: A Global Survey." *The Lancet* 5, no. 12 (Dec. 2021): e863–e873.

Hickman, Leo. "James Lovelock: 'Fudging Data Is a Sin against Science.'" *The Guardian,* Mar. 29, 2010.

Hinton, Elizabeth, LaShae Henderson, and Cindy Reed. *An Unjust Burden: The Disparate Treatment of Black Americans in the Criminal Justice System.* New York: Vera Institute of Justice, 2018.

Hirschmann, Nancy. *The Subject of Liberty: Toward a Feminist Theory of Freedom.* Princeton, NJ: Princeton University Press, 2003.

Hochschild, Arlie Russell. *Strangers in Their Own Land: Anger and Mourning on the American Right.* New York: New Press, 2016.

Holland, Breena. "Environment as Meta-Capability: Why a Dignified Human Life Requires a Stable Climate System." Pp. 145–164 in Allen Thompson and Jeremy Bendik-Keymer, eds., *Ethical Adaptation to Climate Change.* Cambridge, MA: MIT Press, 2012.

Holt-Giménez, Eric. *Can We Feed the World without Destroying It?* Cambridge, UK: Polity Press, 2018.

Hopkins, Andrew. *Disastrous Decisions: Human and Organizational Causes of the Gulf of Mexico Blowout.* Sydney: CCH Australia, 2017.

Horowitz, Sara. *Mutualism: Building the Next Economy from the Ground Up.* New York: Random House, 2021.

Howard, Marc Morjé. *Unusually Cruel: Prisons, Punishment, and the Real American Exceptionalism.* New York: Oxford University Press, 2017.

Howe, Daniel Walker. *What Hath God Wrought: The Transformation of America, 1815–1848.* Oxford, UK: Oxford University Press, 2007.

Human Rights Watch/ACLU. *Racial Discrimination in the United States.* New York: Human Rights Watch/ACLU, 2022.

Hunnicutt, Benjamin Kline. *Free Time: The Forgotten American Dream.* Philadelphia: Temple University Press, 2013.

Hyman, Louis. *Temp: The Real Story of What Happened to Your Salary, Benefits, and Job Security.* New York: Penguin, 2018.

Inglehart, Ronald, and Pippa Norris. "Trump and the Populist Authoritarian Parties: The Silent Revolution in Reverse." *Perspectives on Politics* 15, no. 2 (June 2017): 443–454.

Intergovernmental Panel on Climate Change. *Climate Change 2022: Impacts, Adaptation, and Vulnerability.* Geneva: IPCC, 2022. https://www.ipcc .ch/report/ar6/wg2.

Intergovernmental Panel on Climate Change. *The Ocean and Cryosphere in a Changing Climate: Special Report of the Intergovernmental Panel on Climate Change.* Cambridge, UK: Cambridge University Press, 2022.

Jackson, C. Kirabo. *Does School Spending Matter? The New Literature on an Old Question.* NBER Working Paper Series, no. 25368. Cambridge, MA: National Bureau of Economic Research, 2018. https://www.nber.org /papers/w25368.

Kaiser, Robert G. *So Damn Much Money: The Triumph of Lobbying and the Corrosion of American Government.* New York: Alfred A. Knopf, 2009.

Kaiser Family Foundation, "Policy Tracker: Exceptions to State Abortion Bans and Early Gestational Limits." https://www.kff.org/womens-health -policy/dashboard/exceptions-in-state-abortion-bans-and-early-gesta tional-limits.

Karpman, Michael, Stephen Zuckerman, and Dulce Gonzalez. *Material Hardship among Non-Elderly Adults and Their Families, 2017: Implications for the Social Safety Net.* Washington, DC: Urban Institute, 2018.

Kasakove, Sophie. "Investors Are Buying Mobile Home Parks. Residents Are Paying a Price." *New York Times,* Mar. 27, 2022.

Kateb, George. *Human Dignity.* Cambridge, MA: Harvard University Press, 2011.

Katznelson, Ira. *Fear Itself: The New Deal and the Origins of Our Time.* New York: W.W. Norton, 2013.

Katznelson, Ira. *When Affirmative Action Was White: An Untold Story of Racial Inequality in Twentieth-Century America.* New York: W.W. Norton, 2006.

Kaufman, Arnold. *The Radical Liberal. The New Politics: Theory and Practice.* New York: Atherton Press, 1968.

Keefe, Patrick Radden. *Empire of Pain: The Secret History of the Sackler Dynasty.* New York: Doubleday, 2021.

Kennedy, Dan. *The Wired City: Reimagining Journalism and Civic Life in the Post-Newspaper Age.* Amherst: University of Massachusetts Press, 2013.

Kent, Ana Hernández, and Lowell R. Ricketts. *U.S. Wealth Inequality: Gaps Remain Despite Widespread Wealth Gains.* St. Louis: Federal Reserve Bank of St. Louis, 2024.

Kerwin, Donald, Mike Nicholson, Daniela Alulema, and Robert Warren. *U.S. Foreign-Born Essential Workers by Status and State, and the Global Pandemic.* Washington, DC: Center for Migration Studies, 2020.

Kiatpongsan, Sorapop, and Michael I. Norton. "How Much (More) Should CEOs Make? A Universal Desire for More Equal Pay." *Perspectives on Psychological Science* 9, no. 6 (2014): 587–593.

King, Martin Luther, Jr. *Why We Can't Wait.* New York: Signet Classic, 2000 [1964].

Kirchman, David L. *Dead Zones: The Loss of Oxygen from Rivers, Lakes, Seas, and the Ocean.* New York: Oxford University Press, 2021.

Kirsch, Robert. *The Future of Work in America: Policies to Empower American Workers and Secure Prosperity for All.* New York: Roosevelt Institute, 2014.

Kochhar, Rakesh, and Mohamad Moslimani. *Wealth Surged in the Pandemic, but Debt Endures for Poorer Black and Hispanic Families.* Washington, DC: Pew Research Center, 2023.

Kolhatkar, Sheelah. "What Happens When Investment Firms Acquire Trailer Parks." *New Yorker,* Mar. 8, 2021.

Kommenda, Niko, Shannon Osaka, Simon Ducroquet, and Veronica Penney. "Where Dangerous Heat Is Surging." *Washington Post,* Sept. 5, 2023.

Konisky, David M. "Regulator Attitudes and the Environmental Race to the Bottom Argument." *Journal of Public Administration Research and Theory* 18, no. 2 (Apr. 2008): 321–344.

Koubi, Vally. "Climate Change and Conflict." *Annual Review of Political Science* 22 (2019): 343–360.

Kozol, Jonathan. *Rachel and Her Children: Homeless Families in America.* Rev. ed. New York: Three Rivers Press, 2006.

Lakhani, Nina. "Record Number of Fossil Fuel Lobbyists Get Access to COP 28 Climate Talks." *The Guardian,* Dec. 5, 2023.

Lakhani, Nina. "'They Rake In Profits—Everyone Else Suffers': U.S. Workers Lose Out as Big Chicken Gets Bigger." *The Guardian,* Aug. 11, 2021.

Lakhani, Nina, Maanvi Singh, and Rashida Kamal. "Almost Half a Million U.S. Households Lack Indoor Plumbing: 'The Conditions Are Inhumane.'" *The Guardian,* Sept. 27, 2021.

Law, Ian. *Red Racisms: Racism in Communist and Post-Communist Contexts.* Basingstoke, UK: Palgrave Macmillan, 2012.

Lears, Jackson. *Rebirth of a Nation: The Making of Modern America, 1877–1920.* New York: HarperCollins, 2009.

Leber, Rebecca. "An 'Attack on American Cities' Is Freezing Climate Action in Its Tracks." *Vox,* Sept. 29, 2021.

Lefebvre, Alexandre. *Liberalism as a Way of Life.* Princeton, NJ: Princeton University Press, 2024.

Leonard, Christopher. *The Meat Racket: The Secret Takeover of America's Food Business.* New York: Simon and Schuster, 2014.

Lesk, Corey, Pedram Rowhani, and Navin Ramankutty. "Influence of Extreme Weather Disasters on Global Crop Production." *Nature* 529 (2016): 84–87.

Levin, Sam. "'We Have Failed': How California's Homelessness Catastrophe Is Worsening." *The Guardian,* Mar. 22, 2022.

Levitsky, Steven, and Daniel Ziblatt. *How Democracies Die.* New York: Crown, 2018.

Levitsky, Steven, and Daniel Ziblatt. *Tyranny of the Minority: Why American Democracy Reached the Breaking Point.* New York: Penguin Random House, 2023.

Lewis, Michael. *The Big Short: Inside the Doomsday Machine.* New York: W.W. Norton, 2010.

Lincoln, Abraham. "Address before the Wisconsin State Agricultural Society, Milwaukee, Wisconsin." Pp. 472–482 in Roy P. Basler, ed., *Col-*

lected Works of Abraham Lincoln. New Brunswick: Rutgers University Press, 1953 [1859].

Lindblom, Charles E. "The Market as Prison." *Journal of Politics* 44, no. 2 (May 1982): 324–336.

Liptak, Adam. "Defiance and Threats in Deportation Case Renew Fear of Constitutional Crisis." *New York Times,* Mar. 19, 2025.

Little, Margaret Olivia. "Abortion, Intimacy, and the Duty to Gestate." *Ethical Theory and Moral Practice* 2 (1999): 295–312.

Little, Margaret Olivia. "The Moral Permissibility of Abortion." Pp. 151–159 in Hugh Lafollette, ed., *Ethics in Practice: An Anthology.* New York: Wiley, 2014.

Loury, Glenn. *The Anatomy of Racial Inequality.* Rev. ed. Cambridge, MA: Harvard University Press, 2021.

Lum, Cynthia. "Perspectives on Policing." *Annual Review of Criminology* 4 (2021): 19–25.

Lustgarten, Abrahm. "The Great Climate Migration Has Begun." *New York Times Magazine,* July 26, 2020.

Mahajan, Shiwani, César Carabello, Yuan Lu, Javier Valero-Elizondo, Daisy Massey, Amarnath R. Annapureddy, Brita Roy, et al. "Trends in Differences in Health Status and Health Care Access and Affordability by Race and Ethnicity in the United States, 1999–2018." *Journal of the American Medical Association* 326, no. 7 (2021): 637–648.

Mahone, Jessica, Qun Wang, Philip Napoli, Matthew Weber, and Katie McCollough. *Who's Producing Local Journalism: Assessing Journalistic Output across Different Outlet Types.* Durham, NC: Sanford School of Public Policy, 2019.

Marble, William, and Clayton Nall. "Where Self-Interest Trumps Ideology: Liberal Homeowners and Local Opposition to Housing Development." *Journal of Politics* 83, no. 4 (Oct. 2021): 1747–1763.

Marmot, Michael. *The Status Syndrome: How Social Standing Affects Our Health and Longevity.* New York: Owl Books, 2004.

Massey, Douglas S., and Nancy A. Denton. *American Apartheid: Segregation and the Making of the Underclass.* Cambridge, MA: Harvard University Press, 1993.

Mayer, Jane. *Dark Money: The Hidden History of the Billionaires behind the Rise of the Radical Right.* New York: Anchor Books, 2016.

Mazzucato, Mariana. *Mission Economy: A Moonshot Guide to Changing Capitalism.* London: Penguin, 2020.

McAlevey, Jane F. *No Shortcuts: Organizing for Power in the New Gilded Age.* New York: Oxford University Press, 2016.

McClelland, Mac. "I Was a Warehouse Wage Slave: My Brief, Backbreaking, Rage-Inducing, Low-Paying, Dildo-Packing Time inside the Online-Shipping Machine." *Mother Jones,* Mar./Apr. 2012.

McCloskey, Deidre. *Why Liberalism Works: How True Liberal Values Produce a Freer, More Equal, Prosperous World for All.* New Haven: Yale University Press, 2019.

McGhee, Heather. *The Sum of Us: What Racism Costs Everyone and How We Can Prosper Together.* New York: One World, 2021.

McKibben, Bill. *Deep Economy: The Wealth of Communities and the Durable Future.* New York: Times Books, 2007.

McKibben, Bill. *Falter: Has the Human Game Begun to Play Itself Out?* New York: Henry Holt, 2019.

McQuade, Barbara. *Attack from Within: How Disinformation Is Sabotaging America.* New York: Seven Stories Press, 2024.

McRaney, David. *How Minds Change: The Surprising Science of Belief, Opinion, and Persuasion.* New York: Portfolio/Penguin, 2022.

Medina, Jennifer. "For Minority Working-Class Voters, Dismay with Democrats Led to Distrust," *New York Times,* Nov. 19, 2024.

Mendez, Michael. *Climate Change from the Streets: How Conflict and Collaboration Strengthen the Environmental Justice Movement.* New Haven: Yale University Press, 2020.

Mervosh, Sarah. "Who Runs the Best U.S. Schools? It May Be the Defense Department." *New York Times,* Oct. 10, 2023.

Mettler, Suzanne. *The Submerged State: How Invisible Government Policies Undermine American Democracy.* Chicago: University of Chicago Press, 2011.

Meyer, David S. *The Politics of Protest: Social Movements in America.* 2nd ed. New York: Oxford University Press, 2015.

Michaels, David. *The Triumph of Doubt: Dark Money and the Science of Deception.* New York: Oxford University Press, 2020.

Mill, John Stuart. "Considerations on Representative Government." In Geraint Williams, ed., *Utilitarianism, On Liberty, Considerations on Representative Government.* London: Everyman, 1993 [1861].

Mill, John Stuart. *On Liberty,* ed. Elizabeth Rapaport. Indianapolis: Hackett, 1978 [1859].

Mill, John Stuart. "Utility of Religion." In *Three Essays On Religion,* ed. Louis J. Matz. Toronto: Broadview Press, 2009 [1874].

Miller, Reuben Jonathan. *Halfway Home: Race, Punishment, and the Afterlife of Mass Incarceration.* New York: Little, Brown, 2021.

Mills, Charles. "'Ideal Theory' as Ideology." Pp. 72–90 in Mills, *Black Rights/White Wrongs.* New York: Oxford University Press, 2017.

Mills, Charles. "Racial Liberalism." Pp. 28–48 in Mills, *Black Rights/White Wrongs.* New York: Oxford University Press, 2017.

Minow, Martha. *Saving the News: Why the Constitution Calls for Government Action to Preserve Freedom of Speech.* New York: Oxford University Press, 2021.

Mishel, Lawrence, and Josh Bivens. *Identifying the Policy Levers Generating Wage Suppression and Wage Inequality.* Washington, DC: Economic Policy Institute, 2021.

Mishel, Lawrence, and Julia Wolfe. *CEO Compensation Has Grown 940% since 1978.* Washington, DC: Economic Policy Institute, 2019.

Mitnik, Pablo A., and David B. Grusky. *Economic Mobility in the United States.* New York: Pew Charitable Trusts and the Russell Sage Foundation, 2015.

Moller, Dan. *Governing Least: A New England Libertarianism.* New York: Oxford University Press, 2019.

Moniz, Michelle H., A. Mark Fendrick, Giselle E. Kolenic, Anca Tilea, Lindsay K. Admon, and Vanessa K. Dalton. "Out-of-Pocket Spending for Maternity Care among Women with Employer-Based Insurance, 2008–15." *Health Affairs* 39, no. 1 (2020): 18–23.

Monk, Ellis P., Jr. "The Unceasing Significance of Colorism: Skin Tone Stratification in the United States." *Daedalus* 150, no. 2 (2021): 76–90.

Moore, Kyle K. *State Unemployment by Race and Ethnicity: Softening, but Strong, Labor Market; Robust Growth; Persistent Gaps across Groups.* Washington, DC: Economic Policy Institute, 2024.

Morgenson, Gretchen, and Joshua Rosner. *These Are the Plunderers: How Private Equity Runs—and Wrecks—America.* New York: Simon & Schuster, 2023.

Mounk, Yascha. *The People vs. Democracy: Why Our Freedom Is in Danger and How to Save It.* Cambridge, MA: Harvard University Press, 2019.

Moyn, Samuel. *Liberalism against Itself: Cold War Intellectuals and the Making of Our Times.* New Haven: Yale University Press, 2023.

Muirhead, Russell, and Nancy Rosenblum. *A Lot of People Are Saying: The New Conspiracism and the Assault on Democracy.* Princeton, NJ: Princeton University Press, 2019.

Mullainathan, Sendhil, and Eldar Shafir. *Scarcity: The New Science of Having Less and How It Defines Our Lives.* New York: Picador, 2013.

Müller, Jan-Werner. *What Is Populism?* Philadelphia: University of Pennsylvania Press, 2016.

Murphy, Liam, and Thomas Nagel. *The Myth of Ownership: Taxes and Justice.* Oxford, UK: Oxford University Press, 2002.

Naím, Moisés. *The Revenge of Power: How Autocrats Are Reinventing Politics for the 21st Century.* New York: St. Martin's, 2022.

Napoli, Philip, and Jessica Mahone. *Local Newspapers Are Suffering, but They're Still (by Far) the Most Significant Journalism Producers in Their Communities.* Cambridge, MA: Nieman Lab, 2019.

NASA. "Ocean Warming." NASA.org. https://climate.nasa.gov/vital-signs/ocean-warming/?intent=111.

National Oceanic and Atmospheric Administration (NOAA). *Billion-Dollar Weather and Climate Disasters.* Silver Spring, MD: NOAA, 2023.

National Oceanic and Atmospheric Administration (NOAA). *Technical Report Overview.* Silver Spring, MD: NOAA, 2022.

Nellis, Ashley. *The Color of Justice: Racial and Ethnic Disparity in State Prisons.* Washington, DC: Sentencing Project, 2021.

Nicas, Jack. "A Slow-Motion Climate Disaster: The Spread of Barren Land." *New York Times,* Dec. 3, 2021.

Norris, Pippa, and Andrea Abel van Es, eds. *Checkbook Elections? Political*

Finance in Comparative Perspective. New York: Oxford University Press, 2016.

Norris, Pippa, and Ronald Inglehart. *Cultural Backlash: Trump, Brexit, and Authoritarian Populism.* Cambridge, UK: Cambridge University Press, 2019.

North, Anna. "The Christian Right Is Coming for Divorce Next." *Vox,* June 13, 2024.

Nownes, Anthony. *Total Lobbying: What Lobbyists Want (and How They Try to Get It).* Cambridge, UK: Cambridge University Press, 2006.

Nussbaum, Martha. "Capabilities and Human Rights." *Fordham Law Review* 66 (1997): 273–300.

Nussbaum, Martha. *Sex and Social Justice.* New York: Oxford University Press, 1999.

Organisation for Economic Co-operation and Development (OECD). *OECD Employment Outlook, 2022: Building Back More Inclusive Labour Markets.* Paris: OECD Publishing, 2022.

Oxner, Reese. "Texas Agriculture Commissioner Sid Miller Alleges Aid to Farmers of Color Discriminates against White Farmers in Suit against Biden Administration." *Texas Tribune,* Apr. 27, 2021.

Pace, Fred. "New Coalition Looks to Transform West Virginia's Economy." *Herald-Dispatch,* Feb. 8, 2022.

Parents Involved in Community Schools v. Seattle School Dist. No. 1, 551 US 701 (2007).

Pascale, Celine-Marie. *Living on the Edge: When Hard Times Become a Way of Life.* Cambridge, UK: Polity Press, 2021.

Paul, Mark, Carla Santos Skandier, and Rory Renzy. *Out of Time: The Case for Nationalizing the Fossil Fuel Industry.* Washington, DC: People's Policy Project, 2020.

Payne, Charles M. *I've Got the Light of Freedom: The Organizing Tradition and the Mississippi Freedom Struggle.* Berkeley: University of California Press, 1995.

Perry, Andre M., Hannah Stephens, and Manann Donoghoe. *Black Wealth Is Increasing, but so Is the Racial Wealth Gap.* Washington, DC: Brookings Institution, 2024.

Pettit, Kathryn, G. Thomas Kingsley, Jennifer Biess, Kassie Bertumen, Nancy Pindus, Chris Narducci, and Amos Budde. *Continuity and Change: Demographic, Socioeconomic, and Housing Conditions of American Indians and Alaska Natives.* Washington, DC: US Dept. of Housing and Urban Development, 2014.

Pettit, Philip. *Just Freedom: A Moral Compass for a Complex World.* New York: W.W. Norton, 2017.

Pew Research Center. *Beyond Red vs. Blue: The Political Typology.* Washington, DC: Pew Research Center, 2021.

Pew Research Center. *Biden, Trump Supporters Both Say the U.S. Economic System Unfairly Favors Powerful Interests.* Washington, DC: Pew Research Center, 2024.

Pew Research Center. *Changing Partisan Coalitions in a Politically Divided Nation.* Washington, DC: Pew Research Center, 2024.

Pew Research Center. *Most Americans Point to Circumstances, Not Work Ethic, for Why People Are Rich or Poor.* Washington, DC: Pew Research Center, 2020.

Pew Research Center. *1999 Millennium Survey: Optimism Reigns, Technology Plays Key Role.* Washington, DC: Pew Research Center, 1999.

Pfaff, John. *Locked In: The True Causes of Mass Incarceration—and How to Achieve Real Reform.* New York: Basic Books, 2017.

Philpott, Tom. *Perilous Bounty: The Looming Collapse of American Farming and How We Can Prevent It.* New York: Bloomsbury, 2020.

Pickard, Victor. *Democracy without Journalism? Confronting the Misinformation Society.* New York: Oxford University Press, 2019.

Piketty, Thomas. *A Brief History of Equality.* Cambridge, MA: Harvard University Press, 2022.

Pinto-Rodrigues, Anne. "Microplastics Are in Our Bodies. Here's Why We Don't Know the Health Risks." *ScienceNews,* Mar. 24, 2023.

Piston, Spencer. *Class Attitudes in America: Sympathy for the Poor, Resentment of the Rich, and Political Implications.* New York: Cambridge University Press, 2018.

Polanyi, Karl. *The Great Transformation: The Political and Economic Origins of Our Time.* Boston: Beacon Press, 1957 [1944].

Pollin, Robert. "Nationalize the U.S. Fossil Fuel Industry to Save the Planet." *American Prospect,* Apr. 8, 2022.

Polsby, Nelson. *Consequences of Party Reform.* Oxford, UK: Oxford University Press, 1983.

Pope, Clayne. "Inequality in the Nineteenth Century." Pp. 109–142 in Stanley Engerman and Robert Gallman, eds., *The Cambridge Economic History of the United States,* vol. 2. Cambridge, UK: Cambridge University Press, 2000.

Powis, Carter M., David Byrne, Zachary Zobel, Kelly N. Gassert, A. C. Lute, and Christopher R. Schwalm. "Observational and Model Evidence Together Support Wide-Spread Exposure to Noncompensable Heat under Continued Global Warming." *Science Advances* 9, no. 36 (2023): eadg9297.

Punch, Maurice. "Suite Violence: Why Managers Murder and Corporations Kill." *Crime, Law, and Social Change* 33 (2000): 243–280.

Purdy, Jedediah. *Two Cheers for Politics: Why Democracy Is Flawed, Frightening—and Our Best Hope.* New York: Basic Books, 2022.

Quillian, Lincoln, Devah Pager, Ole Hexel, and Arnfinn H. Midtbøen. "Meta-Analysis of Field Experiments Shows No Change in Racial Discrimination in Hiring over Time." *Proceedings of the National Academy of Sciences* 114, no. 41 (2017): 10870–10875.

Rainie, Lee, Scott Keeter, and Andrew Perrin. *Trust and Distrust in America.* Washington, DC: Pew Research Center, 2019.

Ravenelle, Alexandrea J. *Hustle and Gig: Struggling and Surviving in the Sharing Economy.* Oakland: University of California Press, 2019.

Raymond, Colin, Tom Matthews, and Radley M. Horton. "The Emergence of Heat and Humidity Too Severe for Human Tolerance." *Science Advances* 6 (2020): eaaw1838.

Reece, Robert L. "The Future of American Blackness: On Colorism and Racial Reorganization." *Review of Black Political Economy* 48, no. 4 (2021): 481–505.

Reed, Touré. *Toward Freedom: The Case against Race Reductionism.* London: Verso, 2020.

Rehavi, M. Marit, and Sonja B. Starr. "Racial Disparity in Federal Criminal Sentences." *Journal of Political Economy* 122, no. 6 (2014): 1320–1354.

Reich, Rob, Mehran Sahami, and Jeremy Weinstein. *System Error: Where Big Tech Went Wrong and How We Can Reboot.* New York: HarperCollins, 2021.

Reich, Robert B. *Saving Capitalism: For the Many, Not the Few.* New York: Knopf, 2015.

Reich, Robert B. *The System: Who Rigged It, How We Fix It.* New York: Vintage, 2020.

Reporters Without Borders. "One Month of Trump: Press Freedom Under Siege." Feb. 19, 2025. https://rsf.org/en/one-month-trump-press-freedom-under-siege.

Resnick, Brian. "How to Talk Someone out of Bigotry." *Vox,* Jan. 29, 2020.

Richardson, Heather Cox. *The Death of Reconstruction: Race, Labor, and Politics in the Post-Civil War North, 1865–1901.* Cambridge, MA: Harvard University Press, 2001.

Riedl, Rachel Beatty, Jennifer McCoy, Kenneth Roberts, and Murat Somer. "Pathways of Democratic Backsliding, Resistance, and (Partial) Recoveries." *Annals of the American Academy of Political and Social Science* 712, no. 1 (2024): 8–31.

Robbins, Rebecca. "How a Drug Company Made $114 Billion by Gaming the U.S. Patent System." *New York Times,* Jan. 28, 2023.

Robertson, Derek. "What Would a Socialist America Look Like?" *Politico Magazine,* Sept. 3, 2018.

Robison, Peter. *Flying Blind: The 737 MAX Tragedy and the Fall of Boeing.* New York: Knopf, 2022.

Rogers, Melvin L. *The Darkened Light of Faith: Race, Democracy, and Freedom in African American Political Thought.* Princeton, NJ: Princeton University Press, 2023.

Rojanasakul, Mira, Christopher Flavelle, Blacki Migliozzi, and Eli Murray. "America Is Using up Its Groundwater Like There's No Tomorrow." *New York Times,* Apr. 28, 2023.

Rolnik, Guy, Julia Cagé, Joshua Gans, Ellen Goodman, Brian Knight, Andrea Prat, Anya Schiffrin, and Prateek Raj. *Protecting Journalism in the Age of Digital Platforms.* Chicago: George J. Stigler Center for the Study of the Economy and the State, 2019.

Romanello, Marina, Claudia Di Napoli, Paul Drummond, Carole Green, Harry Kennard, Pete Lampard, Daniel Scamman, et al. "The 2022 Report of the Lancet Countdown on Health and Climate Change: Health at the Mercy of Fossil Fuels." *The Lancet* 400, no. 10363 (2000): 1619–1654.

Roosevelt, Franklin. "Topeka, KS—Campaign Speech. September 14, 1932." Champaign, IL: FDR Library. http://www.fdrlibrary.marist.edu/_re sources/images/msf/msf00510.

Rosenblat, Alex. *Uberland: How Algorithms Are Rewriting the Rules of Work.* Oakland: University of California Press, 2018.

Rosenblatt, Helena. *The Lost History of Liberalism: From Ancient Rome to the Twenty-First Century.* Princeton, NJ: Princeton University Press, 2018.

Rosenfeld, Sophia. *Democracy and Truth: A Short History.* Philadelphia: University of Pennsylvania Press, 2019.

Ross, Jack. "In Los Angeles, A Friendship Grows out of Housing Strife." *USA Today,* Mar. 21, 2023.

Ross, Martha, and Nicole Bateman. *Meet the Low-Wage Workforce.* Washington, DC: Brookings Institution, 2019.

Rothfeder, Jeffrey, and Christopher Maag. "How Wall Street's Fossil-Fuel Money Pipeline Undermines the Fight to Save the Planet." *Fortune,* Feb. 2, 2023.

Rothstein, Richard. *The Color of Law: A Forgotten History of How Our Government Segregated America.* New York: Liveright, 2017.

Roza, Marguerite, Paul T. Hill, Susan Sclafani, and Sheree Speakman. "How Within-District Spending Inequities Help Some Schools to Fail." *Brookings Papers on Education Policy,* no. 7 (2004): 201–227.

Sabl, Andrew. *Ruling Passions: Political Offices and Democratic Ethics.* Princeton, NJ: Princeton University Press, 2002.

Sadowski, Jathan. "Why Silicon Valley Is Embracing Universal Basic Income." *The Guardian,* June 22, 2016.

Saez, Emmanuel, and Gabriel Zucman. *The Triumph of Injustice: How the Rich Dodge Taxes and How to Make Them Pay.* New York: W.W. Norton, 2019.

Saez, Emmanuel, and Gabriel Zucman. "Wealth Inequality in the United

States since 1913: Evidence from Capitalized Income Tax Data." *Quarterly Journal of Economics* 131, no. 2 (2016): 519–578.

Saitō, Kōhei. *Slow Down: The Degrowth Manifesto.* New York: Astra House, 2024 [2020].

Saitone, Tina L., K. Aleks Schaefer, and Daniel P. Scheitrum. 2021. "COVID-19 Morbidity and Mortality in U.S. Meatpacking Counties." *Food Policy* 101 (2021): 102072.

Sandel, Michael. *The Tyranny of Merit: What's Become of the Common Good?* New York: Farrar, Straus, and Giroux, 2020.

Sawhill, Isabel. *The Forgotten Americans: An Economic Agenda for a Divided Nation.* New Haven: Yale University Press, 2018.

Schneider, Daniel, and Kristen Harknett. "Consequence of Routine Work-Schedule Instability for Worker Health and Well-Being." *American Sociological Review* 84, no. 1 (2019): 82–114.

Schor, Juliet. "The (Even More) Overworked American." Pp. 6–11 in John de Graaf, ed., *Take Back Your Time: Fighting Overwork and Poverty in America.* San Fransisco: Berrett-Koehler, 2003.

Schor, Juliet B., William Attwood-Charles, Mehmet Cansoy, Isak Ladegaard, and Robert Wengronowitz. "Dependence and Precarity in the Platform Economy." *Theory and Society* 49 (2020): 833–861.

Schuetz, Jenny. *Fixer-Upper: How to Repair America's Broken Housing Systems.* Washington, DC: Brookings Institution Press, 2022.

Select Subcommittee on the Coronavirus Crisis. *"Now to Get Rid of Those Pesky Health Departments!" How the Trump Administration Helped the Meatpacking Industry Block Pandemic Worker Protections: Staff Report.* Washington, DC: Select Subcommittee on the Coronavirus Crisis, 2022.

Semuels, Alana. "How to Fix a Broken Police Department." *Atlantic Monthly,* May 28, 2015.

Sered, Danielle. *Until We Reckon: Violence, Mass Incarceration, and A Road to Repair.* New York: New Press, 2019.

Shapiro, Thomas M. *The Hidden Cost of Being African American: How Wealth Perpetuates Inequality.* New York: Oxford University Press, 2004.

Sharkey, Patrick. *Stuck in Place: Urban Neighborhoods and the End of Progress toward Racial Equality.* Chicago: University of Chicago Press, 2013.

Sharma, Swati, Aprajita Bhardwaj, Monika Thakur, and Anita Saini. "Understanding Microplastic Pollution of Marine Ecosystem: A Review." *Environmental Science and Pollution Research* 31 (2024): 41402–41445.

Shaw, Al, and Lylla Younes. *The Most Detailed Map of Cancer-Causing Industrial Air Pollution in the U.S.* New York: ProPublica, 2023.

Shaw, Christopher. *Liberalism and the Challenge of Climate Change.* London: Routledge, 2024.

Shearman, David, and Joseph Wayne-Smith. *The Climate Change Challenge and the Failure of Democracy.* Westport, CT: Praeger, 2007.

Shelby, Tommie. *Dark Ghettos: Injustice, Dissent, and Reform.* Cambridge, MA: Harvard University Press, 2016.

Shelby, Tommie. *The Idea of Prison Abolition.* Princeton, NJ: Princeton University Press, 2022.

Shipler, David K. *The Working Poor: Invisible in America.* New York: Vintage, 2005 [2004].

Shklar, Judith. "The Liberalism of Fear." Pp. 21–38 in Nancy Rosenblum, ed., *Liberalism and the Moral Life.* Cambridge, MA: Harvard University Press, 1989.

Shulman, Beth. *The Betrayal of Work: How Low-Wage Jobs Fail 30 Million Americans and Their Families.* New York: New Press, 2003.

Skelley, Geoffrey. "How the Republican Push to Restrict Voting Could Affect Our Elections." *FiveThirtyEight,* May 17, 2021.

Skocpol, Theda. *Diminished Democracy: From Membership to Management in American Civic Life.* Norman: University of Oklahoma Press, 2003.

Skocpol, Theda, and Vanessa Williamson. *The Tea Party and the Remaking of Republican Conservatism.* Updated ed. New York: Oxford University Press, 2016.

Smith, Graham. *Can Democracy Safeguard the Future?* Cambridge, UK: Polity, 2021.

Snyder, Timothy. *On Tyranny: Twenty Lessons from the Twentieth Century.* New York: Crown, 2017.

Song, Lisa, and Lylla Younes. *Air Monitors Alone Won't Save Communities from Toxic Industrial Air Pollution.* New York: ProPublica, 2022.

Starr, Paul. *Freedom's Power: The True Force of Liberalism.* New York: Basic Books, 2007.

Steinzor, Rena. *Why Not Jail? Industrial Catastrophes, Corporate Malfeasance, and Government Inaction.* New York: Cambridge University Press, 2015.

Stevenson, Betsey, and Justin Wolfers. "Bargaining in the Shadow of the Law: Divorce Laws and Family Distress." *Quarterly Journal of Economics* 121, no. 1 (2006): 267–288.

Stiglitz, Joseph E., Nell Abernathy, Adam Hersh, Susan Holmberg, and Mike Konczal. *Rewriting the Rules of the American Economy: An Agenda for Growth and Shared Prosperity.* New York: W.W. Norton, 2016.

Stokes, Leah Cardamore. *Short Circuiting Policy: Interest Groups and the Battle over Clean Energy and Climate Policy in the American States.* New York: Oxford University Press, 2020.

Stone, Katherine V. W., and Alexander J. S. Colvin. *The Arbitration Epidemic: Mandatory Arbitration Deprives Workers and Consumers of Their Rights.* Washington, DC: Economic Policy Institute, 2015.

Stone, Peter. "'Openly Authoritarian Campaign': Trump's Threats of Revenge Fuel Alarm." *The Guardian,* Nov. 22, 2023.

Stout, Jeffrey. *Blessed Are the Organized: Grassroots Democracy in America.* Princeton, NJ: Princeton University Press, 2010.

Stovall, Tyler. *White Freedom: The Racial History of an Idea.* Princeton, NJ: Princeton University Press, 2021.

Strang, Heather, and Lawrence Sherman. "The Morality of Evidence: The Second Annual Lecture." *Restorative Justice: An International Journal* 3, no. 1 (2015): 6–27.

Stratton, Mark. "Carbon-Free Copenhagen: How the Danish Capital Is Setting a Green Standard for Cities Worldwide." *National Geographic,* Mar. 16, 2020.

Strine, Leo E., Jr. *Toward Fair and Sustainable Capitalism.* New York: Roosevelt Insitute, 2020.

Sullivan, Laura, Tatjana Meschede, Thomas Shapiro, Teresa Kroeger, and

Fernanda Escobar. *Not Only Unequal Paychecks: Occupational Segregation, Benefits, and the Racial Wealth Gap.* Waltham, MA: Institute on Assets and Social Policy, 2019.

Sullivan, Margaret. *Newsroom Confidential: Lessons (and Worries) from an Ink-Stained Life.* New York: St. Martin's, 2022.

Sunkara, Bhaskar. *The Socialist Manifesto: The Case for Radical Politics in an Era of Extreme Inequality.* New York: Verso, 2020.

Svajlenka, Nicole Prchal. *Protecting Undocumented Workers on the Pandemic's Front Lines.* Washington, DC: Center for American Progress, 2020.

Sweet, William, Ben Hamlington, Robert E. Kopp, Christopher Weaver, Patrick L. Barnard, David Bekaert, William Brooks, et al. *Global and Regional Sea Level Rise Scenarios for the United States.* Silver Spring, MD: National Oceanic and Atmospheric Administration, 2022.

Tabuchi, Hiroko, Nadja Popovich, Blacki Migliozzi, and Andrew W. Lehren. "Floods Are Getting Worse, and 2500 Chemical Sites Lie in the Water's Path." *New York Times,* Feb. 6, 2018.

Tanden, Neera, Carmel Martin, and Marc Jarsulic. *Toward a Marshall Plan for America: Rebuilding Our Towns, Cities, and the Middle Class.* Washington, DC: Center for American Progress, 2017.

Teachout, Zephyr. *Break 'Em Up: Recovering Our Freedom from Big Ag, Big Tech, and Big Money.* New York: All Points Books, 2020.

Teachout, Zephyr. *Corruption in America: From Benjamin Franklin's Snuff Box to Citizens United.* Cambridge, MA: Harvard University Press, 2014.

Thomson, Judith Jarvis. "In Defense of Abortion." *Philosophy and Public Affairs* 1, no. 1 (1971): 47–66.

Tingley, Kim. "'Forever Chemicals' Are Everywhere. What Are They Doing to Us?" *New York Times Magazine,* Aug. 16, 2023.

Tirado, Linda. *Hand to Mouth: Living in Bootstrap America.* New York: Berkley Books, 2014.

Tomasky, Michael. "Why Does No One Understand the Real Reason Trump Won?" *New Republic,* Nov. 8, 2024.

Toral, Karla Martinez, Catherine Higham, Joana Setzer, Navraj Singh Ghaleigh, Asanga Welikala, and Chiara Arena. "The 11 Nations Heralding a New Dawn of Climate Constitutionalism." Grantham Research Institute for Climate Change and the Environment, London, Dec. 2, 2021. https://www.lse.ac.uk/granthaminstitute/news/the-11-nations-heralding-a-new-dawn-of-climate-constitutionalism.

Tura, Nina, and Ville Ojanen. "Sustainability-Oriented Innovations in Smart Cities: A Systematic Review and Emerging Themes." *Cities* 126 (2022): article 103716.

United Nations. *Our Common Future: Report of the World Commission on Environment and Development.* New York: United Nations, 1987. https://sustainabledevelopment.un.org/content/documents/5987our-common-future.pdf?dtid=oblgzzz000659.

Vaidhyanathan, Siva. *Anti-Social Media: How Facebook Disconnects Us and Undermines Democracy.* New York: Oxford University Press, 2018.

Valls, Andrew. *Rethinking Racial Justice.* New York: Oxford University Press, 2018.

Van Parijs, Philippe, and Yannick Vanderborght. *Basic Income: A Radical Proposal for a Free Society and a Sane Economy.* Cambridge, MA: Harvard University Press, 2017.

Victor, David G., Frank W. Geels, and Simon Sharpe. *Accelerating the Low Carbon Transition: The Case for Stronger, More Targeted and Coordinated International Action.* London: UK Department for Business, Energy, and Industrial Strategy, 2019.

Villavicencio, Karla Cornejo. *The Undocumented Americans.* New York: One World, 2021.

Vosoughi, Soroush, Deb Roy, and Sinan Aral. "The Spread of True and False News Online." *Science* 359, no. 6380 (2018): 1146–1151.

Waldron, Jeremy. "Homelessness and the Issue of Freedom." *UCLA Law Review* 39 (1991): 295–324.

Walker, Robert. *The Shame of Poverty.* Oxford, UK: Oxford University Press, 2014.

Wallace-Wells, David. "Beyond Catastrophe: A New Climate Reality Is Coming into View." *New York Times Magazine,* Oct. 26, 2022.

Walzer, Michael. *Political Action: A Practical Guide to Movement Politics.* New York: New York Review of Books, 2019 [1971].

Warren, Elizabeth. "Companies Shouldn't Be Accountable Only to Shareholders." *Wall Street Journal,* Aug. 14, 2018.

Weathers, Ericka S., and Victoria E. Sosina. "Separate Remains Unequal: Contemporary Segregation and Racial Disparities in School District Revenue." *American Educational Research Journal* 59, no. 5 (2022): 905–938.

Weil, David. *The Fissured Workplace: Why Work Became so Bad for so Many and What Can Be Done to Improve It.* Cambridge, MA: Harvard University Press, 2014.

Weis, Tony. *The Ecological Hoofprint: The Global Burden of Industrial Livestock.* London: Zed Books, 2013.

Weisburd, David, and Malay K. Majmundar, eds. *Proactive Policing: Effects on Crime and Communities.* Washington, DC: National Academies Press, 2018.

Wertheimer, Alan. *Exploitation.* Princeton, NJ: Princeton University Press, 1996.

West, Stasia, Amy Castro Baker, Sukhi Samra, and Erin Coltrera. *Preliminary Analysis: SEED's First Year.* Stockton, CA: Stockton Eonomic Empowerment Demonstration, 2022.

Western, Bruce, and Jessica Simes. "Criminal Justice." Pp. 18–20 in Stanford Center on Poverty and Inequality, *State of the Union.* Palo Alto, CA: Stanford Center on Poverty and Inequality, 2019. https://inequality .stanford.edu/publications/pathway/state-union-2019.

Whittaker, Martin. "The Idea that Raising Wages Destroys Value Is a Fallacy." *Forbes,* Oct. 22, 2020.

Wilkerson, Isabel. *Caste: The Origins of Our Discontents.* New York: Random House, 2020.

Williamson, Vanessa. "Radical Taxation." *Dissent,* Summer 2022.

Williamson, Vanessa. *Read My Lips: Why Americans Are Proud to Pay Taxes.* Princeton, NJ: Princeton University Press, 2017.

Willingham, Leah. "Gender Divide Prominent as Male-Dominated Legis-

latures Debate Abortion." *PBS News Hour,* Sept. 24, 2022. https://www
.pbs.org/newshour/politics/gender-divide-prominent-as-male-domin
ated-legislatures-debate-abortion.

Wolfe, Anna. "'A Profound Betrayal of Trust': Why Jackson's Water System
Is Broken." *Mississippi Today,* Mar. 24, 2021.

Woo, Jong-Min, and Teodor T. Postolache. "The Impact of Work Environment on Mood Disorders and Suicide: Evidence and Implications."
International Journal on Disability and Human Development 7, no. 2
(2008): 185–200.

Wood, Alex. *Despotism on Demand: How Power Operates in the Flexible Workplace.* Ithaca, NY: Cornell University Press, 2020.

Woodly, Deva. *The Politics of Common Sense: How Social Movements Use Public Discourse to Change Politics and Win Acceptance.* Oxford, UK: Oxford
University Press, 2015.

Woodly, Deva. *Reckoning: Black Lives Matter and the Democratic Necessity of
Social Movements.* New York: Oxford University Press, 2022.

Woods, Neal D. "An Environmental Race to the Bottom? 'No More Strin-
gent' Laws in the American States." *Publius: The Journal of Federalism*
51, no. 2 (Spring 2021): 238–261.

Worden, Robert E., and Sarah J. McLean. *Mirage of Police Reform: Procedural Justice and Police Legitimacy.* Oakland: University of California
Press, 2017.

Wu, Tim. *The Curse of Bigness: Antitrust in the New Gilded Age.* New York:
Columbia Global Reports, 2018.

Wu, Tim. "Is the First Amendment Obsolete?" *Michigan Law Review* 117,
no. 3 (2018): 547–581.

Wykstra, Stephanie. "Bail Reform, Which Could Save Millions of Uncon-
victed People from Jail, Explained." *Vox,* Oct. 17, 2018.

Xu, Xiaoming, Prateek Sharma, Shijie Shu, Tzu-Shun Lin, Philippe Ciais,
Francesco N. Tubiello, Pete Smith, Nelson Campbell, and Atul K. Jain.
2021. "Global Greenhouse Gas Emissions from Animal-Based Foods Are
Twice Those of Plant-Based Foods." *Nature Food* 2 (2021): 724–732.

Zakaras, Alex. *The Roots of American Individualism: Political Myth in the Age
of Jackson.* Princeton, NJ: Princeton University Press, 2022.

Zhong, Raymond, and Nadja Popovich. "How Air Pollution across America Reflects Racist Policy from the 1930s." *New York Times,* Mar. 9, 2022.

Zhou, Li. "How Trump's DOJ Could Severely Curtail Oversight of Police." *Vox,* Dec. 6, 2024.

Žižek, Slavoj. *First as Tragedy, Then as Farce.* London: Verso, 2009.

Zuboff, Shoshana. *The Age of Surveillance Capitalism: The Fight for a Human Future at the New Frontier of Power.* New York: PublicAffairs, 2019.

Index

litical culture, 8–9, 246–247; and
basic interests of human beings,
30–35; and citizen engagement, 6,
209–213; and the common good,
203; and concentrated power, 49;
and corporate tyranny, 87–88;
definition of, 5–7; and democracy,
17–18; and equality, 7–8, 37–43, 46,
245–247; as evidence-based, 10, 12;
and freedom, 5–6, 24–25, 231,
246–247; and grassroots power, 6,
209–213; historical roots of, 243;
and human rights, 35–37; institutional foundations of, 10; key
characteristics of, 7–13; and protection of natural resources, 177;
and racial hierarchy, 140–141, 147,
159–160; and realistic assumptions,
10, 12, 230; and social justice, 203;
as theory of human society, 47–48.
See also equal freedom; power-
sharing liberalism
Reagan, Ronald: and privatization of
public services, 82
recognition: as aspect of equality,
38–39, 159; as denied to minority
populations, 150–151, 153; failures
of, 153
Reed, Touré: *Toward Freedom*, 237
regenerative agriculture, 13
regulatory agencies: challenges to,
82–84
religious intolerance: impact of on
freedom, 25
reproductive rights, 172–175
Republican Party: and assault on the
electoral process, 67–69; authoritarian tilt of, 66, 68, 85, 223, 238;
and economic populism, 139;

radicalization of, 223; Trump's
takeover of, 66–67; violent rhetoric
of, 66
restorative justice programs, 13,
169–170
"right-to-work" statutes: repeal of,
131
right-wing activists: voter outreach
by, 234
Roberts, John, 155
Roosevelt, Franklin, 26–27, 243; on
freedom, 27; and the Wagner Act,
115
Roosevelt Institute: and calls for a
21st Century Homestead Act, 167
rule of law: and freedom, 55–56
Russian government: and control
of elections, 51–52; and media
narrative about the war effort,
50; repression of opposition to,
50–52
Russian oligarchs, 51
Rustin, Bayard, 171

Sallie Mae, 218
Sanders, Bernie, 235, 243
Seneca Falls Convention (1848), 172
sexual identity: and freedom of expression, 29
Shapiro, Thomas: on impact of inherited wealth, 158
Shelby, Tommie, 165, 171
Shklar, Judith, 26
Sinclair media, 87
Skocpol, Theda: *Diminished Democracy: From Membership to Management in American Civic Life*,
212–213
social critics: crucial role of, 9